Agent-Based Computational Sociology

Agent-Based Computational Sociology

Flaminio Squazzoni

University of Brescia, Italy

A John Wiley & Sons, Ltd., Publication

This edition first published 2012
© 2012 John Wiley & Sons, Ltd

Registered office
John Wiley & Sons Ltd, The Atrium, Southern Gate, Chichester, West Sussex, PO19 8SQ,
United Kingdom

For details of our global editorial offices, for customer services and for information about how to apply
for permission to reuse the copyright material in this book please see our website at www.wiley.com.

Library of Congress Cataloging-in-Publication Data

Squazzoni, Flaminio.
  Agent-based computational sociology / Flaminio Squazzoni.
    p. cm.
  Includes bibliographical references and index.
  ISBN 978-0-470-71174-3 (cloth)
  1. Sociology–Research–Methodology.   2. Computer simulation.   3. Social interaction.   I. Title.
  HM511.S686 2012
  301.01–dc23
                                                                                        2011046724

A catalogue record for this book is available from the British Library.

ISBN: 978-0-470-71174-3

Typeset in 10/12pt Times by Aptara Inc., New Delhi, India

To Eleonora, my most inspiring agent

Contents

Preface

If you believe that the aim of sociology is to reflect on and delve into the sublime complexity and idiosyncrasy of reality, as for philosophy, history, and literature, I expect this book will disappoint you. In my view, sociology is not a branch of the humanities. Its task is to explain social puzzles by reducing reality to recurrent and simple patterns, as for any other rigorous science. In order to accomplish this task, formalization, modeling and computer simulation can make the same difference here as for physics and evolutionary biology.

Sociology is no exception to this rule, nor does it recognize the immense complication of its investigation object, that is, social interaction. The main message of this book is that formalized models that look at agent behavior and interaction are essential elements for sociology, both for theory building and empirical knowledge.

Some years ago, defending the idea that social sciences need the same kind of rigor and mathematical foundations as 'hard' sciences, the Nobel Prize winner Herbert Simon provocatively suggested that social sciences should be considered the 'real' hard science. Understanding human behavior and interaction is the real challenge for 'hard' scientists, Simon claimed.

I have no doubt that all sociologists share this view. The idea that humans do not follow deterministic laws and that social interaction implies higher levels of complexity is obvious. However, most of them use such a claim to deny the advantages of simplification, reduction, modeling and generalization, following the (wrong) idea that social phenomena are too complex to be understood by standard scientific practices.

As far as I can tell, in this way, we have paralyzed the advance of cumulative science, eroded the explanatory capacity of our investigation and undermined a fruitful combination of theory and observation in our discipline. This has reduced sociology to a well-educated descriptive account of the present or a set of 'broad tent view' philosophical speculations. Indeed, the current situation of our discipline dramatically testifies to this: paradigmatic fragmentation, parochial balkanization of research programs and schools, no epistemological and methodological consensus, low prestige of the discipline, low funds, and poor influence on the public sphere. Everything today suggests that something has gone wrong.

Obviously, the refusal of formalization and modeling cannot be the whole cause of this crisis, but I think it is useful to start from here to contemplate a different type of sociology. If sociology is much less influential than other disciplines, such as economics and psychology, and physicists have started to substitute sociologists in understanding social puzzles, it is because of the type and quality of investigation that we currently undertake, rather than any external conspiracy.

This book refers to the Simonian legacy. It aims to show that formalization and modeling do not necessarily sentence us to excessive reductionism and abstraction or to losing sight of the fundamental ingredients of society. The key point is that from the 1990s onward, some sociologists started to apply sociologically friendly computational techniques to simulate and analyze implications of agent interaction in given social structures. This book reports on this innovation and aims to contribute to its wider recognition.

However, I do not intend to write an apology for this new formalism. This should be clear. First, there is evidence about the dramatic danger in the excessive mythology of the *techné* in science. Secondly, formalization is just one component of sociological investigation, which is a multifaceted set of different interrelated activities. Let me discuss these two points.

I suggest that it is easy to understand the danger of excessive emphasis on formalism for the advance of social science. Looking at mainstream economics is a good example. Generations of well-educated scientists have incrementally developed a fascinating general and abstract model built on complex mathematical scaffolds which does not have any empirical evidence behind it. This book suggests considering formalization and modeling, if and only if they allow us to explain empirical puzzles. This is possible now as agent-based modeling has ontological correspondence with the atoms of social life (i.e., agents) and explicitly addresses agent behavior in social interaction, that is, observable features of our social life.

This ontological correspondence between models and social facts has two relevant consequences. First, agent-based models (from now on ABMs) allow us to prearrange theory towards empirical validation. Indeed, it is easier to empirically validate a well-defined, simple, clear and logically coherent theoretical model which explicitly addresses human behavior and interaction, than un-formalized and descriptive accounts about unobservable social entities, such as 'habitus', 'organizational fields' and 'liquid modernity'. Secondly, by generating artificial data, ABMs can also help to guide empirical research. Indeed, it is easier to question reality and search for empirical data (if available) when research is informed by well-constructed and verified theories about observable entities. This opportunity to discipline and link theory and observation is one of the most important added values of agent-based computational sociology.

That said, it must be clarified that this book does not support any absolutistic view, nor does it aim to add parochialism to an already fragmented discipline such as sociology. I do not want to convey the message that this type of research is the only way, or the most correct way of doing sociology. Other types of sociology, such as qualitative, quantitative, mathematical or critical sociology, can bring plenty of useful findings and intuitions to advance our discipline. With this book, I want only to suggest, first, that considering sociology closer to other types of science in advocating the added value of formalization and modeling is worth pursuing as least as much as other ways. Secondly, I want to emphasize that this type of research may contribute to reducing balkanization by helping to cross-fertilize qualitative and quantitative approaches and deductive and inductive reasoning.

It must also be clarified that the line I have taken in this book does not suggest that the 'analytical' approach typical of agent-based computational sociology is expected to exclude any other type of sociological approach. Observing from statistical data, inquiring into the field in different ways, reasoning and theorizing, describing in qualitative terms, are all important aspects of this endeavor we call science. After all, heterogeneity has an incommensurable heuristic value for our discipline, being an advantage for all species for long-term adaptation and evolution.

If this is so, in my view it is hard to understand why the only type of sociology so largely neglected by most traditional sociologists and so dramatically underrepresented in our community, is that which is closer to the standards of other more influential and reputed sciences. This book aims to suggest turning this page, showing that there are more benefits than disadvantages in doing so.

Let me further expand on formalization. So far, most sociologists have viewed formalized models as synonymous of simplified mathematical approaches, where unrealistic assumptions about human behavior and interaction are made for analytic tractability. The classic example is economics, where the fiction of the representative agent, perfect rationality and no direct interaction between economic agents is assumed to mathematically guarantee equilibrium solutions. Others view modeling as synonymous of a set of assumptions about variables and statistical correlations from empirical datasets. The first approach is more concerned with deduction, the second one with induction.

As I will try to show in this book, agent-based computational sociology is poised to dramatically change these views. ABMs are a new type of formalism that exploit the flexibility of programming languages to model human behavior and social interaction which mimic social reality, with agents who are heterogeneous, rule-followers, boundedly rational, embedded in social structures (e.g., social networks, spatial neighborhoods or institutional scaffolds) and subject to social influence. Therefore, they allow us to relax the abstracted and unrealistic assumptions of analytic models and to work with more realistic models which move deduction closer to observation.

This is not all. By running the model on a computer, macro social aggregates are simulated, which look at complex dynamics impossible to observe directly, either with analytic, statistical or descriptive models. Therefore, computer simulation is used to generate (artificial) data which can be analyzed by induction. This allows us to make intuitions and reveal unforeseen insights from social interaction. It is a technological breakthrough which could have significant implications for social research.

All in all, there is one thing that makes me confident that in this was we are heading in the right direction. Generally, when I meet supporters of mathematics and analytic models, the criticism against ABMs is that they are dirty models, too far from mathematics, too complicated and realistic and not concerned enough with clear and definitive analytic solutions. On the other hand, supporters of qualitative research claim that ABMs are not complex enough to look at social reality in detail, are too abstract and oversimplified.

This leads me to think that agent-based computational sociologists are in an interesting unexcluded middle position where different viewpoints and types of research can ensure good synthesis, providing room for cross-fertilization, which is difficult in sociology.

I hope that the reader will appreciate certain examples reported in this book which builds a bridge between quantification and quality, numbers and insights and raw statistical data and qualitative intuition. In my view, even if only for this reason, agent-based computational sociology deserves a good standing in our discipline.

Finally, let us move on to the presentation of the book's contents. The first chapter introduces agent-based computational sociology and the idea of agent-based modeling. I have defined agent-based computational sociology as *the study of social patterns by computer models of social interaction between heterogeneous agents embedded in given social structures (e.g., social networks, spatial neighborhoods, or institutional scaffolds)*. Particular attention has been given here to the founding fathers of this type of research and to reconstructing its position compared with other approaches. The reader will discover, perhaps surprisingly, that some of the most influential sociologists of the past century are closely associated with agent-based computational sociology. People like James S. Coleman, Raymond Boudon, Thomas Schelling, and Mark Granovetter have all left their mark. It has been surprising to see retrospectively that they were more or less motivated by the same understanding of what sociological research should be like.

After reconstructing predecessors and historical origins, I have presented the six most striking ideas of agent-based computational sociology. These are: the primacy of models over theorizing and descriptive accounts, the generative approach to explanation, a pragmatic approach to the micro–macro link, the importance of process and change as key elements of sociological investigation, the pursuit of an unexcluded middle position between deduction and induction, theory and data and a tendency towards a trans-disciplinary/issue-oriented style of research. These ideas are discussed in detail as they answer certain critical points of current sociology.

The chapter ends with a categorization that can help the reader to understand different ABM usages in sociology. My interest here has been strictly 'analytical' and so I did not address policy issues, nor have I given examples of applied models. However, there are interesting examples which testify to the growing interest of policy makers and business managers in this type of research to solve crucial problems and help manage complex organizations. In my view, sociologists are being called on to play a role in these practical aspects, breaking out of an ivory tower. This is discussed in the last chapter.

In the second and third chapters, I have extensively reviewed the literature. I must confess that this will require a certain amount of patience on behalf of the reader. The detail is to allow the reader to fully understand the premises, working and consequences of the issue. As I want to emphasize the advantage of model replication and extension for sociology development (i.e., in the fourth chapter), I have also reported in detail subsequent studies which originated from exemplary and influential models. I am confident that the game is worth the effort for the reader.

Another caveat is that all examples have been categorized according to the topic investigated rather than to the approach followed by modelers. Generally speaking, these examples follow two approaches, according to their level of analysis. There are (1) studies which investigate the emergence of global macro patterns from local agent interaction (i.e., more micro-to-macro oriented) and (2) others which investigate in more detail the impact of social patterns on agent interaction (i.e., more macro-to-micro oriented). It is worth noting that in some cases both directions were jointly investigated. As a result, these level-concerned explanatory aspects have been distinguished on a case-by-case basis, whereas examples have been grouped around issue specificity.

More specifically, in the second chapter I have reported on cooperation and social norms. Here, the literature is quite ample with examples where ABMs, game theory and experimental research have been fruitfully crossed over. This field allows us to spotlight certain social mechanisms which have wide implications for the spontaneous emergence of social order, one of the most important challenges for sociologists and social scientists in general.

The examples I have selected focus on the following cooperation mechanisms: direct reciprocity, social sanctions, social conventions, cultural transmission, partner selection in dynamic social networks and reputation. They provide a coherent picture of the heterogeneity of human behavior and motivations in social interaction, as well as interesting insights into the role played by social structures on the emergence of pro-social behavior. Most of the examples revolve around abstract models (with more or less experimental foundations), but I hope that the reader will appreciate some which combine experimental data and computational models.

In the third chapter, I have investigated social influence. The focus has been on themes such as residential segregation, collective opinions, culture, and market dynamics. I think that these examples are useful to understand that, when social influence is involved, the explanation of aggregate behavior is largely dependent upon micro details which are difficult to look at without modeling and simulating.

Sociological explanation is more informative, complete and thought provoking when it deals with individual behavior in social interaction, rather than with macro variables and structural factors. I have also included a couple of examples of my own research, which deals with social reflexivity, a complicated typology of social influence. Here, the idea is that the action of other people and specific features of the social contexts where agents are embedded could be the object of cognitive interpretation by agents which could in turn dramatically influence their behavior.

I also want to emphasize that these examples are inspired by a radically different picture of human behavior from economics. Indeed, when social interaction is seriously considered, such as in agent-based computational sociology, social outcomes cannot be understood by assuming representative agents, perfect information and individuals as utility maximizers. Social interaction implies agent heterogeneity, imperfect information, local adaptation and nonlinear effects between agents. Rather than economics and rational choice theory, here the reference for agent-based computational sociology is experimental behavioral science and social psychology. This is a new alliance that agent-based computational sociologists should seriously nurture.

Moreover, the examples of these two chapters help us to zero in on an important point addressed also in the first chapter. Although the book introduces many models, agent-based computational sociology is more than a mere repository of models and examples. Although it does not offer a coherent picture or paradigm of social inter-action yet, it can be considered as a meta-theory which provides precise preliminary foundations for theory building when social interaction is involved. Furthermore, there are social mechanisms which allow us to explain the role played by social interaction to determine social outcomes.

Obviously, only future developments will help to systematize more coherently our knowledge on social interaction and provide a comprehensive picture of the sociological foundations of human behavior. However, although incomplete, I think that for the time being, the picture depicted of agent-based computational sociology is a concrete advance for our discipline.

Having said that, ABMs are performed differently by sociologists and social sci-entists generally. This will be more easily understood as we progress through the book. Some scientists use ABMs as an extension of mathematical conventional models, that is, to complement the impossibility of finding analytic solutions to equation-based models. Some quantitative sociologists use them to bring agent interaction into statistical models, that is, to shift from 'factors to actors'. Some use them to explore the implications of empirical/experimental evidence in more complex, large-scale simulated systems. In general, many of us use them to completely substitute equation models, where agent heterogeneity and complex forms of interaction should be taken into account and no equation can fruitfully represent system behavior. Therefore, although we are all interested in explaining social outcomes in terms of social interaction, there are different approaches and different degrees of distance between conventional science and the ABM approach.

Furthermore, there is not even a common definition of an agent and those irre-ducible properties which make a computer code behave like a social agent. This type of research is still in its infancy and we should expected pluralism and diversity. This also reflects extremely sensitive definitional issues. For instance, some contributions make the difference between ABMs and equation-based models and others speculate on the minimal cognitive requirement which makes a computer code realistically behave like a human being. Some others defend the idea that rich cognitive models are needed to look at social interaction and this distinguishes their approach from reductive, physics-oriented approaches.

I must confess that as time goes by I have become skeptical about the time lost in definitional issues and I have become more catholic on this point. This is why I have not spent too much time on definitional issues in this book. The reader will not find a single word on the minimal cognitive requirements to talk about social agents, nor will he/she find extensive epistemological digressions on emergence, emergent properties, differences between first- and second-order properties, supervenience, immergence and the like.

My only interest has been to show the explanatory capacity of a model of crucial sociological puzzles by looking at agent behavior and interaction in (more or less realistic) social structures. Learned cognitive scientists could call this behavioralism. Some could consider this a rough view, but I wonder whether a model which includes equations or not, and rings ten behavioral parameters instead of three, should definitively matter more than its capacity to explain something.

Obviously, explanation requires methodology and this is the topic of the fourth chapter. It is worth noting that attention to methodological issues has recently improved and most methodological problems have been seriously tackled by the ABM community. Here, I have discussed the main methodological steps, such as the definition of research questions in ABM terms and specification of model building blocks to model reporting and publication.

I have focused especially on two crucial aspects: replication and multi-level validation. Replication is *the process of how a model is independently scrutinized by peers by re-running it*. Multi-level empirical validation is *the process by means relevant model parameters are informed by and simulation findings are evaluated against empirical data*.

In my view, one of the crucial points which makes this type of research so beneficial for sociology, is that ABMs favor inter-subjective tests. This makes finding cumulativeness a truly collective scientific enterprise and disciplines investigation by strengthening logical rigor and openness to peer scrutiny. I have insisted in many parts of this book on this point, as I see that it is a serious weakness in current sociology.

Unfortunately, as most scientists can attest, replication is seldom rewarded. On the contrary, I think that replication is crucial to defend the idea that theoretical findings should be replicable, empirically testable and generalizable. Obviously, there is a lot of work still to be done to make replication an easy, well-organized and an ordinary task in the community, but significant advance has already been made.

To underline this point, I have focused in detail on a couple of recent replication querelles. The first one was published in the *American Journal of Sociology* and dealt with residential segregation. The second one was published in *The Journal of Artificial Societies and Social Simulation* and dealt with trust and cooperation between strangers in markets. In both cases, peers replicated a previous model, discovered limitations and extended original findings. The original authors had the chance to specify important aspects of their model better and improve it. In both cases, the result was a better understanding for everyone on the particular issue at stake.

Another point is that of linking models and empirical data. This means calibrating simulation input and validating simulation output on empirical data. The twofold link is important as in sociology we do not have all-embracing theories about micro level processes and the descriptive adequacy of 'situations' where agents interact (i.e., context-specific macro constraints) is often decisive in discriminating between alternative explanations.

Therefore, the challenge is not only to replicate/generate observed statistical regularities at the macro level, but also to do it starting from empirically well-specified micro assumptions. On the one hand, the advantage here is that ABMs are data-generating tools, that is, they generate artificial data patterns which may be easily compared with real ones. On the other hand, it is always difficult to gather well-controlled and complete data for micro foundations.

To suggest ways to do this, I have listed various methods for data gathering, such as experimental, stakeholder, qualitative and quantitative approaches and provided examples of empirically calibrated and validated ABMs. Obviously, stable methodological and technical standards have not been developed yet, but these examples can provide guidelines and practices for empirically oriented sociologists.

In the last chapter, I have returned to the most important points presented both here and in the first chapter, to provide a prospective view of agent-based computational sociology. I have focused on future challenges for our community. I will outline that we cannot escape from the microscopic nature of sociology. To understand the emergence of social patterns, rather than looking only at the macroscopic scale, we need to discover behavioral and interactional details that really matter. There is a dramatic mismatch between observation scales in social systems.

Agent-based computational sociology helps us to understand that complex social puzzles are not always due to complicated agent behavior, but are the result of agent interaction based on relatively simple behavior. This can help traditional quantitative sociologists to realize that considering seriously the micro foundations does not mean looking at complicated cognitive or psychological investigations without any sociological implication.

Finally, I have added an Appendix that consists of two parts. The first aims to supply additional information to learn about or to do ABM research in sociology. I have provided a list of research centers where this type of research can be done, some associations where to meet ABM scientists, the most representative journals, where ABM research is regularly published and a brief guide to simulation tools, which can help the reader to understand where to start.

The second part includes simulation codes of some models described in the second and third chapters. I have included only examples of my work. To help the reader to practise with other examples, I have created a supporting material book web page, which is accessible at: <www.eco.unibs.it/computationalsociology>. Here, the reader will find more information and descriptions of most of the examples included in this book. I hope this will encourage young scholars to work with ABMs and follow rigorous methodological standard.

I also want to underline that each argument I have developed here has benefited considerably from discussions, opinions and suggestions with many colleagues who were kind enough to share their concerns and enthusiasm with me. Obviously, I cannot thank them all individually, but I would like at least to let them know that they have been incommensurably important for me. I acknowledge comments and suggestions on different chapter drafts or on papers related to some book chapters by Ahmadreza Asgharpour, Giangiacomo Bravo, Rosaria Conte, Peter Davis, Simone Gabbriellini, Nigel Gilbert, David Lane, Gianluca Manzo, Károly Takács, Pietro Terna and Klaus G. Troitzsch. I thank Riccardo Boero and Claudio Gandelli for their help on the simulation codes reported in the Appendix. Besides them, other colleagues have also played an important role for my adventure in this type of research. Among them, I especially thank Giancarlo Provasi who gave me my first introduction to this type of research when I was starting my PhD.

I also want to thank PhD students and young scholars with whom I have had the chance to discuss the main topics of this book over the last few years. They have been important to me and this book is primarily intended for an audience of this kind, that is, those venturing into sociology with enthusiasm and expectation for innovation. First, I would like to thank the PhD students of my annual course on social simulation here in Brescia, who have motivated me to specify any epistemological and methodological implications of this type of sociology and appreciate the benefits of combining ABM with other more traditional social science methods.

I found challenging audiences when I taught 'Complex Systems and Social Simulation' at the CEU Summer University in Budapest, July 2008, when I met a group of Dutch PhD students for the 'Advanced Course on Agent-Based Simulation', held in Utrecht, February 2011 and when I taught 'Experimentally Grounded Social Simulation' at the Second ESSA Summer School in Social Simulation, held in Guildford, July 2011. I would like to thank Laszlo Gulyas, Gyorgy Kampis, Virginia and Frank Dignum and Nigel Gilbert for inviting me.

Finally, special thanks go to Riccardo Boero, Giangiacomo Bravo and Marco Castellani, my colleagues at GECS, where we are combining experimental and ABM research. I am grateful to them for sharing objectives, passions and time, always enriching my understanding of research issues from diverse perspectives. I only hope that this book will contribute to the diffusion of our ideas and allows us to find new fellow travelers.

Finally, given that many parts of this book have been presented in the form of papers and talks at different meetings, I want to list here the most important ones: the 8th Conference of the Society for Computational Economics, Aix-en-Provence, 2002; RASTA 2002 International Workshop on Regulated Agent-Based Social Systems, Bologna, 2002; EMAEE 2003 Conference on 'The Knowledge-Based Economies. New Challenges in Methodology, Theory and Policy', Augsburg, 2003; EPOS 2004 Workshop (Epistemological Perspectives on Simulation), Koblenz, 2004; EMAEE 2007 Conference on 'Globalization, Services and Innovation: The Changing Dynamics of the Knowledge Economy', Manchester, 2007; The Fourth Conference of the European Social Simulation Association, Toulouse, 2007; The Workshop on Computational and Mathematical Approaches to Societal Transitions, Leiden, 2008; The Fifth Conference of the European Social Simulation Association, Brescia, 2008; The First ICORE Conference on Reputation, Gargonza, 2009; The International Workshop on Mechanisms and Analytical Sociology, Torino, 2009; the Sixth Conference of the European Social Simulation Association, Guildford, 2009; and the Third World Congress on Social Simulation, Kassel, 2010.

In these conferences, I have benefited tremendously from discussions with many colleagues who have indirectly or directly influenced my view on sociology, modeling and explanation. I thank them, as they made me understand what it means when we say that science is a truly collective enterprise.

Last but not least, I wish to thank the Wiley team, especially Ilaria Meliconi for her confidence in the idea of this book, Heather Kay for her support, and Richard Davies for being so patient with latecomer writers. Special thanks go to Robert Coates and Judith Gorham for revising my Italianate English and helping me to improve the readability of the text.

1

What is agent-based computational sociology all about?

There is no doubt that the last twenty years have brought radical changes to the use of computers in social research (Heise and Simmons 1985; Gilbert and Abbott 2005). In the past (and even still today), social scientists used computers to provide analytic solutions to complicated equation systems that represented a given system's structure, or more generally to estimate statistical models for data. From the 1990s onward, they started to use advanced computational techniques in an innovative way to simulate and analyze implications of agent interaction in social structures (e.g., Epstein and Axtell 1996; Axelrod 1997a; Epstein 2006; Miller and Page 2007).

Computational sociology, that is, the use of computationally intensive methods to model social phenomena, is not a recent development (Brainbridge 2007). It is a branch of sociology that has a long and, to a certain extent, venerable tradition that goes back to the 1960s. At that time, under the influence of systems theory and structural functionalism, computer simulation was used to model control and feedback mechanisms in systems, such as organizations, cities, or global populations. The idea was to simulate complicated differential equation models to predict population distribution as a function of systemic factors, such as urban traffic, migration, demographic change, or disease transmission. Inspired by Forrester's work on world dynamics (Forrester 1971) and the idea of systems theory and cybernetics, the focus was on systems and aggregates rather than on agents and behavior, and on prediction rather than understanding and explanation (Sawyer 2005).

Nevertheless, against this trend, some pioneers started to use computer simulation to investigate models of micro social processes. In the 1960s, James S. Coleman led the most active research center for computer research in sociology in the US.

Agent-Based Computational Sociology, First Edition. Flaminio Squazzoni.
© 2012 John Wiley & Sons, Ltd. Published 2012 by John Wiley & Sons, Ltd.

At Johns Hopkins University, he published some interesting contributions to plead the cause of simulation models in sociology aiming to investigate agent interaction (Coleman 1962, 1964b). Raymond Boudon also published an article on prosecutions in France with a simulation model as a key element (Davidovitch and Boudon 1964). Some years later, in his famous book on the mathematical approach to sociology, he systematically examined the similarities and differences of equation-based and computer simulation models to understand social processes from a micro–macro perspective (Boudon 1970). Ahead of their times, these leading sociologists pre-empted the agent turn of the 1990s.

Computer simulation approaches and techniques changed over time, as we will see later. From the 1990s onward, sociologists started to analyze macro social aggregates as the resultant properties of micro interaction, by explicitly modeling agents, interaction and environment (i.e., geographical space, institutional settings, and/or social structures). The growth of computational capacity applied to research, as well as its ubiquitous and distributed nature, allowed the creation and diffusion of the first agent-based model (ABM) open-source simulation platforms, easily manageable even with portable computers. This innovation in research technologies set the stage for an 'agent-based turn' in social research and helped agent-based computational sociology to materialize.

The aim of this chapter is to introduce agent-based computational sociology as *the study of social patterns by computer models of social interaction between heterogeneous agents embedded in social structures (e.g., social networks, spatial neighborhoods, or institutional scaffolds)*. The first section identifies predecessors and founding fathers. Herbert Simon, James S. Coleman, Raymond Boudon, Thomas Schelling and Mark Granovetter have been included as they pioneered and/or largely influenced this type of research. As we will see, not only is there a certain coherence between the work of these authors, but also a *fil rouge* links these studies to certain streams of sociology today that revolve around the idea of the 'generative' approach to sociological investigation. These research streams have recently been systematized under the name of 'analytical sociology', where emphasis is given to the explanation of social patterns from agent interaction and where agent-based modeling plays a pivotal role (Hedström and Swedberg 1998; Hedström 2005; Bearman and Hedström 2009; Hedström and Ylikoski 2010; Manzo 2010).

The second section illustrates the main ideas of this new type of sociology. They are as follows: (a) the primacy of models, (b) the generative approach to explanation, (c) a pragmatic approach to the micro–macro link, (d) process and change as key elements of sociological investigation, (e) a reconciliation of deduction and induction, theory and data through models, and (f) a tendency towards a trans-disciplinary/issue-oriented style of research. While ideas from (a) to (e) have application in the literature, (f) is still in the latent phase, though not less important.

The third section illustrates ABMs as the tool that has made this new type of research possible. It is worth noting that agent-based computational sociology does not totally conflate with ABMs, as the latter is used also in physics, biology and computer sciences with different purposes. Here, ABMs specifically target the properties of social behavior and interaction and addresses relevant empirical sociological puzzles. Without entering into technical detail, a comparison between ABMs and other simulation techniques is presented that examines the peculiarities of ABMs for sociological investigation. Finally, the fourth section looks at ABM classification, illustrating differences in its use in research. Certain implications are made to link theory and empirical data treated in detail in Chapter 4. Examples and attention to substantive issues will be looked at in Chapters 2 and 3.

1.1   Predecessors and fathers

Perhaps unexpectedly, the ABM approach has a venerable legacy in sociology. In common with traditional mathematical sociology, it includes the idea that formalized models can make sociology more scientific (Coleman 1964a; Fararo 1969). However, it makes no sacrifice to analytic solutions or top-down deductions. Indeed, the ABM perspective espouses a more complex view of sociological models, where (a) theory should be the result of bottom-up data exploration, and (b) models should look at nonlinear local agent interaction and global out-of-equilibrium system behavior, rather than pre-constituted structural behavior and equilibrium. It shares the idea that computational formalization can help to improve the theory building process, by revealing non-obvious mechanisms and providing for a theory test.

However, the ABM approach aims to develop sociologically rich models that mimic the properties of social behavior and interaction. Indeed, ABMs aim to understand what is taken for granted in more functionalistic, macro-oriented simulation approaches, such as system dynamics, that is, the emergence of social patterns, structures and behavior from agent interaction. This also helps us to understand under which conditions, certain social patterns might emerge in reality.

One of those who has contributed the most to this type of research, is a non-sociologist, the Nobel Prize winner, Herbert A. Simon. One of the most prominent social scientists of the last century, Simon influenced a wide range of disciplines, from artificial intelligence to organization science and psychology. One of his simplest ideas was that there is no isomorphism between the complexity that social systems show at the macro level and their complexity at the micro level. In many cases, the former is nothing more than the result of interaction between simple micro processes. Therefore, computer simulation is pivotal to simplify and model complex social systems from a micro–macro approach (e.g., Simon 1969).

Simon was also interested in understanding what he called 'poorly understood systems', that is, those in which the modeler has poor or no knowledge of the laws that govern inner systems. By suggesting the rationale for simple computer simulation models that look at these types of systems, he argued that:

> resemblance in behaviour of systems without identity of the inner systems
> is particularly feasible if the aspects in which we are interested arise out
> of the *organization* [italics in original] of the parts, independently of all
> but a few properties of the individual components (Simon 1969, p. 17).

The first lesson is that understanding the interaction mechanisms between individual components is pivotal to look at the complex behavior of a social system. The second is that by pinpointing the explanatory power of interaction, sociology can omit detailed knowledge of the behavior of each individual component, at the same time avoiding referring to supposed causal autonomy of macro social entities to understand macro system behavior. The latter should be viewed as fully shaped by organizational micro processes.

Obviously, this was not Simon's only contribution to the ABM approach in social sciences. We can mention his investigation into the foundations of human behavior and his theory on bounded rationality (Simon 1982). He influenced all ABM scientists who have tried to understand how a population of boundedly rational agents can spontaneously and endogenously give rise to patterns of collective intelligence in diverse spheres of the economy and society (e.g., Epstein and Axtell 1996).[1]

The Nobel Prize winner Thomas C. Schelling, with his pioneering work on the micro–macro link and his famous segregation model in the 1970s, has had an incommensurable influence on agent-based computational sociology. In the first pages of his influential book *Micromotives and Macrobehavior* in 1978, he illustrated the crucial challenge of understanding macro behavior from agent interaction by using this simple example:

> There are easy cases, of course, in which the aggregate is merely an ex-
> trapolation from the individual. If we know that every driver, on his own,
> turns his lights on at sundown, we can guess that from our helicopter we
> shall see all the car lights in a local area going on at about the same time.
> [...] But if most people turn their lights on when some fraction of the
> oncoming cars already have their lights on, we'll get a different picture
> from our helicopter. In the second case, drivers are responding to each
> others' behaviour and influencing each other's behaviour. People are re-
> sponding to an environment that consists of other people responding to
> *their* [italics in original] environment, which consists of people respond-
> ing to an environment of people's responses. Sometimes the dynamics
> are sequential [...]. Sometimes the dynamics are reciprocal [...]. These
> situations, in which people's behaviour or people's choices depend on

---

[1] Although not very influential in sociology, the Austrian economist, Nobel Prize winner Fredrick von Hayek was among the first to realize the importance of studying collective social properties which emerge from dispersed, decentralized and local interaction among agents (e.g., Hayek 1976). To a certain extent, he could be considered as one of the founding fathers of the contemporary complex adaptive systems theory, which has much in common with agent-based computational sociology. Indeed, complex adaptive systems theory aims to understand how decentralized and local interactions among boundedly rational and adaptive agents following simple behavior can create collective patterns which have robust, intelligent and evolving properties, such as flexibility and resilience against environmental perturbations (e.g., Anderson Arrow and Pines 1988). Although largely underestimated by sociologists, a system-environment approach might be important as it might help to enlarge the sociological attention from the individual/collective couple to the individual/collective/environment dimension and to reason in an evolutionary perspective. It is worth noting that the latter is dramatically neglected from current sociology.

the behaviour or the choices of other people, are the ones that usually don't permit any simple summation or extrapolation to the aggregates. To make that connection we usually have to look at the *system of interaction* [italics in original] between individuals and their environment [...]. And sometimes the results are surprising. Something they are not easily guessed. Sometimes the analysis is difficult. Sometimes it is inconclusive. But even inconclusive analysis can warn against jumping to conclusions about individual intentions from observations of aggregates, or jumping to conclusions about the behaviour of aggregates from what one knows or can guess about individual intentions (Schelling 1978, pp. 13–14).

The difficulty of mapping micro and macro levels when nonlinear agent interactions are involved is the premise that avoids both conflating or contrasting the various levels of social system analysis (Squazzoni 2008). This was evident in Schelling's famous segregation model, which is now a standard example in ABM literature, where the dynamics of residential mobility and segregation by race and ethnicity, that is, a long lasting pattern of many large cities in the US, were explained not as the result of racist preferences, but in terms of social influence and interaction (we will return to this model in detail in Chapter 3) (Schelling 1971, 1978). Schelling's idea of 'contingent behavior', for example, individual behavior that depends on what others do, emphasizes the relevance of studying agent interaction to understand how individual actions cause unplanned and unexpected social patterns. By looking just at the aggregate level, sociology cannot explain where these patterns come from.[2]

This was confirmed by Mark Granovetter in his contributions to understanding collective behavior in social systems during the late 1970s and early 1980s (e.g., Granovetter 1978; Granovetter and Soong 1983, 1988). Following Schelling, he contributed to current literature on 'critical mass' or 'tipping point' models of collective behavior. The latter also has hit the headlines of popular science in a couple of bestsellers (e.g., Gladwell 2001; Ball 2004).

By modeling riots in a population subjected to social influence and examining the relevance of interaction structure, Granovetter showed that, when interaction and contingent behavior matter, 'it is hazardous to infer individual dispositions from aggregate outcomes' (Granovetter 1978, p. 1425). In his view, the most important point for sociology is the understanding of 'situation-specific' aggregation processes. To put it in Granovetter's words:

By explaining paradoxical outcomes as the result of aggregation processes, threshold models take the 'strangeness' often associated with collective behaviour out of the heads of actors and put it into the dynamics

---

[2] This was also the intuition of the neglected Sakoda's checkerboard model, which was published in the same journal issue of Schelling's, but has been developed by the author in the late 1940s for his PhD dissertation, after an experience in a relocation center for Japanese minorities during World War II in the US (Sakoda 1971).

of situations. Such models may be useful in small-group settings as well as those with large numbers of actors. Their greatest promise lies in analysis of situations where many actors behave in ways contingent on one another, where there are few institutionalized precedents and little pre-existing structure [...] Providing tools for analyzing them [*these situations*] is part of the important task of linking micro to macro levels of sociological theory (Granovetter 1978, p. 1442).

The pivotal role that agent interaction plays in determining social patterns has also been investigated by two leading sociologists, James S. Coleman and Raymond Boudon. In the 1960s, Coleman significantly contributed to developing mathematical sociology (Coleman 1964a), but also worked to extend equation-based models through computer simulation. Against the functionalistic mood of the time, he argued that computer simulation could motivate an agent-based turn in sociology. He correctly predicted that this approach would contribute to 'a shift away' from social systems tradition and their 'large-scale problems of social speculation' to 'problems which can be studied by systematic research' (Coleman 1962, p. 61).

He also provided interesting examples on how to use simulation models both to compensate for the impossibility of looking at social mechanisms in sufficient detail with analytic deductive models, and to include not only quantitative but also qualitative data. In 1964, in a review on equation-based models and computer simulation, he emphasized that through analytic deduction sociologists could only mirror certain components of social interaction, by isolating simple micro processes. Given that social processes are bound up in a complex system, computer simulation would become extremely valuable to synthesize these processes into formalized models to understand their implications for system behavior (Coleman 1964b, p. 1046).

While referring to a Simmel-like case of triadic relationships in social groups, Coleman wrote that 'this example illustrates a general strategy in social simulation: to link together known micro processes in a particular structural configuration, in order to examine consequences at the level of the system' (Coleman 1964b, p. 1054). He emphasized that simulation models could be viewed as a 'bridge between individuals, upon whom most of the sociologist's observations are made, and social systems, which are his objects of interest' (Coleman 1964b, p. 1055). He concluded by prefiguring the agent-based turn: 'much of the social simulation of the future will have purposive actors in roles as its principal elements' (Coleman 1964b, p. 1059).

At the same time, Boudon worked on a simulation model to examine the prosecution rates of abandoned cases by State prosecutors in France between 1879 and 1931. This was a theoretical model aiming to find a precise statistical pattern in historical data. By anticipating one of the main advantages of computer simulation, that is, to generate empirically testable data, he indicated that the model aimed to 'verify a certain set of hypotheses on the mechanisms that were responsible for the empirically observed variations of these rates'. He said that the added value of simulation was to help to formalize models capable of generating certain patterns 'that might be compared with empirically observed statistical patterns [*my translation*]' (Davidovitch and Boudon 1964, pp. 212, 217–218). Specifically, the model was pivotal in revealing the interaction between the seriousness and frequency of crime and changes in the classification of prosecutions over time. This interaction was also responsible for the variation in the rates of abandoned cases empirically observed.

In a subsequent and more systematic contribution on computer simulation of social processes, Boudon explained similarities and differences between analytic and simulation models. Of the similarities, he highlighted the ideas of specification, simplification and reduction as cornerstones of any rigorous sociological investigation. Of the differences, he pointed out that computational methods could help sociologists to overcome the limits of analytic tractability imposed by mathematics, which penalizes disciplines like sociology that deals with complex systems.

Boudon therefore suggested that, while in some cases computational models could be mere extensions of equation-based models, they should be viewed as a completely new formalization method when systems involve complex interactions and there is no possible mathematical counterpart. In these cases, the aim is not to help deduction, but to allow for inductive observation (Boudon 1970, pp. 379–380). By relying on his experience of these models, he also suggested that by looking at interaction effects, simulation models could complete the weaknesses of statistical models in treating these important sociological aspects (Boudon 1970, p. 402).

This contribution was also important for another reason. Boudon quoted an example of a model by Breton, who examined the emergence of collaboration norms in organizational teamwork, to emphasize the powerful 'realism' of these models. By realism, he meant that these models allow sociologists to 'rule out the imprecise concept of norm internalization' and understand that social norms 'can socially dominate [. . .] simply as aggregate consequences of rational individual behavior [*my translation*]' (Boudon 1970, pp. 386–387). As we will see throughout the book, this idea of the added value of 'realism' and a methodological individualism basis are intrinsic to agent-based computational sociology.

Subsequently, Boudon launched the idea of 'generative models' in sociology to study unintended macro consequences of social behavior (Boudon 1979, 1984). In a commentary to Robert Hauser's review of Boudon's famous book on education and social inequality, Boudon depicted the generative approach by contrasting it with descriptive accounts of data, and discussed the limitations of variable-based theorizing in sociology. By using the example of Schelling's segregation model, and so defending the idea of the added value of simplified theoretical models, he wrote that 'we must go beyond the statistical relationships to explore the generative mechanism behind them' (Boudon 1976, p. 1187).

In short, all these authors highlighted one of the key ideas of agent-based computational sociology, that is, the relevance of 'generative models' capable of explaining social patterns from agent interaction, by paying due attention to micro mechanisms. This idea was first suggested by Robert K. Merton in the late 1940s, where he argued that the challenge of sociology was neither to produce broad theories of everything, nor to fill university libraries worldwide with books of detailed and fascinating empirical accounts. The challenge was rather to work with theoretical models capable of looking at causal mechanisms for well-specified empirical puzzles (Merton 1968).

This was also expressed by Coleman in 1962, when he wrote about the added value of simulation models:

> Perhaps simulation is the wrong word, for it suggests that the attempt is to mirror in detail the actual functioning of a social system. Instead, it is very different. The aim is to program into the computer certain theoretical processes, and then to see what kind of a behaviour system they generate. The aim is to put together certain processes at the individual and interpersonal level and then to see what consequences they have at the level of the larger system (Coleman 1962, p. 69).

This idea touches upon a crucial point for the use of simulation in the social sciences. The aim of a simulation model should not be to mirror the complexity of empirical reality, but to abstract certain micro social mechanisms that might be responsible for system behavior.

More recently, one of the leading social scientists who contributed to the popularization of ABMs in social sciences was Robert Axelrod. In 1981, together with the evolutionary biologist W. D. Hamilton, he published an article in *Science* where an ABM was constructed to show the key role of reciprocity for the emergence of cooperation in a population of rational self-interest agents (Axelrod and Hamilton 1981). Some years later, he published his famous ground-breaking book *The Evolution of Cooperation* (Axelrod 1984), which greatly influenced the ABM field of cooperation and social norms and showed the potential of combining experiments, game theory and computer simulation. This ABM field blossomed into a trans-disciplinary approach, receiving recognition in, for example, *Nature*, *Science* and *PNAS* (examples will be provided in Chapter 2).

After Axelrod's initial contributions, the ABM approach started to materialize in social sciences both in the US and in Europe. In the US, the establishment and success of the Santa Fe Institute in New Mexico in the late 1980s and early 1990s, launched a world-wide research program for the study of the common properties of complex systems in many fields, including social sciences. They used the first ABM open source simulation platform ever, that is, SWARM (Minar *et al.* 1996), now maintained by the Swarm Development Group (see: http://www.swarm.org/index.php/Main_Page).

SWARM was first released in 1994 by a multidisciplinary team at the Santa Fe Institute and a large trans-disciplinary community of developers/users started to form. The success of SWARM testified to the presence of a growing and vibrant community interested in ABM research also in the social sciences and opened the door to a rich ABM platform market. The books *Growing Artificial Societies: Social Science from the Bottom-Up*, by Epstein and Axtell (1996) and *The Complexity of Cooperation: Agent-Based Models of Competition and Collaboration*, by Axelrod (1997a), not to mention the proceedings of a workshop on complex systems and economics held at the Santa Fe Institute (Arthur, Durlauf and Lane 1997), gained such popularity as to spread this type of research worldwide.

At the same time in Europe, a series of foundational symposia and workshops on computer simulation in the social sciences, the first in Guildford in 1992, were crucial in creating a scientific community of ABM social scientists. Their proceedings were widely published and provided the first coherent picture of the potential ways through which ABM research could cross disciplinary barriers between social, computer and natural sciences (e.g., Gilbert and Doran 1994; Gilbert and Conte 1995; Hegselmann, Mueller and Troitzsch 1995; Conte, Hegselmann and Terna 1997). The establishment of *The Journal of Artificial Societies and Social Simulation* (*JASSS*) in 1998 was the consecration of this process. Subsequently, special issues published in other important journals testified to the growing maturity of this field.[3]

1.2   The main ideas of agent-based computational sociology

Agent-based computational sociology revolves around the following six ideas: (a) the primacy of models over grand theories and descriptive accounts; (b) the generative approach to explanation; (c) a pragmatic approach to the micro–macro link; (d) the pursuit of an unexcluded middle ground between deduction and induction, theory and data; (e) the focus on dynamics, process and change; and (f) a tendency towards a trans-disciplinary/issue-oriented style of research (Squazzoni 2010).

1.2.1   The primacy of models

A model is a simplified representation – small scale, less detailed, less complex or all of these together – of an empirical target, for example, a social structure, system or phenomenon (Gilbert and Troitzsch 2005, p. 2). Rather than studying the empirical target directly, because it is impossible or difficult, a model is built that can scale down the target, simplify it to make it more tractable or substitute it with analogical examples (e.g., the hydraulic model of an economic system or the computer model of the mind). It can have a theoretical purpose, for example, understanding macro implications of theoretical assumptions about micro processes, or a more empirical one, for example, drawing intuitions from existing raw data (Hartmann and Frigg 2006).

Epstein (2008) reported a detailed list of reasons to build models in social sciences. They are as follows (not in order of importance):

> [predict], explain, guide data collection, illuminate core dynamics, suggest dynamical analogies, discover new questions, promote a scientific habit of mind, bound (bracket) outcomes to plausible ranges, illuminate core uncertainties, offer crisis options in near-real time, demonstrate

---

[3] Here are some of the special issues devoted to ABM research in social sciences: *American Behavioral Science* 1999, *IEEE Transactions on Evolutionary Computation* 2001, *Journal of Economic Dynamics and Control* 2001 and 2004, *Computational Economics* 2001 and 2007, *Proceedings of the National Academy of Sciences* 2002, *Artificial Life* 2003, *Journal of Economic Behavior and Organization* 2004, *Journal of Public Economic Theory* 2004, *Physica A* 2005, *American Journal of Sociology* 2005, *Advances in Complex Systems* 2008, *Journal of Economics and Statistics* 2008, *Nature* 2009, *Synthese* 2009, and *Mind & Society* 2009.

tradeoffs/suggest efficiencies, challenge the robustness of prevailing theory through perturbations, expose prevailing wisdom as incompatible with available data, train practitioners, discipline the policy dialogues, educate the general public, reveal the apparently simple (complex) to be complex (simple) (Epstein 2008, 1.9).

For whatever reason, generally, models make reality more understandable in scientific terms and a significant proportion of research is carried out on them rather than on reality itself (Hartmann and Frigg 2006). They have a learning function, as scientists can learn about the target exactly because they discover features and ascertain facts by manipulating the model. In this case, the model itself becomes the 'real' object of research as it and only it can be subjected to peer scrutiny, extension, testing, and comparison.

Besides the general added value of models for science, there are also specific reasons for formalized models in sociology. By formalizing models, sociologists can discipline discussion and move the dialog out of narrative persuasion to well-founded, organized and really constructive criticism. Models are preliminary exercises of theory and maintain a tight link with empirical reality. As testified by the difficulty of comparing and testing narrative empirical cases and unformalized theoretical accounts, the added value of modeling is that it can guarantee cumulativeness of scientific findings at an inter-subjective level (Giere 1999; Manicas 2006).

This point is of paramount importance. One of the main aims of agent-based computational sociology is to shift the sociological focus from grand theories and descriptive empirical accounts to formalized models of specific social phenomena (Giere 1999; Frank 2002; Buchanan 2007). It is precision, clarity and fine-grained distinctions that are crucial to analyzing complex social phenomena, whereas there is incontrovertible proof that these properties are difficult to obtain from unformalized narrative accounts (Hedström 2005). In championing the cause of models, agent-based sociology also goes beyond the limits of mathematical sociology as it overcomes most of the drastic simplification that the latter assumes for analytic tractability (for more details, see the next section). As such, it can regain the trust of those sociologists who have been frustrated by mathematical modeling and its excessive abstraction (Squazzoni and Boero 2005).

Thinking in terms of models has other relevant advantages for sociology, some of them included in Epstein's list. First, as mentioned above, it exercises our sociological imagination to look at reality and not simply to mirror or replicate it, but to recognize abstract and essential elements. Secondly, it trains sociologists to explain through generalization, that is, seeing common properties in different empirical situations. It must be said that this is a largely and unfortunately neglected activity in our discipline, while it is fundamental for the scientific progress of any discipline. Thirdly, it prearranges sociological analyses towards empirical validation, as it is easier to empirically test model assumptions and findings than ill-structured and unformalized propositions. At the same time, it is also easier to gather interesting and appropriate data when a model guides us in this direction. Moreover, it allows us to work with artificial data where empirical data cannot be gathered for whatever reason (e.g., ethical prohibitions, time or resource constraints, or lack of sources). This is an ABM-specific added value. Finally, models can be a focal point of teams from many disciplines and so favor trans-disciplinary collaboration.

Obviously, these are general properties of formalization and modeling. But, as we will see later, the point is that a more sociologically friendly formalism definitively enters the picture with ABMs.

1.2.2   The generative approach

ABMs are a means of understanding the social mechanisms which are responsible for the macro patterns under scrutiny. The idea is that the macro behavior of social systems can be better understood bottom-up, rather than beginning with a set of variables and their predefined relations. Here lies the real uniqueness of the ABM approach compared with other approaches that investigate social patterns through the computer (Castellani and Hafferty 2009, p. 135).

As we have seen before, the idea of generative explanation is not a recent development (e.g., Boudon 1979; Barth 1981; Hedström and Swedberg 1998; Cederman 2005). It has also been the aim of certain influential sociologists who never used formalized models in their work (e.g., Elster 2007; Gambetta 2009). The point here is that ABMs allow us to put this idea into practice on a large scale and provide incomparable advantages when looking at macro implications of agent interaction, difficult to achieve both in reality and in the sociologist's imagination. Sociological imagination without strong reference to concrete models is often a poor exercise, or at best is productive only when pursued by real genius. The power of sociological imagination can be better exploited when disciplined by models that help us to dispute findings in an organized and productive way, favoring model replicability and testing. All in all, this is extremely difficult to achieve with descriptive and unformalized accounts of social behavior.

Joshua M. Epstein used the idea of the 'generative experiment' to summarize this approach as follows:

> Given some macroscopic *explanandum* [italics in original] – a regularity
> to be explained – the canonical agent-based experiment is as follows:
> Situate an initial population of autonomous heterogeneous agents in a
> relevant spatial environment; allow them to interact according to simple
> local rules, and thereby generate – or 'grow' – the macroscopic regularity
> from the bottom up. [...] In fact, this type of experiment is not new
> and, in principle, it does not necessarily involve computers. However,
> recent advances in computing, and the advent of large-scale agent-based
> computational modelling, permit a generative research program to be
> pursued with unprecedented scope and vigour (Epstein 2006, p. 7).

Suppose that we have to explain a macro pattern k_r. We build an ABM of k_r because we have proof or intuition that k_r is a complex outcome, not completely understandable either by direct observation or by analytic deduction. Suppose that

$A, B, C, \ldots$, are assumptions, micro specifications or model components that we introduce to understand k_r, as we expect that they play a role in determining k_r. They could be as follows: numbers and types of agents, behavioral rules followed by agents, the interaction structure (how agents interact) and the constraints of the macro situation where agents are embedded. Note that we could call them 'model parameters', provided that we bear in mind that they could be both quantitative (e.g., number of agents) and qualitative (e.g., rules of agent behavior).

Now, suppose that $A_1, A_2, A_3, \ldots, B_1, B_2, B_3, \ldots$, and $C_1, C_2, C_3, \ldots$, are all possible variations that the model components could take in principle. The 'generative experiment' lies in exploring which of these variations of components $A, B, C, \ldots$, generate k_a, that is, the simulated pattern that should be compared with k_r, the empirical pattern. The idea is that if A_2, C_1, D_3, N_5 allow us to generate $k_a = k_r$, then A_2, C_1, D_3, N_5 should be seen as 'sufficient generative conditions' for k_r and therefore are a generative explanation of k_r (Boero and Squazzoni 2005).

According to Epstein (2006, p. 8), *being able to generate a macro regularity of interest with an ABM* is to be taken as a necessary condition for the explanation itself. If explaining implies generating (i.e., specifying and showing the generative process through which interacting agents in a given environment combine to produce the pattern under scrutiny), then ABMs are pivotal to identify candidate explanations that can also guide empirical research. As argued in Boero and Squazzoni (2005), Squazzoni (2008), and Frank, Squazzoni and Troitzsch (2009), given the high sensitivity of social patterns to small contextual and contingent micro details, the shift from discovering *sufficient* to identifying *sufficient and necessary* generative conditions calls for the relevance of careful empirical inspection (see Chapter 4 for details). Nevertheless, although insufficient and incomplete, the capability of discovering 'candidate explanations', such as generative explanations, is a crucial step forward in itself for sociology.

It is worth noting that the generative approach is instrumental to understand complex social systems, where top-down analytic deduction is a poor guide. Complex systems are full of intertwining relationships, so that analytic decomposition does not hold. This simply means that breaking down the behavior of systems into the behavior of their parts is unfeasible as it throws away interaction (Casti 1994, 1999). As we will see, the source of 'complexity' of social systems is social interaction, so that the action of individuals does not simply aggregate at the macro level, as though individuals were isolated 'atoms' following universal and predictable behavior.

The embeddedness of individuals in social structures determines a profound nonlinearity in the aggregation processes, which makes macro outcomes extremely difficult to predict and understand, even if in principle we were aware of the behavior of individuals (which in most cases we are not). Furthermore, the intrinsic heterogeneity of individuals, in terms of behavior, information and position in social structure, implies that the law of large numbers and the focus on average behavior are inadequate to understand system behavior (Miller and Page 2007).

If top-down analytic breakdown does not hold, analytic deduction does not inform, as we do not have a strong theory about system behavior. An outlook of average behavior at the micro level for statistical properties at the macro level is a largely imprecise map. So we must take the opposite direction. This means modeling from the bottom-up to explore various micro specifications and observe their macro consequences. This is the idea behind the 'generative experiment' mentioned by Epstein (2006) and is the most important idea of agent-based computational sociology.

1.2.3   The micro–macro link[4]

The debate on micro foundations versus macro properties of social systems is the root of our discipline (e.g., Alexander *et al.* 1987; Ritzer 1990; Huber 1991; Sawyer 2005). On the one hand, many supporters of rational choice and of sociological *subjectivism* argue that explanations of social outcomes should be reduced to individual reason and meaningful action. On the other hand, structural sociologists and the advocates of social system theories argue that sociology should dissociate itself from behavioral sciences to understand the concrete ontologies of social reality (such as 'norms', 'cultures', and 'roles'), in terms of structures and their forms and functions. Accordingly, macro social properties, as well as individual actions, are understood as produced by other macro social properties. In the first approach, the role of social structures and constraints upon individual action is taken for granted. At the opposite extreme, supporters of social ontologies over-emphasize the importance of social structures, while under-representing the relevance of individual heterogeneity and action (Granovetter 1985).

The strength of these arguments can also explain the twofold and contradictory meaning that sociologists attach to the term 'emergence'. Authors such as Coleman stressed the relevance of understanding how individual actions combine to generate emergent properties at a macro social system level. Introducing the concept of 'emergence', Coleman firmly stated that 'the only action takes place at the level of individual actors, and the "system level" exists solely as emergent properties characterizing the system of action as a whole' (Coleman 1990, p. 28). This perspective is close to what epistemologists call 'weak emergence', 'epistemological emergence', or 'supervenience' to mean that macro behavior is a resultant property of micro behavior, although often the causal link is difficult to clearly identify (e.g., Bedau 1997; Silberstein and McGeever 1999; Kim 2006).

On the other hand, authors such as Archer (1995) and, more recently, Sawyer (2005), stressed that emergent social structures at a macro level can exercise causal power (and consequently can act) on individuals at a micro level. In this case, the macro social level is viewed as a 'social stratum' populated by ontological entities that are distinct from lower entities, that is, individuals. This perspective is close to what epistemologists call 'ontological emergence', 'strong emergence', or 'downward causation' (Silberstein and McGeever 1999).

It is worth noting that recently, respective positions in sociology have become less clear-cut than in the past. First of all, advocates of methodological and ontological

---

[4] This section extensively drew on Squazzoni (2008).

individualism now seem more inclined to take into account institutions and social structures as macro constraints upon individual action (Coleman 1990; Udehn 2001; Hedström 2005). Institutions, in their formal and informal/regulative and constitutive meaning, for example, the rules of the game, incentives embodied in institutional setting, or cognitive and cultural behavioral (and identity) frameworks of social actors, are all seen as the main features of the 'social situation' that simultaneously constrain and make individual action possible (e.g., Scott 1995; North 2005).

Furthermore, following Boudon and Coleman, the influence of social structure on individual behavior and in particular that of position within the interaction context, are generally acknowledged as an important explanatory factor by most supporters of methodological individualism (e.g., Boudon 1984, 1992; Coleman 1990; Hedström 2005).

Secondly, some macro sociologists seem more inclined than in the past to recognize the need to combine macro analysis and generative mechanism-based explanations (e.g., Manzo 2007). For instance, in his ambitious attempt to combine empirical research and theory, statistical macro sociology and the theory of individual action, Goldthorpe (2007, p. 16) emphasized that 'the explanation of social phenomena is sought not in terms of the functional or teleological exigencies of social systems, but rather in terms of the conduct of individuals and of its intended and unintended consequences'.

To favor this convergence and understand how micro and macro are concretely linked to determine social systems' behavior, the recourse to formalized models and ABMs is essential (Raub, Buskens and Van Assen 2011). Conversely, the debate tends to perpetuate an ontological 'chicken and egg' dispute between primacy of micro or macro levels without any concrete explanatory achievement.

In this respect, one of the main ideas of agent-based computational sociology is that ABMs can strengthen links and integrative frameworks and 'secularize' the debate between micro and macro levels. This is because it brings the debate away from a foundational and philosophical level to a more pragmatic one. The constraints and rigor imposed by ABM formalism implies that micro and macro levels, rather than being merely theoretical constructions, refer to clear-cut model-grounded concepts. Implications of micro social processes for large-scale macro patterns can be investigated and consequently understood in due detail. The same is true for micro influences of macro patterns (examples will be provided in the following chapters).

Equipped with ABMs, sociologists can therefore study the micro mechanisms and local processes that are responsible for macro patterns, as well as the impact of the latter on the former over time, so that the self-organized nature of social patterns can be subject to modeling, observation, replication and understanding. This relationship between processes at different levels, which is always difficult to empirically examine in sociology, can now be investigated in fine detail (Squazzoni 2010).

To sum up, agent-based computational sociology allows us to approach social interaction modeling as a problem of abstraction and scales (i.e., local interaction vs. global outcomes) more than a problem of ontology and categorical levels (i.e., 'individual' or 'social' primacy) (Petri 2011).

1.2.4   Process and change

One of the traditional problems of sociology is to have methods and tools to understand the evolving nature of social structures and institutions. Most sociologists acknowledge the process nature of social phenomena, but for the sake of tractability or for lack of appropriate modeling tools, they use theories and models that do not seriously reflect this belief. The long ignored German sociologist Norbert Elias (1987) brilliantly emphasized the risk of what he called 'the retreat of sociologists into the present', both for theory development and empirical research. His antidote was a 'processual perspective' capable of putting current social patterns into the appropriate space–time dimension, so as to discover the influence of historical change, dynamics and processes to understand the present.

ABMs are a crucial means of putting process, change and long-term dynamics at the very core of sociology. Thanks to their capability of reproducing, synthesizing and visualizing space–time dynamics through the computer, they allow sociologists to think of social patterns in terms of processes that emerge from agent interaction and change over time. Instead of being the consequence of fixed structures or linear variables, social patterns are the result of nonlinear interaction processes that resemble concrete social reality, where agent behavior is subjected to social influence and contributes to it. 'Rewinding the tape' and exploring different scenarios are activities that are impossible without simulation and are pivotal to study complex social dynamics in the long-term (e.g., Frank, Squazzoni and Troitzsch 2009).

With a few exceptions, unfortunately this perspective seems to be more advanced in anthropology or archeology than in sociology (e.g., Costopoulos and Lake 2010). For example, in anthropology, Lansing and Kremer (1993) modeled a Bali farming community, subject to crisis from the 1960s onwards caused by the Green Revolution. At the time, top-down planners criticized the old social structures used by farmers to manage irrigation and agriculture, in favor of mass agriculture technology progress. Using an empirically grounded ABM, they showed that sociocultural Bali structures were co-evolving with their environmental constraints into a self-organized sustainable path over time.

The simulation findings helped to show how past social structures were more adaptive than Green Revolution inspired mass agriculture technologies, so the farmers' resistance was not driven just by religious conservatism as the planners had claimed. The persuasiveness of this model and its results also helped policy makers change their approach. This is a brilliant example of how much explanatory achievement can be gained if a model looks at dynamics, evolution and social changes over time.

Another well-known example is the Anasazi model, less relevant for policy implications, but exemplary for various types of empirical data, from environmental to social factors, used to calibrate important model parameters. Developed by a trans-disciplinary team at the Santa Fe Institute, this model investigated the history of an ancient community that inhabited the Four Corners area in the American Southwest between the last century BC and 1300 AD. This disappeared from the region in a few years, without any evidence of enemy invasion or dramatic environmental catastrophes (Dean et al. 2000).

Simulation helped to rewind the tape and prove that previous claims about the relevance of environmental factors to explain the Anasazi story were false. Similarly, Berger, Nuninger and van der Leeuw (2007) built an empirically grounded model of the Middle Rhône Valley between 1000 BC and 1000 AD to study how particular sociocultural structures could explain the evolutionary resilience of these ancient social systems against environmental perturbations (see also Kohler *et al.* 2007; Varien *et al.* 2007; Wilkinson *et al.* 2007).

By examining specific mechanisms that determine the evolution of complex social structures or institutions in the long-term and using simulation to reconstruct particular histories in detail, investigation can provide evolutionary explanations and combine quantitative findings and qualitative insights (Lane *et al.* 2009).

1.2.5   The unexcluded middle

One of the main problems of sociology is that theory and empirical work are rarely mutually reinforcing or even mutually comprehensible. Robert K. Merton was among the first to emphasize the danger of excessive hiatus between theory and empiricism for sociology development (Merton 1968). The modeling attitude of ABMs can have potentially innovative consequences for this, as it can reconcile empirical evidence and theory (Squazzoni and Boero 2005).

First, ABMs allow us to pursue a kind of 'third way of doing science', which combines deduction and induction (Axelrod 1997b). Like deduction, modelers start with a rigorously specified set of assumptions regarding a system under scrutiny, but they are not intended to giving analytic proof of theorems. Rather, models generate (artificial) data suitable for analysis by induction, which help to fully understand logical implications of the assumptions, as well as to develop intuition about macro consequences of interaction processes. At the same time, in contrast to typical induction, data come from an artificial observed system rather than from direct measurement of the real world (e.g., Axelrod 1997b; Gilbert and Terna 2000).

This is important as sociologists are often compelled to investigate reality without the chance of gathering empirical data. On the other hand, by generating 'real' data, the validation of findings against empirical data (if any) is favored and the empirical data gathering process can be more productively guided. In doing this, it is also possible to empirically validate, as well as to derive theoretical implications from empirical data.

The fact that ABMs position research in this unexcluded middle between deduction and induction is shown by ways in which it has affected various social sciences, depending on the prevalence of deductive or inductive practices currently in use. In areas where mathematical formalism, abstraction and deduction are the pillars of a discipline's research style, as in economics, ABMs have been a means to bringing more empirically based hypotheses into theory, relaxing a body of highly abstracted assumptions.

In particular, ABMs have opened the possibility of introducing complexity based upon bounded rationality of agents and out-of-equilibrium dynamics (e.g., Tesfatsion and Judd 2006). In disciplines where qualitative evidence, narrative descriptions and induction form the dominant research style, as in anthropology, ABMs have increased rigor through formalism, simplifying complex narrative constructs and amplifying empirical evidence through theoretical tests (Squazzoni 2010). Given that sociology basically includes this difference within its own field, this approach could help bridge the gap between qualitative and quantitative communities in our discipline.

1.2.6   Trans-disciplinarity

ABMs have raised the possibility and even the promise of a trans-disciplinary re-configuration of the disciplinary borders between sciences (e.g., Kohler 2000). This is because models can be focal points for various experts, promoting integrative approaches where relevant aspects can be synthesized into the same model (Epstein 2008). A good example is one of the first popular models in the ABM literature, namely *Sugarscape* by Epstein and Axtell (1996). This model included agents that left pollution, died, reproduced themselves, inherited resources, shared information, traded, transmitted disease, and interacted in spatial structures. Therefore, demographic, economic and social aspects and their implications for collective behavior were jointly examined.

The original idea of 'artificial societies' that permeated some initial examples of ABMs in the social sciences in the 1990s (see Section 1.4 for details), was to view computer simulation as a means to explore uncommon connections between disciplinary fields and to favor dialog between various specialists around relevant issues (e.g., Conte, Hegselmann and Terna 1997).

This reconfiguration also revolves around the idea of 'working together' and cross-fertilizing different research methods, starting from the primacy of the issues investigated rather than from disciplinary specialties. This is important as problems in reality do not have disciplinary boundaries. In this process, ABMs are not the only method, but they have a leading role as they help to connect qualitative and quantitative findings, micro evidence and macro implications. A good example of this is the type of research done in socioecological systems and common resource management. Here, qualitative case studies, quantitative surveys, field and laboratory experiments and ABMs are linked or even jointly pursued (e.g., Poteete, Janssen and Ostrom 2010).

This process of reconfiguration is still in its infancy and disciplines will naturally tend to follow their own path. However, it could have important consequences for sociology. First, given that it focuses on broad-range issues, involving different entities, processes and levels, trans-disciplinarity increases the possibility of achieving theoretical generalization and formulating taxonomies.

For instance, in the trans-disciplinary field of cooperation (see Chapter 2), it is now possible to distinguish, compare and order explanatory mechanisms at the level of atoms, molecules, individuals, societies, and ecologies, so that researchers have started to thoroughly understand general features, as well as peculiarities that arise at any particular level. This can improve reciprocal understanding among specialists and provide a more coherent picture of the global implications of an individual phenomenon or levels of interest.

Secondly, trans-disciplinarity favors the sharing of modeling approaches, techniques and best practices in methods which can help innovation to spread. This reduces the self-reference and parochialism of disciplinary fields and is important in sociology, which is a rather conservative discipline where innovation in research technologies and methods is not always the rule. Therefore, it is reasonable to expect that it is only by sharing attitudes and methods with others, that sociologists will participate in such a truly collective enterprise.

Obviously, this aspect is still latent as such research is a recent innovation. We cannot today forecast all the epistemological and institutional consequences that the growing collaboration between specialists, who in the past were confined in their narrow particular fields, may eventually entail. However, it is already evident that the ABM perspective tends to favor this process. In fact, there is no doubt that the knowledge frontier presently revolves around intrinsically trans-disciplinary issues, such as cooperation, socioecological systems, and socially inspired computing, just to name a few, where different specialists are collaborating and share attitudes, methods and concepts on the ground.

1.3   What are ABMs?

An ABM can be defined as a 'computational method that enables a researcher to create, analyze, and experiment with models composed of agents that interact within an environment' (Gilbert 2008, p. 2). From a technical point of view, this modeling tool represents a turning point in the history of artificial intelligence and its application to social sciences.[5]

The rise of distributed artificial intelligence and the diffusion of the object-oriented programming paradigm, on which ABMs are based, started in the 1990s. This allowed researchers to model agents as separate or distinct parts of a computer program which could contain heterogeneous variables, parameters, and behavior. Agents could interact by exchanging information and via communication protocols, and can react to the environment, learn, adapt, and change rules of behavior. Modelers can therefore equip computational agents with cognitive and behavioral properties typical of human agents, while the environment (i.e., social structures and institutions) can be programmed to mimic the real social world in varying degrees of detail.

Unlike equation-based, statistical and standard simulation models, ABMs allow sociologists to: (i) achieve an ontological correspondence between the model and the real-world, since individual agents can be modeled which mimic cognitive and social characteristics of real-world actors; (ii) include agents' heterogeneity, for example, in terms of behavioral rules, information, resources, position in given social structures, whereas standard equation-based models generally assume homogenous representative agents, or no agents at all, for analytic tractability; (iii) study nonlinear

---

[5] For a technical analysis of computer simulation in the social sciences, where a comparison of different simulation tools is thoroughly developed, the best reference is Gilbert and Troitzsch (2005). For a technical analysis of ABM, see Gilbert (2008).

agent interaction (in various forms) and its (long-term) consequence at the macro level, so that macro patterns can be diachronically studied as bottom-up emergent properties from local interaction (Fararo and Hummon 2005); (iv) provide an explicit representation of the environment (i.e., geographical space, institutional rules, and/or social structures) and the constraints they impose on agents' behavior and interaction; (v) provide sophisticated visualization techniques that allow us to observe and investigate complex interaction dynamics (Epstein and Axtell 1996; Gilbert 2008).

Thanks to these properties, ABMs differ from their computer simulation forerunners such as system dynamics, microsimulation and cellular automata (e.g., Troitzsch 1997). While system dynamics looks at social system behavior as the result of interaction between social structures, microsimulation, although based on micro units, such as households or individuals, cannot look at social interaction. Finally, although similar to ABMs in many respects, cellular automata provide a too simplified picture of human behavior and social interaction. Let us look at the features of these computer simulation techniques in detail.

System dynamics was originally developed in the 1950s to help corporate managers to understand industrial processes better, and now is generally used to support policy analysis and management in the public and private sector. Although it can include nonlinear interaction, as the change of any given system variable depends upon the behavior of other variables, system dynamics starts from the assumption that the system behavior is the result of circular and time-delayed relationships between structural components, factors or variables (Randers 1980; Hanneman and Patrick 1997; Gilbert and Troitzsch 2005).

Therefore, it does not allow for modeling heterogeneous micro behavioral aspects, only interdependence and feedback among macro variables. As such, it presupposes full *ex-ante* knowledge and description of system structures, which conversely are exactly the real *explanandum* of agent-based computational sociology (Grüne-Yanoff and Weirich 2010).

Microsimulation is a modeling technique that focuses on individual units, such as people, households, vehicles or firms, which are treated as a record containing a unique identifier and a set of associated attributes. If the unit is a list of individuals, records could be relative to age, sex, marital and employment status and are derived from empirical surveys or datasets. The modeler assumes certain deterministic transition probabilities that change the state and behavior of each model unit. This might be a change in taxation or stochastic processes that predict the probability of marrying. The purpose is to estimate the impact of these transition probabilities on certain aggregate variables of interest. Although it includes agent heterogeneity, at least in terms of distribution parameters (but not in terms of behavior), microsimulation does not include interaction between units, and consequently cannot provide insight into social interaction (Gilbert and Troitzsch 2005).

Cellular automata are used in a variety of disciplines to model local interaction between units and observe macro implications. They consist of a regular grid of cells, each in one of a finite number of states, such as 'on' and 'off', changing states over time according to the states of their neighboring cells. They have many overlapping properties with ABMs, but reducing the problem of interaction between dispersed micro entities to a single homogenous parameter. The idea of synchronous updating of agent behavior is a poor approximation to understanding complex social interaction (Hegselmann 1996; Troitzsch, 1997, 2009; Gilbert and Troitzsch 2005).

This being said, it will not surprise the reader that sociologists have found ABMs to be a suitable modeling tool to look at the emergence of social patterns from agent interaction in complex social systems (Gilbert 1996). Nevertheless, there is not yet any general consensus on a common way of using ABMs in sociology, or generally in all social sciences.

We can ideally identify two approaches, which have different implications for the relationships between ABMs and conventional analytic research (Axtell 1999). A first group of researchers use ABMs to support and complement analytic models. The aim here is to exploit computational power to extend deductive analysis where certain fixed close solutions are possible *in principle* and *de facto*, but impossible or very hard to find via differential equation systems. As such, ABMs have been conceived as an extension of math models, with object-oriented programming languages used to reproduce or translate equation-based objects.

A second group of researchers use ABMs to completely substitute analytic models, when these do not apply. In this case, object oriented programming languages and their logic are used to model a system of autonomous and heterogeneous agents (Liebrand 1998), where the macro system behavior is not known in advance, and no fixed close and equilibrium solutions are attainable. It is by exploiting the logic and power of these programming languages and by simulating the model, that behavior of the system can be concretely observed and understood (Bedau 1997). In this way, this approach exploits at best the isomorphism between the language of ABMs (i.e., object-oriented, based on logic, instructions and rules) and the language in which most sociological theory is expressed (e.g., Gilbert and Terna 2000).

As we will see, these two ideal-typical approaches coexist in agent-based computational sociology and this makes clear-cut technical distinctions between models a poor guide to understanding the evolution of this field and its long-term potential. The first approach lends itself more to generalization and is often associated with conventional theoretical frameworks, such as game theory. Therefore, ABM sociologists here come closer to conventional formalized science.

The second is more suitable to build sophisticated and empirically grounded models, where the level of empirical details of agent heterogeneity of behavior is more important. ABM sociologists here come closer to empirical social scientists. Given the relative novelty of the ABM approach in sociology, it is reasonable to expect that these differences will not diminish in the future. Perhaps, this could also be beneficial as sociology will continue to be a strongly diversified discipline called to investigate phenomena with different approaches, methods, and levels of detail.

1.4   A classification of ABM use in social research

In the perspective of the model's purpose and the link between model and empirical reality, we can distinguish five types of ABMs in social research (see Table 1.1):

Table 1.1   A map of ABM use in sociology.

	Synthetic models		Analytical models		Applied models
	Artificial societies	*Abstract models*	*Middle-range models*	*Case-based models*	*Applied simulation*
Definition	*In-silico* social system surrogates	Theoretical models on general social phenomena	Theoretical models with a well-specified explanatory empirical range that refers to a specific class of empirical phenomena	Models on (space–time) well-circumscribed empirical phenomena	Replication of a given real system with the due detail
Purposes	Synthesizing components of social life realistically so as to explore intuitions on important aspects of the evolution of social behavior and structures that cannot be studied empirically or experimentally	Theory building and development through models that do not reflect any concrete and specific empirical instance	Improving knowledge on differences and similarities between different empirical instances of a specific class of empirical phenomena Favoring comparison between empirical cases for theory building on specific empirical puzzles	Achieving a fine grained representation of the systems under scrutiny Appreciating complexity of social systems	Obtaining knowledge on a given system's functioning to solve problems, assist planners and decision makers, or improve the knowledge of agents involved about the system's behavior and the consequences of their decision

(Continued)

Table 1.1 A map of ABM use in sociology. (Continued)

	Synthetic models		Analytical models		Applied models
	Artificial societies	*Abstract models*	*Middle-range models*	*Case-based models*	*Applied simulation*
Positive conse-quences	New insights might be incorporated/tested in more precise studies. Favoring new connections between specialized knowledge might help a big picture view on social puzzles	Findings' generalization. Revealing non-obvious properties of social systems. Exploring explanatory hypotheses. Providing theoretical frameworks for empirical studies	Strengthening the link of theory and empirical evidence. Progressively develop and coherently articulate theoretical explanations about well-specified empirical puzzles	Relevant and illustrative case studies can provide intuitions for theory building that might be extended. Providing examples for middle-range theories	Promoting research/action methods. Improving the learning of real agents. Adjusting pre-existing theories through stakeholders' involvement
Critical points	Difficult to transform results into empirically testable findings	Easy to lose sight of real empirical *explanandi*	Difficult to generalize findings and to empirically test them against singular cases	Theoretical generalization	Theoretical generalization

artificial societies, *abstract models*, *middle-range models*, *case-based models*, and *applied simulations*. Abstract models, middle-range models, and case-based models are all examples of an analytical use of ABMs, in order to shed light on well-specified social phenomena (although at a different level of empirical detail and theoretical generalization). Artificial societies have more to do with a 'synthetic' and explorative approach to computer simulation, and applied simulation with a research/action approach.

Before going into the details of each type of model, it is worth noting that, in order to provide a map of ABM use in sociology, we will not focus on the relationships between different types of model. By providing the example of fish market models, in Boero and Squazzoni (2005), we have suggested that the different analytical use of ABMs should be viewed as 'types in a continuum'. This has more to do with general epistemological problems of model generalization and validation that are not relevant here (see Chapter 4 for details).

Another important point to mention is that, obviously, not all these types have been equally explored, as analytic use is dominant in sociology. Moreover, this does not disqualify the added value of each type of model and its potential for the development of our discipline.

Artificial societies are *in-silico* social system surrogates. Here, the modeler's aim is to recreate forms of social life realistically with the computer so as to investigate social phenomena which cannot be looked at in empirical or experimental research for various reasons, for example, ethical/time/budget constraints or absence of data. As such, these types of models do not have precise empirical puzzles to explain or empirical data to look at. They are explorations on surrogates of real social systems. Creating a surrogate means synthesizing basic components of social life by following the original idea of 'artificial life' research (e.g., Langton 1997): *in-silico* systems can help to explore intuitions on important aspects of the evolution of social behavior in real systems.

These models are therefore intrinsically trans-disciplinary as they include aspects that usually pertain to different fields and disciplines, such as demography, linguistics, sociology, economics, environmental and cognitive sciences (e.g., the influence of linguistics on this type of research in Cangelosi and Parisi 2002). At present, this type of research has been poorly developed in social sciences (an exception is Gilbert *et al.* 2006). However, it is important as, by connecting previously unrelated specialized knowledge, it can give the big picture, which could help to give new perspectives for more precise studies. Furthermore, it can provide 'what-if' scenarios which might reveal non-obvious features of reality.

Abstract models focus on social phenomena of a general range. They are neither fine-grained representations of circumscribed empirical phenomena, nor models of specific classes of empirical phenomena. They aim to support theory building and development, generalization being one of their main features. According to Carley (2002), if case-based models are 'veridicality' based, abstractions are 'transparency' based, as they aim to abstract details away under Occam's razor for simplicity which favors inter-subjective scrutiny. As we will see, by working with abstract models, modelers can discover non-obvious properties of social interaction and also provide theoretical frameworks which can be used for empirical study.

Middle-range models are empirically grounded theoretical models intended to investigate specific social mechanisms that account for a variety of empirical phenomena that share common features. They can be based on stylized facts or direct empirical evidence. In another work, we used the concept of 'typifications' to mean that these are models in a Weberian sense, namely heuristic models which allow us to understand certain social mechanisms that operate within a specific class of empirical phenomena, for example, innovation in biotechnology clusters, common resource management in local communities or institutional settings in fish markets (Boero and Squazzoni 2005).[6]

Thanks to their heuristic and pragmatic value, these models should not fully correspond to empirical reality, which is the target of their explanation (Willer and Webster 1970), as they are not designed to represent all possible empirical instances of the class itself. Therefore, qualities which are important for case-based models, such as accuracy, precision, and veridicality, are less important in this case.

According to Weberian 'ideal type', these models synthesize 'a great many diffuse, discrete, more or less present and occasionally absent *concrete individual* phenomena, which are arranged according to those one-sidedly emphasized viewpoints into a unified *analytical* construct' (Weber 1904). The principle is that the further these models are from the empirical instances which the class refer to, the stronger their heuristic value.

Here we call them middle-range models to suggest their Mertonian function, as they point to well-specified explanatory ranges or objectives, are located between abstract models and thin empirical accounts, tend to create a bridge between theory and empirical analyses, and favor the systematization of the theoretical findings in specific empirical fields.

They help to improve understanding of differences and similarities between empirical instances of a common class of phenomena (e.g., Hedström and Udehn 2009). Merton (1968) argued that these types of models are important both to develop well-specified theories to derive testable findings, and to develop and articulate theoretical explanations from the ground up.

Case-based models have an empirical space–time circumscribed target domain. This is because the phenomenon under scrutiny is characterized by idiosyncratic and individual features, that is, what Max Weber called 'a historical individual' (Weber 1904). The aim of the modeler is to achieve fine grained knowledge of the empirical situation, with accuracy, precision, and reliability. As Ragin (1987) argued, case-based models are aimed at 'appreciating complexity' rather than

---

[6] As Coser stressed (Coser 1977), there are at least three kinds of 'ideal types' in the Weberian sense. The first is historical routed ideal types, such as the well known cases of 'protestant ethics' or 'capitalism'. The second one refers to abstract concepts of social reality, such as 'bureaucracy', while the third one refers to a rationalized typology of social action. The latter is the case of economic theory and rational choice theory. These are different possible meanings of the term 'ideal type'. In our view, the first two meanings refer to heuristic theoretical constructs which aim to understand empirical reality, while the third one refers to 'pure' theoretical (as well as normative) purposes. Such a redundancy in the meaning of the term has been strongly criticized. According to our classification, middle-range models include only the first two meanings, while the third one refers to what we call abstract models.

'achieving generality'. Certain methodological traditions in sociology, such as ethnomethodology, over-emphasized the difference between theoretical models and 'a-theoretical descriptions', for example, where investigations try to be subjective and express the direct experience of agents. It is obvious that case-based models cannot be conceived as 'a-theoretical' models. Indeed, they are built upon pre-constituted theoretical hypotheses and often exploit general modeling frameworks. Fragments of theoretical findings or well-known theories are often used both to approach the empirical puzzle and to build the model.

There is no doubt that, following Weber (1904), a case-based model sometimes allows us to say nothing more than a 'particular story'. However, it is also true that its relevance, as well as its possibility, strongly depends on its relationship to a theoretical framework. This means that cases in science are mostly nothing but instances of a broader class of phenomena, for example, part of a middle-range theory. In order to generalize a local explanation, case-based findings have to be extended to other similar phenomena and abstracted at a more general theoretical level, for example, by being compared with, or contributing to a middle-range model.

For instance, returning to the example of the Anasazi model mentioned above, it is worth noting that by reconstructing the particular history of the ancient population who inhabited the Four Corners, the findings helped to say something about the historical and environmental problems encountered by similar populations during similar historical periods. Therefore, relevant and illustrative case studies can provide insights for theory building. For this purpose, different standard methods can be used to generalize case studies towards middle-range theories (e.g., King, Verba and Keohane 1994; George and Bennett 2004).

Last but not least, *applied simulations* are replications of given real systems with sufficient detail to obtain knowledge on how to solve important practical problems, assist planners and decision makers, support re-engineering options, in the case of organizations, or improve the knowledge and reflexivity of individuals involved in real systems.

Here, analysts build *ad hoc* models that should map real systems as closely as possible, as policy and re-engineering conclusions have to be customized to concrete situations. Largely explored in applied social and environmental sciences, as well as in management and organization sciences, these models promote a research/action method, improve real agent learning and in some cases help to adjust pre-existing theories through stakeholder involvement (e.g., Squazzoni and Boero 2010). Moreover, they can contribute to helping people to appreciate the direct contribution of scientific investigation in solving real problems.

Finally, it is worth noting that recently, other authors have suggested classifications similar to ours. Grüne-Yanoff and Weirich (2010) have suggested a similar analytical use of ABMs. They distinguished between 'full explanations', when models are claimed to explain concrete empirical phenomena (e.g., our case-based models), 'partial explanations', when typification of empirical phenomena is involved (e.g., our middle-range models), and 'potential explanations' to mean theoretical abstractions with large scale explanatory domain (e.g., our abstract models). As in our case, this classification tried to connect specificities of the model's target and of the explanation.

In the same way, Gilbert (2008) suggested distinguishing between 'abstract', 'middle-range', and 'facsimile' models.

To conclude, each type of model has its own positive peculiarities and critical problems. *Artificial societies* can support exploration about difficult-to-observe sociological puzzles, promote counterfactual thinking and overcome disciplinary barriers. Unfortunately, it is hard to transform their findings into something empirically testable. *Abstract models* are of paramount importance for the progress of science, but abstract research can easily lose sight of empirically relevant aspects. *Middle-range models* can do a great deal to connect evidence and theory and to focus on well-specified social mechanisms. However, both their empirical validation in single important cases and their theoretical generalization are extremely challenging to achieve. *Case-based models* might help to refine the validity domain of general theories and provide histories that might inspire theory building, but their theoretical generalization requires an enormous and well-organized collection of evidence, not always at hand. Finally, *applied simulations* might help to fill the gap between representation and reality and to promote customized solutions to challenging social problems. Unfortunately, it is generally hard to translate their findings into scientific investigations.

References

Alexander, J.C., Giesen, B., Münch, R., and Smelser, N.J. (eds) (1987) *The Micro-Macro Link*, University of California Press, Berkeley.

Anderson, P.W., Arrow, K.J., and Pines, D. (eds) (1988) *The Economy as an Evolving Complex System*, SFI Studies in the Sciences of Complexity, Addison-Wesley, Reading, MA.

Archer, M.S. (1995) *Realist Social Theory: The Morphogenetic Approach*, Cambridge University Press, New York.

Arthur, W.B., Durlauf, S.N., and Lane, D.A. (eds) (1997) *The Economy as an Evolving Complex System II*, Addison-Wesley, Reading, MA.

Axelrod, R. (1984) *Evolution of Cooperation*, Basic Books, New York.

Axelrod, R. (1997a) *The Complexity of Cooperation: Agent-Based Models of Competition and Collaboration*, Princeton University Press, Princeton.

Axelrod, R. (1997b) Advancing the art of simulation in the social sciences. *Complexity*, **3**(2), 16–22.

Axelrod, R. and Hamilton, W.D. (1981) The evolution of cooperation. *Science*, **211**, 1390–1396.

Axtell, R. (1999) Why agents? On the varied motivations for agent-based computing in the social sciences, in *Proceedings of the Agent 1999 Workshop on Simulation: Applications, Models, and Tools* (eds C.M. Macal and D.L. Sallach), Argonne National Laboratory Report, Chicago, pp. 3–24.

Ball, P. (2004) *Critical Mass. How One Thing Leads to Another*, Arrow Books, London.

Barth, F. (1981) *Process and Form in Social Life: Selected Essays of Fredrik Barth*, Routledge & Kegan Paul, London.

Bearman, P. and Hedström, P. (eds) (2009) *The Oxford Handbook of Analytical Sociology*, Oxford University Press, Oxford.

Bedau, M.A. (1997) Weak emergence. *Philosophical Perspectives*, **11**, 375–399.

Berger, J.-F., Nuninger, L., and van der Leeuw, S. (2007) Modeling the role of resilience in socioenvironmental co-evolution. The Middle Rhône Valley between 1000 BC and AD 1000, in *The Model-Based Archaeology of Socionatural Systems* (eds T.A. Kohler and S. van der Leeuw), SAR Press, Santa Fe, NM, pp. 41–59.

Boero, R. and Squazzoni, F. (2005) Does the empirical embeddedness matter? Methodological issues on agent-based models for analytical social science. *Journal of Artificial Societies and Social Simulation*, **8**(4), accessible at: http://jasss.soc.surrey.ac.uk/8/4/6.html.

Boudon, R. (1976) Comment on Hauser's review of *Education, Opportunity, and Social Inequality*. *American Journal of Sociology*, **81**, 1175–1187.

Boudon, R. (1970) *L'analyse Mathématiques des Faits Sociaux*, 2nd edn, Plon, Paris.

Boudon, R. (1979) Generative models as a research strategy, in *Qualitative and Quantitative Social Research: Papers in Honor of Paul F. Lazarfield* (eds R.K. Merton, J.S. Coleman, and P.H. Rossi), The Free Press, New York, pp. 51–64.

Boudon, R. (1984) *La place du Désordre. Critiques des Théories du Changement Social*, Presses Universitaires de France, Paris.

Boudon, R. (1992) Action, in *Traité de Sociologie* (ed. R. Boudon), Presses Universitaires de France, Paris, pp. 21–55.

Brainbridge, W.S. (2007) Computational sociology, in *Blackwell Encyclopaedia of Sociology* (ed. G. Ritzer), Blackwell Reference Online.

Buchanan, M. (2007) *The Social Atom. Why the Rich Get Richer, Cheaters Get Caught, and Your Neighbor Usually Looks Like You*, Bloomsbury, New York.

Cangelosi, A. and Parisi, D. (2002) *Simulating the Evolution of Language*, Springer, London.

Carley, K.M. (2002) Simulating society: the tension between transparency and veridicality, in *Proceedings of the Agent 2002 Conference on Social Agents: Ecology, Exchange and Evolution* (eds C. Macal and D. Sallach), Argonne National Laboratory, Arbonne, IL, pp. 103–114.

Castellani, B. and Hafferty, F.W. (2009) *Sociology and Complexity Science. A New Field of Inquiry*, Springer-Verlag, Berlin Heidelberg.

Casti, J. (1994) *Complexification: Explaining a Paradoxical World through the Science of Surprise*, John Wiley & Sons, Ltd, New York.

Casti, J. (1999) The computer as a laboratory: toward a theory of complex, adaptive systems. *Complexity*, **4**(5), 12–14.

Cederman, L.-E. (2005) Computational models of social forms: advancing generative process theory. *American Journal of Sociology*, **110**(4), 864–893.

Coleman, J.S. (1962) Analysis of social structures and simulation of social processes with electronic computers, in *Simulation in Social Science* (ed. H. Guetzkow), Prentice Hall, Englewood Cliffs, NJ, pp. 63–69.

Coleman, J.S. (1964a) *Introduction to Mathematical Sociology*, MacMillan Publishing Co., New York.

Coleman, J.S. (1964b) Mathematical models and computer simulation, in *Handbook of Modern Sociology* (ed. R.E.L. Faris), Rand McNally and Company, Chicago, pp. 1027–1062.

Coleman, J.S. (1990) *Foundations of Social Theory*, The Belknap Press of Harvard University Press, Cambridge, MA.

Conte, R., Hegselmann, R., and Terna, P. (eds) (1997) *Simulating Social Phenomena*, Springer, Berlin Heidelberg.

Coser, L.A. (1977) *Masters of Sociological Thought: Ideas in Historical and Social Context*, Harcourt Brace Jovanovich, New York.

Costopoulos, A. and Lake, M.W. (eds) (2010) *Simulating Change: Archaeology into the Twenty-First Century*, The University of Utah Press, Salt Lake City.

Davidovitch, A. and Boudon, R. (1964) Les mécanismes sociaux des abandons de poursuites: Analyse expérimentale par simulation. *L'année sociologique*, **3**, 111–244.

Dean, J.S., Gumerman, G.J., Epstein, J.M., *et al.* (2000) Understanding Anasazi culture change through agent-based modeling, in *Dynamics in Human and Primate Societies: Agent-Based Modeling of Social and Spatial Processes* (eds T.A. Kohler and J.G. Gumerman), Oxford University Press, New York, pp. 179–205.

Elias, N. (1987) The retreat of sociologists into the present. *Theory, Culture and Society*, **4**(2), 223–247.

Elster, J. (2007) *Explaining Social Behavior: More Nuts and Bolts for the Social Sciences*, Cambridge University Press, New York.

Epstein, J.M. (2006) *Generative Social Science. Studies in Agent-Based Computational Modeling*, Princeton University Press, Princeton.

Epstein, J.M. (2008) Why model? *Journal of Artificial Societies and Social Simulation*, **11**(4), accessible at: jasss.soc.surrey.ac.uk/11/4/12.html.

Epstein, J.M. and Axtell, R. (1996) *Growing Artificial Societies. Social Science from the Bottom Up*, The MIT Press, Cambridge, MA.

Fararo, T.J. (1969) The nature of mathematical sociology. *Social Research*, **36**, 75–92.

Fararo, T.J. and Hummon, N.P. (2005) The Emergence of Computational Sociology. *Journal of Mathematical Sociology*, **20**(2–3), 79–87.

Forrester, J.W. (1971) *World's Dynamics*, Wright-Allen Press, Cambridge, MA.

Frank, R. (2002) *The Explanatory Power of Models. Bridging the Gap between Empirical and Theoretical Research in the Social Sciences*, Kluwer Academic Publishers, Dordrecht.

Frank, U., Squazzoni, F. and Troitzsch, K.G. (2009) EPOS-Epistemological perspectives on simulation: an introduction, in *Epistemological Aspects of Computer Simulation in the Social Sciences* (ed. F. Squazzoni), Springer-Verlag, Berlin Heidelberg, pp. 1–11.

Gambetta, D. (2009) *Were They Pushed or Did They Jump?. Individual Decision Mechanisms in Education*, Cambridge University Press, New York.

George, A.L. and Bennett, A. (2004) *Case-Studies and Theory Development in the Social Sciences*, The MIT Press, Cambridge, MA.

Giere, R.G. (1999) *Science Without Laws*, University of Chicago Press, Chicago.

Gilbert, N. (1996) Holism, individualism and emergent properties. An approach from the perspective of simulation, in *Modelling and Simulation in the Social Sciences from the Philosophy Point of View* (eds R. Hegselmann, U. Mueller, and K.G. Troitzsch), Kluwer Academic Publishers, Dordrecht, pp. 1–27.

Gilbert, N. (2008) *Agent-Based Models*, Sage Publications, London.

Gilbert, N. and Abbott, A. (2005) Introduction. *American Journal of Sociology*, **110**(4), 859–863.

Gilbert, N. and Conte, R. (eds) (1995) *Artificial Societies: The Computer Simulation of Social Life*, UCL Press, London.

Gilbert, N. and Doran, J. (eds) (1994) *Simulating Societies: The Computer Simulation of Social Phenomena*, UCL Press, London.

Gilbert, N. and Terna, P. (2000) How to build and use agent-based models in social science. *Mind and Society*, **1**, 57–72.

Gilbert, N. and Troitzsch, K.G. (2005) *Simulation for the Social Scientist*, 2nd edn, Open University Press, Maidenhead.

Gilbert, N., den Besten, M., Bontovics, A., *et al.* (2006) Emerging artificial societies through learning. *Journal of Artificial Societies and Social Simulation*, **9**(2), accessible at: http://jasss.soc.surrey.ac.uk/9/2/9.html.

Gladwell, M. (2001) *Tipping Point. How Little Things Can Make a Big Difference*, Abacus, London.

Goldthorpe, J.H. (2007) *On Sociology. Volume One: Critique and Program*, Stanford University Press, Stanford.

Granovetter, M. (1978) Threshold models of collective behavior. *American Journal of Sociology*, **83**(6), 1420–1443.

Granovetter, M. (1985) Economic action and social structure: the problem of embeddedness. *American Journal of Sociology*, **91**, 481–510.

Granovetter, M. and Soong, R. (1983) Threshold models of diffusion and collective behavior. *Journal of Mathematical Sociology*, **9**, 165–179.

Granovetter, M. and Soong, R. (1988) Threshold models of collective behavior: Chinese restaurants, residential segregation, and the spiral of silence. *Sociological Methodology*, **18**, 69–104.

Grüne-Yanoff, T. and Weirich, P. (2010) The philosophy and epistemology of simulation: a review. *Simulation & Gaming*, **41**(1), 20–50.

Hanneman, P. and Patrick, S. (1997) On the uses of computer-assisted simulation modelling in the social sciences. *Sociological Research Online*, **2**(2), accessible at: www.socresonline.org.uk/2/2/5.html.

Hartmann, S. and Frigg, R. (2006) Models in science, in *The Stanford Encyclopedia of Philosophy* (ed. E.N. Zalta), Stanford University, Stanford, accessible at: http://plato.stanford.edu/entries/models-science/.

Hayek von, F. (1976) The New Confusion about Planning. *The Morgan. Guarantee Survey*, January, pp. 4–13, reprinted in *New Studies in Philosophy, Politics, Economics and the History of Ideas*, **232**, 236 [1978].

Hedström, P. (2005) *Dissecting the Social. On the Principles of Analytical Sociology*, Cambridge University Press, Cambridge, MA.

Hedström, P. and Swedberg, R. (eds) (1998) *Social Mechanisms. An Analytical Approach to Social Theory*, Cambridge University Press, Cambridge.

Hedström, P. and Udehn, L. (2009) Analytical sociology and theories of the middle range, in *The Oxford Handbook of Analytical Sociology* (eds P. Bearman and P. Hedström), Oxford University Press, Oxford, pp. 25–47.

Hedström, P. and Ylikoski, P. (2010) Causal mechanisms in the social sciences. *Annual Review of Sociology*, **36**, 49–67.

Hegselmann, R. (1996) Cellular automata in the social sciences: perspectives, restrictions, and artefacts, in *Modelling and Simulation in the Social Sciences from the Philosophy Point of*

View (eds R. Hegselmann, U. Mueller, and K.G. Troitzsch), Kluwer Academic Publishers, Dordrecht, pp. 209–233.

Hegselmann, R., Mueller, U. and Troitzsch, K.G. (eds) (1996) *Modelling and Simulation in the Social Sciences from the Philosophy Point of View*, Kluwer Academic Publishers, Dordrecht.

Heise, D.R. and Simmons, R.G. (1985) Some computer-based developments in sociology. *Science*, **228**, 428–433.

Huber, J. (ed.) (1991) *Macro-Micro Linkages in Sociology*, Sage, London.

Kim, J. (2006) Emergence: core ideas and issues. *Synthese*, **151**, 547–559.

King, G., Verba, S., and Keohane, R.O. (1994) *Designing Social Inquiry: Scientific Inference in Qualitative Research*, Princeton University Press, Princeton.

Kohler, T.A. (2000) Putting social sciences together again: an introduction to the volume, in *Dynamics in Human and Primate Societies: Agent-Based Modeling of Social and Spatial Processes* (eds T.A. Kohler and J.G. Gumerman), Oxford University Press, New York, pp. 1–18.

Kohler, T.A., Johnson, C.D., Varien, M., *et al.* (2007) Settlement ecodynamics in the prehispanic Central Mesa Verde region, in *The Model-Based Archaeology of Socionatural Systems* (eds T.A. Kohler and S. van der Leeuw), SAR Press, Santa Fe, NM, pp. 61–104.

Lane, D., Denise, P., van der Leeuw, S.E., and West, G. (eds) (2009) *Complexity Perspectives in Innovation and Social Change*, Springer-Verlag, Berlin.

Langton, C.G. (ed.) (1997) *Artificial Life. An Overview*, The MIT Press, Cambridge, MA.

Lansing, J.S. and Kremer, J.N. (1993) Emergent properties of Balinese water temple networks: coadaptation on a rugged fitness landscape. *American Anthropologist*, **95**(1), 97–114.

Liebrand, W.B.F. (1998) Computer modelling and the analysis of complex human behavior: retrospect and prospect, in *Computer Modeling of Social Processes* (eds W.B.F. Liebrand, A. Nowak, and R. Hegselmann), UCL Press, London, pp. 1–14.

Manicas, P. (2006) *A Realist Philosophy of Social Science: Explanation and Understanding*, Cambridge University Press, Cambridge.

Manzo, G. (2007) Le modèle du choix éducatif interdependant. Des mécanismes théoriques aux données empiriques françaises et italiennes. *Archives Européennes de Sociologie*, **48**, 3–53.

Manzo, G. (2010) Analytical sociology and its critics. *European Journal of Sociology*, **51**(1), 129–170.

Merton, R.K. (1968) *Social Theory and Social Structure*, The Free Press, New York.

Miller, J.H. and Page, S.E. (2007) *Complex Adaptive System. An Introduction to Computational Models of Social Life*, Princeton University Press, Princeton.

Minar, N., Burkhart, R., Langont, C., and Askenazi, M. (1996) The Swarm Simulation System: A Toolkit for Building Multi-Agent Simulations. Santa Fe Institute, NM, accessible at: http://www.santafe.edu/media/workingpapers/96–06-042.pdf.

North, D.C. (2005) *Understanding the Process of Economic Change*, Princeton University Press, Princeton.

Petri, Y. (2011) Micro, macro and mechanisms, in *The Oxford Handbook of Philosophy of the Social Sciences* (ed. H. Kincaid), Oxford University Press, New York.

Poteete, A.R., Janssen, M.A., and Ostrom, E. (eds) (2010) *Working Together: Collective Action, the Commons, and Multiple Methods in Practice*, Princeton University Press, Princeton.

Ragin, C.C. (1987) *The Comparative Method: Moving Beyond Qualitative and Quantitative Strategies*, University of California Press, Berkeley.

Randers, J. (1980) *Elements of the System Dynamics Method*, The MIT Press, Cambridge, MA.

Raub, W., Buskens, V., and Van Assen, M.A.L.M. (2011) Micro-macro links and microfoundations in sociology. *Journal of Mathematical Sociology*, **35**, 1–25.

Ritzer, G. (1990) Micro-macro linkage in sociological theory: applying a metatheoretical tool, in *Frontiers of Social Theory. The New Syntheses* (ed. G. Ritzer), Columbia University Press, New York, pp. 347–370.

Sakoda, J.M. (1971) The checkerboard model of social interaction. *Journal of Mathematical Sociology*, **1**(1), 119–132.

Sawyer, R.K. (2005) *Social Emergence: Societies as Complex Systems*, Cambridge University Press, Cambridge, MA.

Schelling, T. (1971) Dynamic models of segregation. *Journal of Mathematical Sociology*, **1**, 143–186.

Schelling, T. (1978) *Micromotives and Macrobehavior*, W. W. Norton, New York.

Scott, R.W. (1995) *Institutions and Organizations*, Sage, London.

Silberstein, M. and McGeever, J. (1999) The search for ontological emergence. *The Philosophical Quarterly*, **49**, 182–200.

Simon, H. (1969) *The Sciences of the Artificial*, The MIT Press, Cambridge, MA.

Simon, H. (1982) *Models of Bounded Rationality, Volumes 1 and 2*, The MIT Press, Cambridge, MA.

Squazzoni, F. (2008) The micro-macro link in social simulation. *Sociologica*, 2(1), doi: 10.2383/26578, accessible at: http://www.sociologica.mulino.it/journal/article/index/Article/Journal:ARTICLE:179.

Squazzoni, F. (2010) The impact of agent-based models in the social sciences after 15 years of incursions. *History of Economic Ideas*, **XVIII**(2), 197–233.

Squazzoni, F. and Boero, R. (2005) Towards an agent-based computational sociology: good reasons to strengthen cross-fertilization between complexity and sociology, in *Advances in Sociology Research. Volume II* (ed. L.M. Stoneham), Nova Science Publishers, New York, pp. 103–133.

Squazzoni, F. and Boero, R. (2010) Complexity-friendly policy modelling, in *Innovation in Complex Social Systems* (ed. P. Arhweiler), Routledge, London, pp. 290–299.

Tesfatsion, L. and Judd, K.L. (eds) (2006) *Handbook of Computational Economics. Agent-Based Computational Economics. Volume II*, North Holland, Amsterdam.

Troitzsch, K.G. (1997) Social science simulation: origins, prospects, purposes, in *Simulating Social Phenomena* (eds R. Conte, R. Hegselmann and P. Terna), Springer, Berlin Heidelberg, pp. 41–54.

Troitzsch, K.G. (2009) Multi-Agent Systems and Simulation: A Survey from an Application Perspective, in *Multi-Agent Systems. Simulation and Applications* (eds A.M. Uhrmacher and D. Weyns), CRC Press, Boca Raton, pp. 53–75.

Udehn, L. (2001) *Methodological Individualism: Background, History and Meaning*, Routledge, London-New York.

Varien, M.D., Ortman, S.G., Kohler, T.A., *et al.* (2007) Historical ecology in the Mesa Verde Region: results from the village project. *American Antiquity*, **72**(2), 273–299.

Weber, M. (1904) Objectivity of social science and social policy, in *The Methodology of the Social Sciences* (eds E. Shils and H. Finch), Free Press, New York [1949].

Wilkinson, T.J., Christiansen, J.C., Ur, J.A., *et al.* (2007) Urbanization within a dynamic environment: modeling bronze age communities in Upper Mesopotamia. *American Anthropologist*, **109**(1), 52–68.

Willer, D. and Webster, M. (1970) Theoretical concepts and observables. *American Sociological Review*, **35**, 748–757.

2

Cooperation, coordination and social norms

If we look at human affairs from a long-term evolutionary perspective, there is one thing that differentiates us from other species: the complex forms of cooperation between unrelated individuals through social norms and institutions. After all, would financial markets, charitable trusts, social services, and blood donation exist without social norms and institutions that help us to overcome free riding and encourage cooperation? The point is that, unlike cooperation between social animals (e.g., bees and termites) driven by kin selection, human cooperation is mostly based on moral motives and cultural forces that are less easily defined, robust or predictable than kin selection (e.g., de Waal 2005).

Certain social mechanisms have been investigated that account for this and close cross-fertilization between experimental findings and simulation models have been established. Recently, various specialists have racked their brains to understand the cooperation puzzle, sometimes collaboratively, sometimes indirectly through model test, replication, or extension. As disciplinary barriers become more and more blurred, inter-scientific collaboration proliferates, which is more problem- than discipline-oriented. It is probable that this interaction will be innovative for many disciplines, including sociology, as it could restructure the present patchwork of disciplinary specializations.

This chapter looks at cooperation and coordination in social interaction. I have started here for a number of reasons. First, these examples spotlight mechanisms that have wide implications in explaining the emergence of social order, the most striking sociological key puzzle ever. The understanding of how social institutions and large social structures spontaneously and endogenously emerged from agent interaction is one of the foundational debates for sociologists and social scientists, generally speaking. This debate has so far been conducted without relying on well-controlled

---

Agent-Based Computational Sociology, First Edition. Flaminio Squazzoni.
© 2012 John Wiley & Sons, Ltd. Published 2012 by John Wiley & Sons, Ltd.

data, or on modeling techniques, which are now possible. Secondly, even when not directly involving sociologists, these examples emphasize important sociological factors, such as the role of agent interaction and the power of social structures in determining outcomes at the macro level.

Last but not least, certain examples allow us to understand the potential of cross-methodological research, combining empirical data and models. Indeed, by starting from relatively simplified and abstract models of agent interaction, sociologists can prearrange their research for empirical calibration and validation. In doing so, these examples place ABMs between inductive and deductive logic, an area where sociological investigation is presently weak.

Obviously, most of these examples are extensions or modifications of the game theory framework. Game theory is extremely useful for studying social interaction (e.g., Kollock 1998). It can be easily translated into, and tested through, laboratory experiments. Therefore, it can be an important source of data to understand individual behavior in well-controlled interactions. Furthermore, a road map of the unification of behavioral and social sciences around common game-theory concepts and modeling-oriented research styles has recently taken great steps forward (e.g., Gintis 2009).

It is also worth noting that ABM scientists follow a different and more sociological approach than conventional game theory to social interaction modeling. First, they do not focus on perfect rationality and equilibrium. Rather, they focus on bounded rationality, heterogeneity and social influence, that is, a more realistic picture of social behavior and interaction. Secondly, they consider the influence of social structure on collective outcomes. These examples allow us to answer the criticism against game theory by sociologists such as Swedberg (2001), who believed it was too economics-oriented with poor sociological implications.

Generally, the following examples testify to the high plasticity of ABMs. ABMs can be used to make up for the impossibility of finding analytic solutions with standard mathematical models, thereby extending the analytic approach (e.g., Axelrod's and Bowles and Gintis' examples). However, they can also substitute it, leaving simplification and math constraints to look at out-of-equilibrium and complex patterns. Moreover, they emphasize the added value of observation other than analytic solutions (e.g., Boero *et al.*'s examples).

There is another important difference between these examples and scholars carrying out ABM research on cooperation and social norms. Some researchers are motivated by the attempt to find minimal conditions that explain cooperation in social systems composed of self-regarding rational agents. This idea is twofold. On the one hand, given that we conceive cooperation as a ubiquitous empirical phenomenon, the understanding of minimal conditions for cooperation can help us both to identify common properties and to distinguish specificities of human and non-human populations.

This could even allow us to explain the origin of human society (e.g., Sigmund 2010). In this context, it is important to remove supplementary conditions that might empirically account for the prevalence of cooperation in social systems, such as reputation, formal agreements, and institutional enforcement, which are human-specific and essentially social.

In doing so, attention can be focused on core ingredients of cooperation that might apply for a large set of interactions, not just confined to social phenomena. By comparing and contrasting, these investigations could enable us to find what makes social behavior really human-specific. On the other hand, the search for minimal conditions could help us to promote cooperation in a broad range of social spheres (e.g., markets, workplaces, and the political arena) by fostering those conditions, so that societies can reverse natural selection and 'nice guys can really finish first', to paraphrase Dawkins (1989).

Others are motivated by the idea of considering exactly those aspects excluded by the former at the expense of generalization (e.g., Conte *et al.* 2001; Conte and Paolucci 2002). In both cases, the explanatory hypotheses of these studies are of paramount importance in understanding how social groups can develop spontaneously self-reinforcing norms which regulate interaction for collective benefits. This is an important issue particularly today, in an era characterized by individualism and autonomous self-regulation of groups and communities in society and the economy.

Finally, there is an important difference for methodological issues about ABMs in sociology and social sciences. Although most examples are abstract models, two examples suggest tighter ways to combine evidence and ABMs by building and calibrating models using empirical data. These cross-methodological examples suggest how to use computer simulation to generalize laboratory findings and understand implications of social interaction for larger and more complex social systems (e.g., Boero, Bravo and Squazzoni's model on partner selection and Boero *et al.*'s model on reputation). We will return to these points in Chapter 4.

The following sections focus on various social mechanisms that can explain cooperation. Section 2.1 illustrates the strength of direct reciprocity and the persistence of interaction for favoring cooperation in a variety of situations where individuals tend to interact frequently, such as families, friendship networks, and the new social media.

Section 2.2 enlarges the perspective from dyadic interaction to n-person social dilemma, investigating the relevance of social sanctions. This helps us to realize the idea that selection in human societies could operate in more subtle and complex ways than in the rest of nature. That is, not only at an individual level, but also within and between social groups (e.g., Boyd and Richerson 2009). It is worth noting that the possibility of multi-level selection has important implications to understand the evolution of nature and society, as it may revise the dictates of Darwinian thought and consider more complex endogenous selective forces (e.g., Fodor and Piattelli-Palmarini 2010).

Section 2.3 reports on the cultural transmission of cooperative behavior and gives two extensions and replications of a previous model offering a clear idea about the added value of models for theory building. Section 2.4 pinpoints the importance of dynamic social networks, investigates the relevance of partner selection as a driving force for fostering trust-based cooperation and provides an example of how to combine data and theory. Section 2.5 looks at cooperation in a market situation where agents are subject to reputation mechanisms. Finally, Section 2.6 changes the perspective from competitive to coordination games and looks at findings on the emergence of social conventions, where the emphasis is on agent behavior more than social structure. Here, the aim is to examine social mechanisms which can account for norm equilibrium and understand their consequences at a micro level.

It is worth noting that none of these examples definitively demonstrate or support general laws on cooperation in social interaction. Everything is open to discussion and improvements are needed, as always in science. These examples offer a clear idea about two of the most important advantages of agent-based computational sociology. First, they improve our knowledge of the link between social behavior and the 'situation' (i.e., specific conditions of a social context where agent interaction takes place). Secondly, they allow us to evaluate scientific achievement in a collaborative, constructive and productive way.

2.1   Direct reciprocity and the persistence of interaction

After Axelrod (1981, 1984, 1997) and Axelrod and Hamilton (1981), it is well established that the repetition of dyadic interaction can create evolutionary conditions for cooperation in many social situations, thanks to reciprocity. Axelrod established this in the early 1980s, when he published his famous iterated Prisoner's Dilemma round-robin tournament. This was held in the late 1970s, where different strategies submitted by a variety of experts were pitted against each other.

The Prisoner's Dilemma is a well-known game that models a variety of social interactions where individuals might not cooperate even if this could guarantee better payoffs for all. The game is summarized in Table 2.1, where T stands for *temptation to defect*, R for *reward for mutual cooperation*, P for *punishment for mutual defection*, and S for *sucker's payoff*. Players' behavior is mutually referred to mimic a strategic interaction where their reward is dependent on each other, and the structure of the game is based on an inequality of payoffs. The equilibrium outcome is therefore defection, as $T > R > P > S$ (for an extensive description, see Kuhn 2007).

Axelrod's tournament assumed that players repeated the game for a finite number of times, so as to explore the emergence of the best suitable strategies over time. The winner of the tournament was dubbed the TIT-FOR-TAT strategy that stated 'cooperate initially, then reciprocate what your counterpart did'. This was originally

Table 2.1   The Prisoner's Dilemma payoff matrix. The first letter is the row player's payoff. The second is for the column player.

	Cooperate	Defect
Cooperate	R, R	S, T
Defect	T, S	P, P

submitted by Anatol Rapoport, a famous Russian-born mathematical psychologist, and was one of the simplest strategies with only four lines of code.[1]

The reason for TIT-FOR-TAT's success was ascribed to certain positive features of this strategy. Indeed, it was *nice*, as it started with a presumption of trustworthiness of the counterpart, *retaliatory*, as it promptly reacted in response to a defection, *forgiving*, since it could restore mutual cooperation, and easily *intelligible* by agents, as it was simple to understand (when opponents were playing it) and learn (when players were called to play).

Axelrod coined the term 'shadow of the future' to mean that as long as the probability of interaction repetition was sufficiently great, individuals expected that their present action affected the future behavior of others and consequently less rewarding behavior in the short term, such as cooperation, could be justified in view of long-term higher rewards (Axelrod 1984).

A variety of extensions, applications and empirical, experimental and simulation tests on the relevance of this type of reciprocity strategy in repeated interaction have been explored in various disciplines. For instance, Kogut (1989) successfully applied it to understand joint ventures in business, Hanson (1991) to understand the promotion of ethical conduct in private companies, and Condlin (1992) to understand dispute settlements between lawyers.[2] On the other hand, others, including some sociologists, have highlighted its limitations, as it compels agents to keep relationships in balance, therefore leading to a potentially long sequence of retaliation (Nowak and Sigmund 1992).

By using a computer simulation model, Kollock (1993) found that the possibility of misperception of mutual strategies required more flexible reciprocity strategies than TIT-FOR-TAT, for example, more capable of positively reacting to the errors of others. Axelrod himself, in a recent contribution (2011), stated that the viability of cooperation through TIT-FOR-TAT could be reinforced by certain social mechanisms that accounted for cases of noisy environments. Here, agents made mistakes, misunderstanding or misimplementing other strategies, so that their action was not what they intended (e.g., Fudenberg and Maskin 1990; Bendor, Kramer and Stout 1991). Indeed, by following TIT-FOR-TAT, which dictated a prompt reply to a defection with a defection, whether this was unintended or not, agents were condemned to a sequence of mutual defections.

---

[1] Recently, Axelrod made some personal comments about his early work and in particular how he came to the idea of a computer tournament for the iterated Prisoner's Dilemma. When he reconstructed his interest in computer chess and artificial intelligence, he mentioned his idea of using more or less expert human players to discover best strategies against the computer. It is worth noting that one of the first players recruited was James S. Coleman and that he was asked to play with TIT-FOR-TAT. Axelrod wrote that the discussion with Coleman at the end of the game confirmed the potentials of the Prisoner's Dilemma to explore the subtleties of strategic interaction in human affairs (Axelrod 2009b).

[2] A commendable annotated bibliography of articles and books that applied, extended or criticized Axelrod (1984) until 1996, prepared by Robert Axelrod and Lisa D'Ambrosio, can be accessed at the following address: http://www.cscs.umich.edu/old/research/Publications/Evol_of_Coop_Bibliography.html. For a severe criticism to the game-theory foundations of Axelrod's models, see Binmore (1998).

Other strategies with less restricted retaliation components were found and tested that outperformed TIT-FOR-TAT especially in maintaining cooperation once established, such as 'generous TIT-FOR-TAT' (i.e., cooperate although the counterpart defected, with a given probability), and 'win-stay, lose-shift' (i.e., repeat your previous decision whenever you are doing well) (Nowak and Sigmund 1993). Bowles and Gintis (2004) questioned the strength of direct reciprocity and TIT-FOR-TAT to explain cooperation in all n-person dilemmas, where interactions were repeated but not dyadic (see below).

The point is that most of these examples questioned the validity domain of reciprocity strategies in randomly mixed populations. A more sociology-friendly point of view on this issue should analyze the impact of social structures in creating evolutionary conditions favorable to cooperation, since it is unlikely that agents interact with everybody else in real situations. Spatial models, where agents play social dilemma games in local neighbors of different size, have been suggested. These take into account the relevance of local interactions to create structural conditions more or less favorable to cooperation.

In a simulation of an iterative Prisoner's Dilemma between cooperators and defectors, Nowak and May (1992) showed that by allowing agents to interact in neighborhoods across a two-dimensional space, cooperators could spatially cluster around mutual help that drastically reduced exploitation opportunities by cheaters. More recently, Santos, Pacheco and Lenaerts (2006) investigated different social dilemmas, including Prisoner's Dilemma, where agents were embedded in social networks and capable of selecting social ties.

Simulation results demonstrated that cooperators wiped out defectors when agents could modify the network topology of their social ties towards high average connectivity with associated single-to-broad heterogeneity. It is worth noting that these topological features characterize social networks in a variety of empirical situations, such as collaboration networks between scientists, links across boards of directors of large companies or ties between Hollywood actors (e.g., Watts 1999; Barabási 2002; Ohtsuki et al. 2006).

This being said, in our view, the most interesting attempt to understand the impact of social structure on cooperation was that proposed by Cohen, Riolo and Axelrod (2001). Largely inspired by Nowak and Sigmund (1992), their model looked at social interactions where certain features of the social structure provided 'context preservation' for cooperation in hostile environments, where defection was likely to dominate. The authors simulated a finite iterated Prisoner's Dilemma game, where N agents ($N = 256$) each played against four other agents each period (see the payoff matrix in Table 2.2). The payoff matrix followed Table 2.1 with T (temptation to defect) = 5, R (reward for mutual cooperation) = 3, P (punishment for mutual defection) = 1, and S (sucker's payoff) = 0. There were three strategies possible, according to a probability function: always defect, TIT-FOR-TAT, always cooperate (for details on the function, see below). Social influence was assumed so that agents were allowed to copy the strategy of the highest fitted player with whom they were matched, with possible emulation errors.

Table 2.2   Cooperation in different simulation scenarios (adapted from Cohen, Riolo and Axelrod 2001, p. 9). The fixed random scenario, in its original version without rewiring, was tested in three different rewiring probabilities. In each period a new randomly chosen agent of each group was substituted with given probability. As the probability approaches 1, the fixed random network is more similar to a randomly mixed population. Note that, to check for possible stochastic processes, each single scenario was simulated for 30 runs for each combination of parameter values, each run beginning with a different seed for the random number generator. Therefore, the second column from the left shows the run proportion of each scenario where cooperation largely prevailed. Mean payoff means the average score per decision for the whole population over the last 1000 steps of all runs. The last column on the right shows the proportion of time agents remained in high levels of cooperation. This gives an idea of the robustness of cooperation over simulations in each scenario.

Simulation scenarios	Proportion of run with high levels of cooperation	Mean payoff	Proportion of time in high cooperation equilibrium
Randomly mixed encounters	0.30	1.091	0.015
Spatial embeddedness	1.00	2.557	0.997
Small-world network	1.00	2.575	0.995
Fixed random network	1.00	2.480	0.942
Fixed random network with rewiring probability 0.1	1.00	2.385	0.884
Fixed random network with rewiring probability 0.3	1.00	2.100	0.402
Fixed random network with rewiring probability 0.5	0.93	1.257	0.061

Seven simulation scenarios were created where various social structures more or less related to spatial embeddedness were assumed as follows (for social structure, it meant 'who interacted with whom'): (1) a *randomly mixed encounters* scenario, where each agent was matched with four others chosen with equal probability from the entire population each period; (2) a *spatial embedded structure* scenario, with a 16 × 16 two-dimensional toroidal lattice where each agent had fixed neighbors of four other agents (those were located north, south, east and west) and was correlated with neighbors of neighbors; (3) a *small-world-like social network* scenario,[3] with a 16 × 16 two-dimensional toroidal lattice as before, but where agents' neighbors of neighbors were not correlated but randomly chosen each round, so that agents were

---

[3] A small-world network is a type of network where most nodes are not neighbors but can be reached from everyone else by a small number of steps. Sociologically, this means that individuals embedded in this type of networks are linked by mutual acquaintance (e.g., Watts 1999).

linked by mutual acquaintance (Watts 1999; for details on how the structure was built see the Appendix of Cohen, Riolo, Axelrod 2001, pp. 30–32); (4) a *fixed-random network* where neighbors were randomly assigned but remained fixed over time, according to a probability function (see Table 2.2 for details).

Simulation findings showed that it is the persistence of interaction patterns rather than neighbors' spatial embeddedness that favors cooperation (see Table 2.2). While it is well-known that cooperation could be promoted by spatial embeddedness alone (e.g., Nemeth and Takács 2007), this would suggest that cooperation is equally encouraged by different types of social networks, without assuming spatial correlation. However, cooperation collapses in situations of randomly mixed encounters. The point is that the spatial nature of embeddedness does not imply qualitatively different behavior, although it does require further conditions, such as a fixed correlation of agents across space.

The point is that interaction persistence is sufficient to create a context where agents with mutually compatible behavior are kept together by emulating each other. By looking at the individual scenarios, the authors suggested certain mechanisms that accounted for such findings.

In the model, each agent strategy was represented by three parameters, y, p, and q, where $0 < y, p, q < 1$. The parameter y indicated the probability that agents cooperated on the first move of the game, p the probability that they cooperated after cooperation by others, and q the probability that they cooperated after a defection by others. Therefore, agent strategies with high values of p were strongly cooperative, whereas those with low values of q were highly retaliatory, as they returned defection with defection.

In situations of randomly mixed encounters, strategies with high p values are vulnerable to exploitation, since defectors can take advantage of other cooperators, achieving higher scores and so spreading socially through imitation. If so, the diffusion of strategies of low q is probable as a reaction and consequently agents are trapped into mutual defection.

However, fragile periods of high cooperation are still possible by chance. In situations of randomly mixed encounters, at any increase of q, a decrease of p is expected (Figure 2.1), as each remaining strategy with low level of p and q outperforms any cooperative strategies. For instance, a strategy with low levels of p and q always defected and scored 5 against the opposite and comparatively better than other cooperative variants it was combined with, such as TIT-FOR-TAT, because it exploited none of them. The randomness of encounters increases the chance that these conditions are perpetuated against occasional bursts of cooperation driven by emulation errors, when q is extremely low.

In more structured conditions, such as spatial embeddedness and social networks, a transition towards cooperation is possible. This is because, after an initial phase of mutual defection, an increase of the average value of p implies that cooperative strategies play each other, achieving higher scores than other strategies (and other combinations of strategies) and are reproduced over time.

Figures 2.1 and 2.2 show a $p–q$ plot in two illustrative scenarios, that is, randomly mixed encounters (Figure 2.1) and random fixed network scenarios (Figure 2.2). In

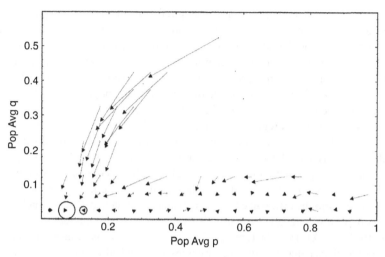

Figure 2.1   The p−q *plot in the randomly mixed encounters scenarios (adapted from Cohen, Riolo and Axelrod 2001, p. 18). The figure depicts changes in parameters* p *and* q *averaged on the entire population. Arrows point to the average values. The circles indicate the amount of time that the entire population spent in the various regions of the parameter space. The larger the circle, the more time that agents spent in that region. The other circles are scaled relative to the largest one. The higher left-hand side arrows show the drastic fall in average* p *parameters when an occasional burst of cooperation was wiped out.*

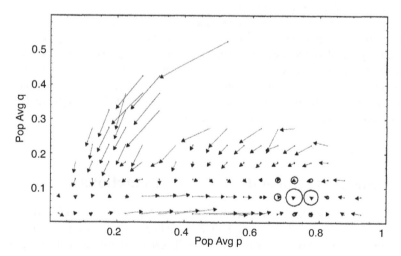

Figure 2.2   The p−q *plot in the random fixed network scenarios (adapted from Cohen, Riolo and Axelrod 2001, p. 18).*

a randomly mixed encounters scenario, the attractor of the parameter space revolves around a region of low levels of both p and q (i.e., the left region of the space downwards), whereas the attractor of the random fixed network scenario points to higher levels of both (i.e., the right region of the space). Furthermore, in the latter, the bottom line arrows point right instead of left and are in a higher position. This means that, at the same level of q value on average in the population, in the random fixed network scenario, agents show higher levels of p.

If we focus on crucial regions of space, that is, the interval between 0.30–0.35 of p and 0.05–0.10 of q, the social network scenarios gave different results compared with the randomly mixed encounters scenario. While in the latter, the average value of p for the whole population tended to be below 0, in this case p values tended the other way. Other data not reported here showed that, while in the randomly mixed encounter scenario the difference between p values of matched agents largely varied, in others there was a tighter correlation between the values of interacting agents (see Cohen, Riolo and Axelrod 2001, pp. 22–24). Therefore, the randomness of encounters increases the chance that cooperative strategies are matched with exploitational ones, so that the population is attracted into a region of lower p values.

In other scenarios, cooperative strategies were emulated by neighbors. The persistence of interaction created contexts where cooperation was more protected against defection. This was because defectors were matched to situations where they could only reciprocate to other defections and were then eliminated over time.

This model was further extended by Axelrod, Riolo and Cohen (2002) who tested various social structures to show that cooperation may be robust even if not supported by spatial embeddedness. Reciprocity and frequent interactions can therefore explain why we see people who largely cooperate in despatialized social networks, such as social blogs, Facebook, and other social media.

There is no doubt that certain restrictive conditions imposed in these examples, such as dyadic interaction, the 'shadow of the future', interaction overloading and no game exit, undermine the generalization of their findings. However, the important point is that these investigations allow us to understand the link between social behavior (e.g., selfishness and reciprocity) and the features of 'the situation' (e.g., dyadic interaction, frequent encounters, and no exit), which is an essential aspect of any sociological analysis on social interaction.

2.2   Strong reciprocity and social sanctions

Everyone can understand that social order, especially in large social systems, is guaranteed by sanctions, but sometimes we forget that sanctions always come at a cost that someone has to pay. Even when we formally establish institutional arrangements to regulate a given interaction (e.g., contracts and fines), so that monitoring and punishment costs can be socially shared and their effect largely magnified, and when sanctions are supported by supervision and monitoring, as in organizations, someone has to pay for them (e.g., taxpayers in the first case and shareholders in the second).

In many situations, such as families, friendship networks, scientific collaboration and social groups, sanctions are informally established and guaranteed only by peers, without sophisticated monitoring or cost-sharing mechanisms. In this case, they are 'social sanctions', since they have more to do with social disapproval based on moral motives, as their effect cannot be easily calculated or translated into monetary fines.

Let us take the example of what happens in public goods games, where most of the restrictions mentioned above often do not hold. A public goods game is a game where agents can choose how much of their money to put into a public pot, knowing that the pot is used to buy goods for everyone, even for those who did not contribute, and that the consumption of these goods by someone does not reduce availability for others. For example, private companies incurring high expenses to buy green technology are playing a game of this kind. In these situations, the logic is that the large prevalence of nice guys in a group is not enough to reduce the opportunities for cheaters, if there is no availability of agents to take responsibility for punishment costs.

Thankfully, experimental findings indicate that many individuals are willing to pay a personal cost to punish wrongdoers (e.g., Ostrom, Walker and Gardner 1992; Fehr and Gätcher 2000; Gintis *et al.* 2005; Hauert *et al.* 2007). This has been explained by emotional and moral factors, such as the empathy towards the victims of unfair behavior or anger against cheating, as well as by sociocultural factors, such as the deliberate protection of group-beneficial social norms. These are motivations that make us retaliate against indecent behavior that penalizes some or all members of our group, although this means decreasing our own fitness for the benefit of others without any certainty about present or future material rewards, with no certainty that others will do this in turn for us. This has been confirmed also by neuroscientific investigations (e.g., de Quervain *et al.* 2004).

Such behavior has been called 'altruistic punishment' and the individuals behaving in this way 'strong reciprocators' (Gintis 2000; Fehr and Gätcher 2002; Bowles and Gintis 2004). These terms convey the idea that this behavior is *altruistic*, as it confers benefits on other members of a group, even on those who do not obey the norm and/or those who do not punish norm violators. It is also *strong* as it has serious consequences on norm violators and comes at significant personal expense for punishers. It is different from 'indirect reciprocity' (i.e., we help another individual, expecting that others will help us in turn) and cannot be fully understood in terms of evolutionary theories of cooperation, such as the shadow of the future, kin selection, or reciprocal altruism arguments, as we will see later (e.g., Gintis 2000; Boyd *et al.* 2003).

The most interesting ABM example on this issue was reported by Bowles and Gintis (2004), who investigated strong reciprocity by relying on empirical studies on mobile hunter-gatherer groups in the late Pleistocene, i.e., our ancestors. An n-player Prisoner's Dilemma model ($n = 400$) was built, which looked at the most essential elements of this sociohistorical context, where individuals participated in public good initiatives, such as hunting, food sharing and common defense, without relying on centralized institutions, precise monitoring, organizational roles and formal sanctions as in modern societies. Therefore, the typical interaction of these groups was dominated by the strategy of contributing very little or nothing to public goods provision.

The model started from the following assumptions, based on empirical literature: (a) individuals lived in middle-sized groups (20 members on average); (b) there was no centralized governance structure, so sanctions were put into action by peers; (c) many unrelated individuals made up the social groups so that altruism could not be fully supported by kin selection; (d) there were poor status differences, so that individuals were relatively homogeneous in terms of power and influence; (e) the economy was based on sharing and immediate consumption of goods, not on accumulation; (f) ostracism was the main social sanction; (g) individuals followed a subjective assessment of a sanction's probability and impact; and (h) there was inter-group mobility.

In more detail, the authors assumed that groups were composed of three types of agents: *strong reciprocators, selfish agents* and *cooperators*. Strong reciprocators unconditionally contributed to the public good (according to the expected contribution level of the group), monitored others (although only randomly) and punished shirkers at the expense of their own fitness. Selfish agents choose a level of shirking that maximized their fitness, given the probability of being caught shirking (depending on how many strong reciprocators there were in their group) and of the cost of being punished (i.e., depending on the length of time agents were forced to abandon the group, which in turn was dependent upon the distribution of the population between group members and isolated agents changing over time). Cooperators unconditionally contributed to the public good (according to the expected contribution level of the group) but never punished shirkers.

The contribution level of the group depended on the size of the group and the fitness of each member. Once the punishment cost and effort lost by shirkers were subtracted, this gave rise to an output shared equally by group members (for details, see Bowles and Gintis 2004, p. 19). The probability and the cost of being punished were heterogeneous and endogenous. Selfish agents with a high value in terms of cost of punishment behaved like cooperators except that, if there were zero strong reciprocators in the group, they did not contribute. Punishment meant being ostracized from the group and then not participating in the public good benefit, that is, fitness lost. Evolutionary mechanisms, such as behavioral inheritance and mutation, were assumed to pass behavioral traits between agents inter-generationally (e.g., Bowles and Gintis 2004, p. 19).

The number of groups and the total population were fixed, but groups changed by admitting new members (equal to a fraction of the total members), both from isolated agents and from other groups. An immigration rate of 12% of agents per generation and a desired emigration rate were assumed. Groups disbanded when they fell below a minimum size of six members and their place was taken by new groups composed of randomly selected agents from the most populous groups that restored the initial size of the group. It is worth noting that at the beginning of the simulation the whole population was composed of selfish agents. The simulation parameters are shown in Table 2.3.

Table 2.4 shows the simulation statistics. The first result is that the three types of behavior coexist over time in a kind of dynamic equilibrium. More importantly, strong reciprocators were pivotal in sustaining groups, as the higher their presence in

Table 2.3   Simulation parameters (Bowles and Gintis 2004, p. 21).

Value	Description
0.2	Output for agent, no shirking
0.1	Cost of working, no shirking
0.1	Cost of punishment
0.05	Emigration rate
0.03	Immigration rate
20	Initial group size
20	Number of groups
−0.1	Fitness in pool
6	Minimum group size
[0,1]	Initially seeded expected cost of ostracism
0.01	Mutation rate

the group, the lower the shirking. Selfish agents and cooperators were more likely to be in disbanded groups (see fractions of agent types in the pool in Table 2.4). Figure 2.3 shows the evolution of the distribution of agent types and the average shirking rate in a typical run. The pattern confirmed that a co-existence of the three agent types in the population is functional to reduce shirking levels balanced by the presence of strong reciprocators.

The dynamics of agent types and groups can be observed in more detail by focusing on a typical story of a group, as depicted in Figure 2.4. Let us suppose that

Table 2.4   Simulation results. Values are averages of the last 1000 simulation periods of a 50 000 period simulation averaged over 25 simulations (Bowles and Gintis 2004, p. 21).

Value	Description
37.2%	Fraction of reciprocators
24.6%	Fraction of cooperators
38.2%	Fraction of selfish agents
11.1%	Average shirking rate
4%	Fraction of population in pool
0.38%	Fraction of reciprocators in pool
0.48%	Fraction of cooperators in pool
10%	Fraction of selfish agents in pool
4%	Fraction of pool who are reciprocators
3%	Fraction of pool who are cooperators
93%	Fraction of pool who are selfish agents
1.21	Ratio of cooperators to reciprocators in disbanded groups
3.4	Ratio of selfish agents to reciprocators in disbanded groups

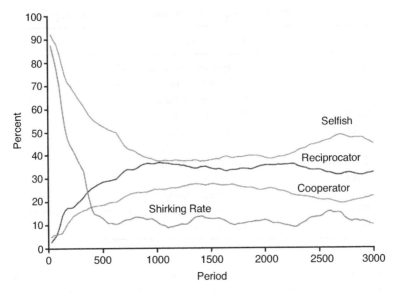

Figure 2.3   Dynamics of behavior and shirking rate in a typical simulation run (Bowles and Gintis 2004, p. 21).

each group was made up of a certain level of selfish agents, cooperators and strong reciprocators. In a Darwinian selective environment, cooperators could outperform reciprocators, as they take advantage of the effect of shirkers' punishment, accumulating resources against both shirkers and reciprocators. Now, suppose that cooperators replaced strong reciprocators in the group, as they become fitter than the latter (as occurred after 330 and 340 periods in Figure 2.4). With a few strong reciprocators present in the group, the expected cost of shirking decreased. Therefore, selfish agents started to shirk exploiting cooperators, who unconditionally continued to contribute to the public good. The former received higher payoffs and eventually replaced the latter. When this occurred, the average fitness of the group dramatically fell and the group disbanded (e.g., see 390 period in Figure 2.4).

This story provides a logical explanation of the relevance of strong reciprocity in a public good dilemma situation that also takes into account multi-level selection, for example, a selection that operates both at an individual and a group level. Indeed, the simulation results show that cooperators can drive out strong reciprocators within individual groups where they co-exist but cannot do so at a population level.

Given that driving out strong reciprocators provides a context for selfish agents to increase shirking levels within groups (by exploiting cooperators' contribution) and this then reduces group fitness, the groups in question tend to disband more readily. However, simulations show that strong reciprocators outperform cooperators in the population (see fractions in Table 2.4), because average group fitness and frequency of cooperators are negatively correlated (see Price's equation in Bowles and Gintis 2004, p. 23). Therefore, selection in social systems can also include groups. This in

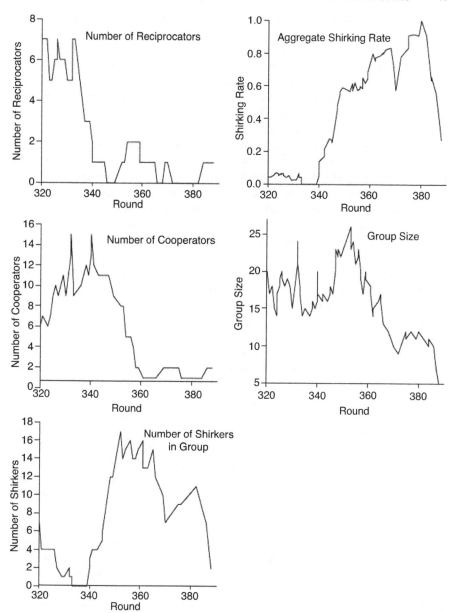

Figure 2.4   The dynamics of a typical group from birth to dissolution (Bowles and Gintis 2004, p. 22).

turn suggests that strong reciprocators are functional to social order and that this is typically human, as it requires a high-level cognitive capability of monitoring the behavior of others and socially organized punishment technologies (see below).

Following this logic, Carpenter *et al.* (2009) extended Bowles and Gintis' model to the case of team work in organizations, by exploring the impact of group size and productivity on punishment and cooperation. They also provided an experimental test of the impact of strong reciprocity through a public goods game played by a subject pool from the University of Massachusetts.

Results showed that social sanctions promote highly productive work collaboration as parts of a self-policing process that lowers supervision costs, favors more precise monitoring of behavior (therefore legitimating peer sanctions), and sends appropriate signals to organization members about appropriate behavior. Unlike material incentives that might backfire by promoting selfish behavior (e.g., Bowles 2008), social sanctions tend to preserve the moral aspect of social interaction and are less demanding in terms of costs, for example, monitoring and information.

It is worth noting that two contingent conditions were still important: the presence of a considerable frequency of strong reciprocators in the groups and a not-too-large group size. This meant, first, that reciprocators were pivotal in reducing opportunities for cheaters to exploit cooperators, as indicated in the original model and secondly, that cooperation in large groups requires the establishment of enforcement institutions.

Boyd, Gintis and Bowles (2010) further elaborated the power of sanctions for cooperation by modeling coordinated punishment, that is, the capability of agents to collectively punish wrongdoers. There is evidence in many fields, from ethnography to experimental behavioral sciences, that norm abiders use gossip, reputation and other communication channels to coordinate punishment, when this is viewed as a legitimate way to increase cooperation by most group members (e.g., Dunbar 1996, 2004; Wiessner 2005; Piazza and Bering 2008). By giving agents the possibility of signaling their willingness to punish and the capability of implementing effective punishment collectively, increasing returns to scales on sanctions tend to favor cooperation, although a high number of strong reciprocators who agree to punishing is still a necessary condition.

In conclusion, the model of Bowles and Gintis allows us to spotlight some important aspects about reciprocity and cooperation, underestimated by examples such as Axelrod's studies. First, the repeated nature of interaction alone might fail to guarantee cooperation in cases where groups are unstable, permeable and threatened by dissolution. In such cases, the so-called 'shadow of the future' makes room for the 'shadow of the abyss', where groups could dissolve and consequently any altruistic behavior could be viewed as a dramatic sacrifice with no probability of future reciprocity benefits. The likelihood of punishment decreases when others are not reciprocating sanctions as the group is expected to break up.

The same is true when interactions are not dyadic (as in Axelrod's examples) but between *n*-players. This is the case in a public goods dilemma and in many empirical situations, where reciprocity is not expected to play a crucial role, unless indirectly, that is, mediated by third-party reputation, tags, stereotypes or prejudices (e.g., Nowak and Sigmund 2005). Secondly, sanctions are based on strong reciprocity among peers, without institutional arrangements, monitoring or enforcement, relying on cognitive and communication capabilities that are uniquely social. These include formulating and sharing social norms, agreeing on common values, and monitoring behavior, even through reputation and gossip.

Logically, these findings show that complex institutional arrangements are deeply rooted in human predisposition towards altruistic punishment and therefore might have originally evolved through this (e.g., Ostrom 2000). According to Boyd, Gintis and Bowles (2010), it is reasonable to argue that, as soon as social groups grew in size, as in modern societies, new institutions were established to exploit economies of scale on sanctions (e.g., police and other social control institutions) helped by technological progress. At the same time, monitoring society probably became paramount in less cohesive and more heterogeneous social groups. Therefore, such developments provided the context for the establishment of formal institutions.

Obviously, these are just intuitions and traditional non ABM studies might have come to the same conclusions, although unsupported by experimental or simulation verification. However, it is important to see that a formal model can also motivate qualitative intuition about the evolution of society and therefore inspire further empirical investigations.

2.3   Disproportionate prior exposure

Social agents are probably influenced by the cultural transmission of behavioral models through social interaction. This happens in childhood, youth, friendship or workplaces. Culture is a set of knowledge socially transmitted by intergenerational inheritance and social interaction. Unlike genetic transmission, cultural transmission involves complex forms of social interaction from different influential figures, such as parents, teachers, high status colleagues and friends, not to mention the mass media. These interactions are the pillars of social learning, by imitation, emulation, instruction, and interpretation.

One of the mechanisms that accounts for the influence of culture on cooperation is 'disproportionate prior exposure'. The idea is simple: agents who behave in a certain way (e.g., cooperative or self-interest) have been disproportionately exposed to this behavior prior to acquiring it (Mark 2002, p. 328). Although the roots of this idea can be traced back to classical sociology, for example, Durkheim and Parsons, the relevance of this mechanism was first formally investigated by Noah Mark (2002) in a differential equation model.

Mark's model was based on a large population of agents playing a sequence of one-shot Prisoner's Dilemma games where: (i) agents had an initial fixed behavior (cooperative or selfish); (ii) they were randomly paired; (iii) they compared their respective fitness; (iv) they behaved, according to (i); (v) they received their respective payoffs according to the interaction; and (vi) they adopted the partners' behavior if the partners' fitness at step (iii) was higher than their own. At the end of the sequence, they acquired a new fitness level and a new behavior and the game restarted. The payoff matrix followed Table 2.1 with T (temptation to defect) = 3, R (reward for mutual cooperation) = 2, P (punishment for mutual defection) = 1, and S (sucker's payoff) = 0.

Mark assumed that each time cooperators were paired with defectors and did not switch behavior, their fitness was 0 in the next round, whereas it was 2 when they were paired with cooperators. Each time defectors were paired with other defectors, their fitness level was 1 in the next round, whereas it was 3 when they were paired with cooperators and did not switch behavior. Mark's assumption was that defectors always became cooperators after interacting and benefiting from well fitted cooperator behavior. For instance, if defectors with a fitness level of 1 were paired with cooperators with a fitness level of 2, defectors became cooperators with a fitness level of 3.

Mark showed that, under these conditions, cooperation is likely to emerge given any distribution of agents across all combinations of behavior and fitness levels. For instance, even if initially 99% of agents were defectors with fitness levels of 3 and 1% of agents were cooperators with a fitness level of 0, the population moved towards full cooperation in about 100 000 simulation rounds. This brought Mark to conclude that disproportionate prior exposure could explain the prevalence of cooperation in human societies, where agents have a unique predisposition for cultural transmission.

The generalization of Mark's results has been questioned by subsequent work. Following replication by Bienenstick and McBride (2004; see also Mark 2004's reply),[4] Welser, Gleave and Vaughan (2007) tested through an ABM certain extensions of Mark's model that looked at the disproportionate prior exposure mechanism more convincingly.[5]

As a matter of fact, Mark's generalization of cooperation in human society contrasted with the fragility of cooperation revealed by many ABM studies on the evolution of cooperation, such as those mentioned above. The problem was that Mark did not seriously take into account incentives towards self-interested behavior. Given that sociologists have put forward plenty of theories that account for cooperation by emphasizing over-socialization and norm internalization, the most crucial challenge for ABM scientists is to understand conditions that make cooperation probable in a population of rational agents that do not passively absorb norms but rather behave

---

[4] Bienenstick and McBride (1996) clearly showed that Mark's results strongly depended upon a set of unspecified assumptions and problematic contradictions. First, the mechanism that accounted for the dominance of cooperation in Mark's model was based on a decoupling of fitness and behavior. This meant that in many cases, defectors paired with higher fitness cooperators became cooperators, even if the fitness of the latter was due to a prior defection. Secondly, cooperation was dependent on the large size of the population assumed in Mark's version, whereas in smaller finite populations defection was more likely. Bienenstick and McBride correctly suggested that an ambitious general theory of cooperation in human societies should first explain the evolution of cooperation within small groups. Finally, they questioned that cultural transmission could be appropriately framed as a mixed motive game, as it is more similar to a coordination game where both parties benefited from converging towards the same behavior. It is worth noting that this criticism was supported by the results of a model replication. We will return to the importance of replication in Chapter 4.

[5] I gratefully acknowledge valuable information and the model codes provided by the authors.

strategically. Besides removing this bias from the original model, Welser, Gleave and Vaughan significantly improved the model towards more sociology-friendly attention to social mechanisms of cultural transmission and social learning, missing in the original model.

Welser, Gleave and Vaughan first replicated Mark's version and then introduced heterogeneity at an agent behavior level and interaction. This was achieved by assuming the presence of 'short-sighted' emulative agents who, initially cooperative, were susceptible to defection if burned by the defection of other agents. To do so, they extended the decision rules that characterized the agent learning of the Mark model. Agents emulate the behavior of others as in Mark's version, but they could also follow a different learning sequence where partners' fitness was compared with concrete behavior in the game. This was called 'short-sighted' emulation and connected fitness and behavior, as suggested by Bienenstick and McBride (2004).

So, now the population was mixed according to two different social learning mechanisms. However, in Mark (2002), agents did not calculate the material consequence of emulating other behavior as if they were simply adhering to role models without understanding the material consequences of adopted behavior. In the 'short-sighted' case, on the other hand, agents could behave selfishly, following short-term material outcomes, that is, they had a clear understanding of individual interest.

The model consisted of three parameters: (1) fitness level (0, 1, 2, 3); (2) initial behavior (cooperation or defection); and (3) learning mechanism (emulation or short-sighted emulation).[6] All parameters were changed and tested in different simulation scenarios. While in one scenario the proportion of cooperators was between 0 and 0.20 (initial prevalence of defection) in another one, the proportion was between 0.8 and 0.99 (initial prevalence of cooperation). The proportion of the 'short-sighted' emulators varied for the third parameter between 0 and 0.15 and was tested in all scenarios. The model included 400 agents and simulation ended after 10 000 rounds or until the entire population converged towards cooperation or defection.

Two simulation scenarios, respectively, a cooperation scenario, with initial prevalence of cooperators, and a defection scenario, with initial prevalence of cooperators, were tested while the percentage of short-sighted emulators varied in both. The results showed that, even when cooperators are initially prevalent and although all short-sighted emulators are initialized as cooperators, even a small fraction of persistent defectors (12% of the population) establishes evolutionary forces that undermine cooperation. As shown in Figure 2.5, cooperation was robust against defectors' exploitation when the percentage of defectors was in the 0–10% range, but defection dominated across most of the parameters' space, since the presence of a small minority of persistent defectors transformed the emulation force into a diffusion mechanism of defection.

---

[6] It is worth noting that the authors first built a system-level model that followed Mark's differential equation version and then created an ABM that replicated and extended the original model and added agent heterogeneity and more subtle social learning mechanisms. This confirms the added value of ABM compared with macro functionalistic simulation approaches, such as system dynamics.

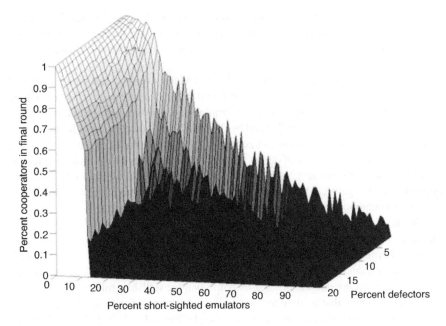

Figure 2.5   End of the cooperation scenario simulation run (Welser, Gleave and Vaughan 2007, p. 187).

These results demonstrated that Mark's assumptions imposed very restrictive conditions to explain cooperation under cultural influence, specifically the absence of any incentive towards defection. This made it impossible to understand the conditions that could have made emulation a cooperation channel.

To fill this gap, Welser, Gleave and Vaughan elaborated on the previous model by focusing on how agents could learn about other behavior in social interactions where sociocultural influences matter. They added three supplementary cognitive properties to agent learning: (1) memory; (2) more intelligent social observation; and (3) more intelligent fitness comparisons. Agents were able to record the behavior and fitness of interaction partners, comparing the amount of fitness associated with cooperation and defection they experienced. They adopted the type of behavior they had been disproportionally exposed to over time. Fitness comparison meant that agents were capable of evaluating their fitness relative to others in the social environment, not just to interaction partners. In this way, authors allowed agents to develop more intelligent social observations.

They explored three scenarios: one where agents could only observe the fitness of interaction partners (as in the original version), one where agents could calculate the average fitness of a sample of ten other agents (including current and past interaction partners as well as themselves), and a mixed scenario where partners and sample were combined. It is worth noting that these supplementary properties were especially important to look at disproportionate prior exposure in a more sociologically precise

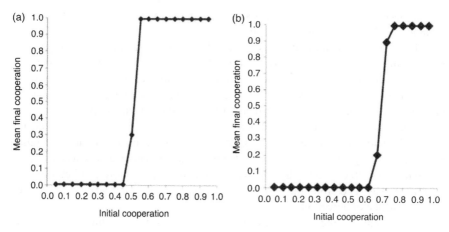

Figure 2.6   Simulation outcomes with frequency of exposure (a) and world-beating (b) mechanisms (adapted from Welser, Gleave and Vaughan 2007, p. 194).

way, by basing the model on sociologically rich agents. They could monitor others and evaluate the respective fitness of different behavioral models which populated the context.

The authors explored three different disproportionate prior exposure mechanisms, that is, the *frequency of exposure* (the more agents see others defecting, the more likely it is they switch to defection), the *world-beating* (agents evaluate higher fitness behavior and switch towards it) and the *disqualified loser* (agents evaluate lower fitness behavior and switch towards the opposite) (for details see Welser, Gleave and Vaughan 2007, p. 190). Therefore, nine different simulation scenarios were tested for all combinations of parameters, that is, source of exposure (partners, sample, combined), and prior exposure mechanisms (the three above mechanisms).[7]

Simulation provides us with a more precise picture of the impact of disproportionate prior exposure mechanisms on cooperation (see Figure 2.6, where some results have been selected where partners were the source of exposure). The frequency of exposure, the simplest cultural learning mechanism, generated logical results, where initial conditions were absolutely dominant on outcomes. For instance, when partners were the source of exposure, the prediction was that agents who cooperate would be those who have been exposed to them. At every level of initial cooperation except 50%, the majority behavior of the initial population became the universal behavior (Figure 2.6).

Therefore, whenever defectors were an initial majority, supplementary mechanisms, such as social network effects, were needed which distorted interaction and interpretation of other behavior to turn them into cooperators. As we will see in Chapter 3, social influence can explain why small differences in initial conditions can nonlinearly amplify, creating counter-intuitive and unpredictable behavior, with

---

[7] The rest of the model followed the previous version with some changes in minor details (Welser, Gleave and Vaughan 2007, p. 191).

transitions from, let us say, all defectors to all cooperators situations, around particular parameters. We will return to this point later.

The world-beating mechanism generated the same overall patterns as the previous mechanism, except that cooperation required more than 50% of initial cooperators and was strongly influenced by the source of exposure. Results showed that, when the population is mixed, defectors still have a fitness advantage, whereas if the proportion of cooperators is greater than 50%, cooperative behavior becomes the role model and outperforms defection. When restricted to partners, the source of exposure tended dramatically to favor defection, because higher levels of initial cooperation were needed to guarantee cooperation [Figure 2.6(b)]. This was because the joint distribution of fitness and behavior made defection appear more profitable than it eventually was. Therefore, the less the source of exposure was restricted, the higher was the chance of defection.

It is evident that the imposed exceptions limited the force of this mechanism to promote cooperation. Again, other additional mechanisms might be considered to turn a prevalence of defection into all cooperation, such as well-educated families, socialization practices, good schools, and well-being oriented workplaces where individuals would have less exposure to high fitness defectors and conversely low fitness cooperators. The disqualified loser mechanism did even worse than the others, by providing a context where defection dominated, since in a randomly mixing population defectors received comparative benefits from the presence of cooperators and high fitness, so becoming the dominant behavior.

To sum up, besides indicating important methodological lessons on the added value of replication, these findings pinpoint two important conclusions. First, the interaction structure of the model was based on randomly mixed interaction and this is a context where defection definitively pays. When defection was ruled out, this was because initially, rare defectors did not have the chance to be paired with short-sighted emulators, so they quickly converted to cooperation.

This was due to random mixing and gives us an important insight: it is probable that those social contexts where social structures and institutions systematically impose rules about who interacts with whom, are more likely to include the disproportionate prior exposure effects originally investigated by Mark (2002). On this, the following example adds new insights. Secondly, it might be that disproportionate exposure depends on social mechanisms of cultural transmission that largely distort the perception of the fitness of selfish behavior. Probably, this happens when parents, teachers, and church leaders tell impressive stories where nice guys finish first, in families, schools, and churches.

2.4   Partner selection[8]

A prominent social mechanism that allows agents to decrease the risk of being cheated in many real social interactions is partner selection. It is likely that in concrete social

---

[8] This section extensively drew on Boero, Bravo and Squazzoni (2010).

situations, individuals have a preferential choice and can opt out of given interactions (e.g. Slonim and Garbarino 2008). Partner selection is not just a means for individuals to make good preferential choices, but also provides an incentive for the partner to be reliable and committed to others so as to avoid social isolation (Ashlock *et al.* 1996). Joyce *et al.* (2006) built an ABM, largely inspired by Axelrod's well-known tournament previously mentioned. This showed that a conditional association strategy (i.e., agents left partners who defected against them and stayed with cooperative partners) can outperform TIT-FOR-TAT. A similar finding on the relevance of contingent strategies which discriminated good and bad partners was also found by Aktipis (2004) and Helbing and Yu (2008). To sum up, the exclusion from social interaction is a low cost form of social sanction that can damage cheaters by reducing exploitation opportunities.

These interactional aspects have been explained by two arguments: strategic uncertainty reduction and commitment bias. While the former emphasizes rational strategic aspects, the latter points to intrinsic other-regarding or emotional motivations. The first position was stressed by Kollock (1994) in an experimental study on market transactions. Here, the challenge to deal with information asymmetries and uncertainty about the trustworthiness of others made long-term interaction partners look more attractive than others. Podolny (2001) suggested that investment bankers who operated in markets characterized by a higher degree of uncertainty were likely to interact with colleagues they had interacted with in the past. Gulati (1995) found the same in an empirical study on corporate alliances.

More recently, Beckman, Haunschild and Phillips (2004) conducted an empirical study on interlocking and alliance networks for the 300 largest US firms during the period 1988–1993. They found that there was a strong correlation between the type of market uncertainty and the stability or instability of partner selection networks: organizations facing firm-specific uncertainty were less selective and more open to new ties than those facing collective market uncertainty. Hauk (2001) developed a simulation model of an iterated Prisoner's Dilemma where partner selection was a learning strategy for agents in uncertain environments. Agents learnt how to discriminate between trustworthy and untrustworthy partners and to reward/punish others. By revising strategies according to selected partners, cooperators learnt how to stop the exploitative strategies of cheaters in the population.

In two experiments conducted in the US and Japan, Yagamashi, Cook and Watabe (1998) also found that uncertainty promoted commitment between partners. In particular, individuals who trusted others more established committed relationships less frequently than skeptics, as they relied more on generalized trust.

The second point stated that the risk and uncertainty of exchange provided partners the opportunity to demonstrate their trustworthiness. Therefore, behavioral commitment and trust signals sustained cooperation in an informal and spontaneous way, without negotiations, bargaining or binding agreements as assumed in social exchange research (e.g., Molm, Takahashi and Peterson 2000). Recent simulation studies indicated that partner selection could generate a 'commitment bias', so that people's commitment to existing partners increases beyond instrumental reasons. This is due to the strength of intrinsic other-regarding motivation (Back and Flache 2006, 2008).

Back (2010) tested this hypothesis in a laboratory commitment-dilemma game based on a market exchange between subjects who played the role of an artist selling paintings and computer-simulated collectors buying them, in six locations in three countries, that is, the Netherlands, China, and the US. He showed that the initial commitment of buyers has a positive effect on partner selection, even when controlling for uncertainty and material benefits.

Although full of important insights, these studies did not seriously consider the relevance of complex social structures. In particular, they undervalued the consequences of partner selection within certain social structure configurations. Most of the experimental literature on partner selection has typically investigated the internal aspects of the selection decision, rather than its consequences over time (e.g., Kagel and Roth 2000; Haruvy *et al.* 2006).

Recently, Slonim and Garbarino (2008) investigated the relevance of partner selection for trust and altruism in the laboratory by playing an investment game and a variant of the dictator game.

Here, partners were exogenously imposed or endogenously chosen. Nevertheless, they underestimated the relevance of studying partner selection sociologically, that is, within network formation processes and investigating how network structure and partner selection could influence each other. The point is that partner selection is a driving force for network formation, stability and change (e.g., Beckman, Haunschild and Phillips 2004; Chiang 2008).

On the other hand, all studies on network formation which explain important aspects of cooperation in social and economic situations are more analytically oriented than explicitly based on experimental data. Moreover, they do not seriously consider complex and large social systems (e.g., Jackson and Wolinksy 1996; Calvó-Armengol 2001; Jackson and Watts 2002; Dutta *et al.* 2005) or the crucial role of partner selection as a driving force for network dynamics (e.g., de Vos, Smaniotto and Elsas 2001).

To fill this gap, we worked on an experimentally grounded ABM that investigated the link of social interaction and social structure in trust situations. Our assumption was that although an Axelrod-like 'shadow of the future' situation can provide a reason for cooperation, it is more likely that agents select each other in reality. This could explain why social interaction structures, especially in strategic and economic exchange situations, have certain ordered shapes and properties, rather than random encounters. Given that we could not test complex social interaction structures in the laboratory, we created an ABM that extended laboratory findings to map the consequences of experimentally grounded behavior for more complex interaction social structures.

First, we played a repeated version of an investment game in the laboratory with N subjects ($N = 108$), who anonymously interacted through a computer network in pairs, randomly recoupled each round (e.g., Berg, Dickhaut and McCabe 1995). The investment game is a standard experimental framework well-suited to investigate trust in economic interaction characterized by information asymmetries and uncertainty, as it mirrors a typical social interaction where *ego* is called to trust *alter* and *alter* to honor trust.

The rules of the game were simple. Each round, participants were coupled and randomly assigned to two different roles, called player A (the investor) and player

B (the trustee). Both players received an initial endowment, E_1 and E_2 expressed in ECU (Experimental Currency Unit) with a fixed exchange rate in real money.

First, investors had to decide whether to send all, some, or none of their endowment to trustees with whom there were paired, keeping the rest, if any. The amount sent by A, denoted M_1, was multiplied by a factor m by the experimenter (in this case, $m = 3$) and sent to trustees, in addition to the endowment. The parameter m should be interpreted as the returns trustees made due to the investors' investment.

Then, trustees decided whether to return to investors all, some, or none of the amount received. The amount returned by trustees, denoted K_2, was not multiplied. Each round ended with the payoffs communicated to the players. Each round, the payoff earned by investors (V_1) was: $V_1 = E_1 - M_1 + K_2$, whereas the payoff earned by trustees (V_2) was: $V_2 = E_2 + mM_1 - K_2$. The parameter M_1 indicated the extent to which investors trusted trustees. The parameter K_2 represented the extent to which trustees were trustworthy (Barrera 2008, pp. 10–11).

At the end of the game, the final payoff of each player was the sum of the payoffs of N rounds. The game was called the 'investment game' as the rule of multiplying the amount sent by investors implied that (a) investors dealt with the uncertainty of paying a cost at the beginning of the interaction to possibly gain higher revenues at the end, and (b) trustees had a return from investors' decisions.

The game was a sequence of one-shot games with no information on past behavior, the players knew the structure of the game and could anticipate the behavior of the opponent by backward induction. The prediction of the rational choice theory was that, as trustees were expected to maximize their utility by choosing $K_2 = 0$, investors maximized their revenue by choosing $M_1 = 0$. Therefore, sending and returning nothing were the equilibrium choices. This led to a Pareto-suboptimal perfect equilibrium, where both players kept their entire endowments. On the contrary, Pareto improvements were possible if $M_1 < E_1$, the pie reached its maximum efficiency when an investor sent everything, that is when $M_1 = E_1$, and the outcome was fair when trustees returned more than what investors sent, that is, when $K_2 > M_1$ (Barrera 2008, p. 11).

It was not surprising that, in spite of rational choice predictions, our results basically conformed to recent literature (e.g., Berg, Dickhaut and McCabe 1995; Ortmann, Fitzgerald and Boeing 2000). Subjects invested on average 35% of their initial endowment and returned slightly less.

We used these robust experimental data to calibrate an ABM that reproduced the behavior of subjects in the laboratory to investigate the impact of more complex interaction structures. First, we estimated a coefficient β_i that indicated how much investors modified their investment each round as a function of the difference between the amount invested and the amount received by trustees in the previous round. For any player i and round t, we calculated the difference $X_{it} = R_i - I_i$, where I_i and R_i were the amounts that i invested and received as return from their investment in the previous round, respectively. Then, we came up with the model:

$$Y_{it} = \alpha_i + \beta_i X_{it} + \varepsilon \qquad (2.1)$$

where Y_{it} was the amount invested by player i in round t, so that the two parameters α_I and β_I were obtained for each subject when playing as investors. Equation (2.1) took into account the fact that investors could have had an individual constant propensity to trust represented by the individual intercept α_I, but also the capability of reacting upon past experiences, which was represented by the β_I coefficient. While the first parameter reflected general attitudes of subjects, the second one was more related to what actually occurred during the game. It is worth noting that the correlation between α_i and β_i was significant and positive ($r = 0.44$, $p < 0.001$). This means that trusting subjects were also trustworthy.

Secondly, we built a baseline version (called 'experimentLike') of the ABM that exactly replicated the experiment with experimentally calibrated parameters. In each period, agents were coupled and played an investment game either as investors or trustees, by following the behavior measured by coefficients α_i and β_i (for details, see Boero, Bravo and Squazzoni 2010). The average investment and return of the baseline were, respectively, 3.57 and 2.76 ECU. A t test over individual investments/returns confirmed that the model did not significantly differ from the experiment (respectively, $t = 0.288, p = 0.774$ two-sided, and $t = -0.085, p = 0.933$ two-sided).

We then designed other scenarios where we modified the interaction structure. We increased the periods, tested the two-way interactions, with agents playing in both roles during the same interaction ('TwoWays' scenario), tested different static interaction structures, such as fixed couples, dense networks, small worlds and scale-free networks (for details, see Boero, Bravo and Squazzoni 2010). Then, we introduced the possibility that agents broke and created links according to a simple happiness threshold function: investors were happy when trustees returned more or the same as in the previous interaction.

In one scenario ('dynamic1'), broken links were replaced only when agents were isolated, according to the rule that a new link could be formed between isolated agents and new agents. In another scenario ('dynamic2'), once a link was broken, one of the two formerly coupled agents was randomly chosen to initiate a new link, with agents who could become isolated.

This last assumption was to keep the number of links fixed over the rounds. We tested these last two scenarios starting from randomly coupled and fully connected networks (for details, see Boero, Bravo and Squazzoni 2010). All scenarios are summarized in Table 2.5.

Simulations showed that static interaction structures did not alter the experimental results. The results were different with dynamic networks, where partner selection was introduced (Table 2.6). By separately analyzing simulation periods, it is evident that the possibility that cooperators link more and interact more provides room for higher profitability of investments and more robust cooperation. This was especially evident in the 'dynamics2Couples' and 'dynamics2k10' scenarios, where higher payoffs were significantly correlated with trusting and trustworthy behavior (see parameters α_i, which estimated the trust propensity of each agent and y_i, which was calibrated on the returns of each B player in the experiment, in Table 2.7).

Table 2.5   The simulation scenarios (Boero, Bravo and Squazzoni 2010).

Scenario	Description
experimentLike	• Random coupling in each period • One-way interaction
twoWays	• Random coupling in each period • Two-way interaction
fixedCouples	• Fixed couples • Two-way interaction
denseNetwork	• Fixed fully connected network • Two-way interaction
smallWorld	• Fixed small-world network • Two-way interaction
scaleFree	• Fixed scale-free network • Two-way interaction
dynamic1Couples	• Dynamic network • Broken links were replaced only for isolated agents • Two-way interaction • Initial random coupling
dynamic1Dense	• Dynamic network • Broken links were replaced only for isolated agents • Two-way interaction • Initial dense network
dynamic2Couples	• Dynamic network • Broken links were replaced only by one of the two agents formerly linked • Two-way interaction • Initial random coupling
Dynamic2k10	• Dynamic network • Broken links were replaced only by one of the two agents formerly linked • Two-way interaction • Initial regular network of degree 10

Figure 2.7 shows the network shape after 30 periods of a typical run of 'dynamics2Couples' [Figure 2.7(a)] and 'dynamics2k10' [Figure 2.7(b)], with clusters around cooperative agents and a plethora of isolated agents in the first case, and cooperative agents with a larger number of links even without isolated agents in the latter. It is worth noting that the average value of α_i (trust propensity) of agents who had five or less links was 2.73, against 4.17 for agents who had more than five links. In short, in the first case, cheaters were isolated and others clustered around

Table 2.6 Average investment and returns in the original experiment and in the dynamic network scenarios. Standard deviations are in parentheses. Averages significantly different from the experiment (at the 10% level) are marked in bold (Boero, Bravo and Squazzoni 2010).

Model name	Period 1–10		Period 11–20		Period 21–30	
	A invest.	B returns	A invest.	B returns	A invest.	B returns
dynamic1	3.65	2.92	3.67	2.95	3.68	2.96
Couples	(2.58)	(2.96)	(2.60)	(2.90)	(2.62)	(2.93)
dynamic1	3.79	**3.32**	3.66	2.96	3.68	2.97
Dense	(2.67)	(3.20)	(2.60)	(2.96)	(2.62)	(2.94)
dynamic2	3.82	**3.37**	**4.48**	**5.02**	**4.63**	**5.58**
Couples	(2.68)	(3.42)	(3.01)	(4.50)	(3.11)	(5.12)
dynamic	**4.11**	**4.00**	**4.43**	**4.85**	**4.49**	**5.02**
2k10	(2.82)	(3.59)	(3.01)	(4.30)	(3.04)	(4.50)
Experiment	3.48	2.79	–	–	–	–
	(2.69)	(3.58)				

highly cooperative agents. In the latter, cheaters were bound to have a few links and only between each other. This means that cooperation can arise as an effect of social structure even without imitation, interpersonal commitment, and reputation, that is, social mechanisms that could naturally foster it.

These results have implications on understanding the limits of reciprocity strategies. Doubtlessly, the Axelrod-like 'shadow of the future' is an important factor that

Table 2.7 Correlation between average payoffs per run and agent parameters. *** $p < 0.001$, ** $p < 0.01$, * $p < 0.05$ (Boero, Bravo and Squazzoni 2010).

Model name	Period	α_i	β_i	γ_i
dynamic1 Couples	1–10	−0.18***	0.11	−0.80***
	11–20	−0.78***	0.16	−0.67***
	21–30	−0.68***	0.21*	−0.66***
dynamic1 Dense	1–10	0.02	−0.18	0.64***
	11–20	−0.72***	0.17	−0.66***
	21–30	−0.66***	0.15	−0.61***
dynamic2Couples	1–10	−0.13	−0.05	0.53***
	11–20	0.37***	−0.14	0.96***
	21–30	0.37***	−0.14	0.95***
dynamic2k10	1–10	0.32***	−0.19	0.87***
	11–20	0.36***	−0.18	0.96***
	21–30	0.35***	−0.19	0.97***

(a)   (b)

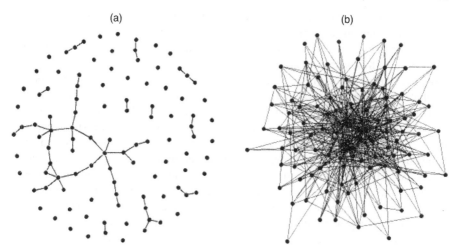

Figure 2.7 Networks after 30 periods in the 'dynamics2Couples' (a) and 'dynamics2k10' (b) scenarios (Boero, Bravo and Squazzoni 2010).

explains cooperation in hostile contexts. The point is that when applied to static social networks and once trust has been eroded by cheating, the stability of the links between agents following conditional strategies can only cause a never-ending sequence of mutual defection. Partner selection in dynamic networks reduces exploitation opportunities for cheaters so that cooperators are not bound to reciprocate defection, because they can find new partners with whom to start cooperative interaction.

Our understanding is that this finding is of particular interest for the nature and evolution of markets, particularly considering the historical and institutional picture suggested by North (2005). First, particular market scaffolds might be more efficient that others exactly because they have institutionalized partner selection as a relatively low-cost sanctioning for cheaters. This can be true not only where interaction is between producers and consumers, but also when production partners collaborate in the co-design or co-production of goods. Secondly, if the argument about markets as networks stressed by White (2004) is correct, particular market structure configurations might have historically evolved out of partner selection mechanisms, and complex market structures could be viewed as a magnification of relatively simple social mechanisms, such as those investigated in our experimentally grounded model.

Obviously, to look at these implications in due detail, models that focus on the co-evolution of individual action and interaction structures are needed. Our experimentally grounded model is an example of this, as we focused on partner selection as a social mechanism that can guide self-reinforcing co-evolution between action and structure. Our findings are also important in that they can guide us in designing new experiments that investigate these issues in the laboratory, to understand, for example, the specific conditions upon which individuals decide to break relationships in typical trust situations. Therefore, the relationship between models and experiments can be twofold: not only can models help to generalize experimental findings, they can also allow us to adjust the experimental design to examine new aspects.

That said, other social mechanisms, such as tags and interpersonal commitment, can boost partner selection and make networks more stable. Every day we make large use of tags to classify and identify others, as well as to signal certain personal attributes to others. In sociological terms, tags can be viewed as socially shared communication signals that connote certain attributes of individuals or groups. For instance, they can include speaking dialects or particular accents, dressing elegantly, driving garish customized sports cars or publishing a self-important ethical code in a company's web site. These attributes or actions might be used socially as predictors of the behavior of others, in particular when we interact with unknown partners. Although they can channel unintentional, inaccurate, arbitrary or false information, tags can favor cooperation in the absence of past interaction experience, memory, reciprocity motives or reputational signals. Therefore, they can substitute past direct experience of partner selection. As such, they have been widely investigated in ABM literature under different social interaction situations (e.g., Hales 2000; Riolo, Cohen and Axelrod 2001; Edmonds and Hales 2003; Hammond and Axelrod 2006; Kim 2010).

The same is true for interpersonal commitment, that is, the building of long-term cooperative links among partners, based on unconditional cooperation. This cannot directly help partner selection when relationships are formed, but can help to maintain them over time. As shown by de Vos, Smaniotto and Elsas (2001) and Back and Flache (2006), interpersonal commitment can exert more robust evolutionary pressures towards cooperation than reciprocity and conditional cooperation, in selective environments where cheaters are likely to exploit cooperators.

For instance, by modeling an exchange dilemma game of mutual help, Back and Flache (2006) showed that interpersonal commitment outperformed conditional cooperation strategies against defection exactly because it avoided the vicious cycle of 'keeping the books balanced' of the latter. Obviously, it is essential that the bundles of these mechanisms are more precisely dissected in future laboratory experiments which could guide new simulations.

2.5 Reputation[9]

In real life, we do not decide what to do simply by relying on market signals, our personal experience or common knowledge, as we often communicate with and are influenced by qualified people. For instance, when we look for competent and trustworthy builders to restore our holiday home, opinions, suggestions and rumors from people living in the neighborhood can make a difference. Communicating with others can help reduce the gap between what we know and what we should know and provides us with good reason to risk interacting with unknown partners. Therefore, the social sharing and circulation of individual judgement about other

---

[9] This section extensively drew on Boero et al. (2010).

people's trustworthiness is a fundamental information source to compensate for lack of personal interaction experience.

The increasing tendency of markets, groups and communities to self-organize in virtual settings, where individuals do not have the chance to know each other personally has highlighted the relevance of reputation. Reliability rankings are endogenously shaped by transaction partners to guarantee cooperation.

Recent experimental findings on a series of different market situations have confirmed that humans are extremely sensitive both to their reputation and to gossip and information about the reputation of others. This is so even when it is not expected to directly affect their material payoff (e.g., Sommerfeld *et al.*, 2007; Piazza and Bering, 2008; Boero *et al.* 2009a, 2009b). The explanatory hypothesis for this is that reputation is an important normative reference for humans which increase the likelihood of trust and cooperation. These could be the value of social approval for personal well-being and the importance of showing commitment to other people's interests.

The study of reputation for cooperation has given rise to a prominent field of ABM and experimental research, with interesting applications also for online community management. Two aspects have been specifically investigated: reputation as a *social order* pillar and reputation as a *social learning* scaffold (Buskens and Raub 2002).

The first aspect was investigated by Conte and Paolucci (2002) through an ABM that indicated the strength of reputation in allowing society to count on a low-cost form of social sanction that helps to discriminate cheaters and defend norm abiders. Reputation is the social sharing of third-party evaluations about agent trustworthiness that, although inaccurate, arbitrary and subjective, makes cheating a risky strategy, especially when interactions are repeated. Agents are embedded in social networks and the shadow of the future is a cogent force against self-interest temptation.

We investigated this second aspect in Boero *et al.* (2010) with an experimentally grounded model. On account of its methodological insights, I have decided to focus on this last example.

The reputation model of Boero *et al.* (2010) was based on data gathered from a laboratory experiment, where 64 individuals were asked to take investment decisions in an uncertain environment. This experiment was explicitly designed to generate a dataset to calibrate an ABM and derive macro implications in more complex systems from microscopic agent interaction. The purpose was to test the impact of other people's opinion on agent investment and the relevance of reputation as a learning scaffold in economic markets characterized by uncertainty.

The experimental game was organized as follows. Subjects had an initial endowment of 1000 ECU with a fixed exchange rate in Euros, and a randomly assigned security with a given yield. The environment consisted of 30 securities with unknown yields. Subjects were allowed to ask for a new security each round. The order of security exploration was a fixed sequence. The game ended after 17 rounds, but subjects knew just that it was supposed to end with a probability $= 0.1$ on each round. In each round subjects knew only the securities discovered in the previous rounds. The search for new securities was a risky investment and subjects bore an exploration cost. The expected final profit at the end of the game was dependent on the yields of the security discovered by subjects.

Each subject was paired with three automata players with predetermined behavior with whom they exchanged information about their already discovered securities. Instructions indicated that they were interacting anonymously with other players in the experiment, called A, B and C. This was to simplify the interaction and increase our control over subject behavior.

Information concerning the securities' yields could have been true or false, for example, subjects could under- or overrate yields or communicate the true yield of their best security (for details, see Boero *et al.* 2010, 2.3., 2.4 and the caption of Figure 10). Therefore, one of the crucial challenges for subjects was to distinguish trustworthy partners from others. Investment strategies were as follows: (1) randomly searching for new securities in the environment (given uncertain yields); (2) buying securities following other hints (perhaps true, maybe not); or (3) exploiting already discovered securities.

First, we explored the experimental data. Through a two-step cluster analysis, we traced certain coherent behavioral patterns: subjects who followed other agents' hints suggested true hints in turn to others; subjects who did not follow hints and preferably adopted exploiting or random exploring investment strategies suggested in turn false hints. Once behavioral patterns were traced from experimental data, an ABM was made that replicated the number of agents, the structure of the game and environment features. The model was calibrated according to the cluster distribution of subject behavior found in the experiment (Table 2.8). The simulation parameters are shown in Table 2.9 (for small differences between the experiment and the model, see Boero *et al.* 2010, 5.2).

Table 2.8   Distribution of agents in the ABM according to experimental clusters (adapted from Boero *et al.* 2010, 5.1).

Information	Investment			
	Explorative subjects who invested by following hints	Subjects who preferred to explore randomly even in presence of reliable hints	Subjects who followed hints when they were reliable	Total
Cooperative subjects who transmitted true hints	12.50%	1.56%	12.50%	26.56%
Reciprocators who transmitted true hints to trustworthy agents and false hints to cheaters	17.19%	4.69%	28.13%	50.00%
Cheaters who always transmitted false hints to everybody	1.56%	7.81%	14.06%	23.44%
Total	31.25%	14.06%	54.69%	100.00%

Table 2.9   The simulation parameters (Boero *et al.* 2010, 5.2).

Simulation parameters	Values
Agents	100
Securities	1 million
Standard deviation of yields' distribution	500
Initial endowment	1000 ECU
Exploration cost	8000 ECU
Number of interactions	495

We followed the experimental idea of treatments, that is, creating some baseline scenarios, introducing incrementally precise parameter modifications and comparatively measuring their impact on certain variables. We then created seven simulation settings that modified the mechanisms of partners' trustworthiness evaluation. In particular, we tested the impact of personal experience (settings 4 and 5) and reputation (settings 6 and 7), in terms of collective sharing of personal evaluations.

In the first case, agents were capable of recognizing other agents they had met before, to form an opinion about their trustworthiness and to remember it for future encounters. The rule of feedback of partners' trustworthiness was that, when agents met a partner who proved to be unreliable (i.e., who suggested securities with false yields), they recorded the cheater in their memory. Agents constantly updated their memory according to a very simple rule: (i) they calculated the sum of true/false hints that the agent had transmitted to them; and (ii) if the sum of true hints was higher than the total average, this agent was considered trustworthy.

In the second case, we added a social reputation layer to trustworthiness evaluation. That is, we introduced a memory at the system level where agents' evaluations (trustworthy/cheater) were individually formed but made public, homogeneous and available for all agents. In short, now each agent contributed to updating their memory about each other's behavior and the evaluation was constantly shared by all agents. Therefore, there was no need for a personal interaction experience, to have an opinion of the partner (Table 2.10).

Simulation results focused on the impact of these assumptions on certain relevant aggregate variables, such as the agents' final profit, exploration capabilities and resource stock. First, results confirmed the intuition that communication and circulation of social information can improve an agent's profit better then exploration and exploitation of individual strategies. As shown in Figure 2.8, although agents were not capable of evaluating partners' trustworthiness, trusting everybody (also false hints) guaranteed higher profit than atomistic strategies, that is, exploration and exploitation without the influence of other agents' hints (for details, see Boero *et al.* 2010, 6.1, 6.2).

This was further confirmed by comparing settings without trustworthiness evaluation (i.e., 'explore_only') and settings where we introduced more sophisticated cognitive capabilities of trustworthiness evaluation (i.e., 'individual_J_pos') and reputation social mechanisms (i.e., 'collective_J_pos') (for details, see Boero *et al.*

Table 2.10   The simulation settings (adapted from Boero *et al.* 2010, 5.7).

Simulation settings	Rules
Baseline settings	
1 'exploit_only'	Pure exploitation: agents can simply exploit the securities randomly distributed at the beginning of the simulation
2 'explore_only'	Pure exploration: agents can simply explore via a random search, when they have enough resources to do so
No trustworthiness evaluation	
3 'listen_always'	No trustworthiness evaluation: agents communicate information as observed in the experiment and trust everybody
Trustworthiness evaluation at the individual level	
4 'individual_J_pos'	Agents explore partners' trustworthiness without sharing any personal experience with others and with a 'positive attitude' towards unknown partners (presumption of partner trustworthiness)
5 'individual_J_neg'	Agents explore partners' trustworthiness without sharing any personal experience with others and with a 'negative attitude' towards unknown partners (presumption of partner untrustworthiness)
Trustworthiness evaluation is shared at the system level (reputation)	
6 'collective_J_pos'	Agents know the partners' reputation (trustworthy/cheater) if any and follow a 'positive attitude' towards unknown partners (presumption of partner trustworthiness)
7 'collective_J_pos'	Agents know the partners' reputation (trustworthy/cheater) if any and follow a 'negative attitude' towards unknown partners (presumption of partner trustworthiness)

2010, 6.3, 6.4, 6.5). Results confirmed that a reputation mechanism which allows agents to share cognitive evaluation on partners' trustworthiness and the social sharing of information in general guarantee higher profits for agents (Figure 2.9).

This is not a trivial result, in particular since there is no general law or undisputed experimental evidence that clearly demonstrates that reputation mechanisms allow agents to cope with uncertain environments better than other simpler micro atomistic mechanisms, not influenced by potentially false information.

The crucial point is that while evaluations about partners' real trustworthiness in the 'individual_J_pos' and 'individual_J_neg' settings were based on personal experience, cumulated and adjusted over time by agents, this was not true for

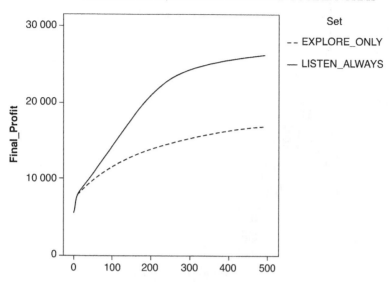

Figure 2.8   Dynamics of final profit of agents in 'explore_only' and 'listen_always' simulation settings (Boero et al. 2010, 6.2).

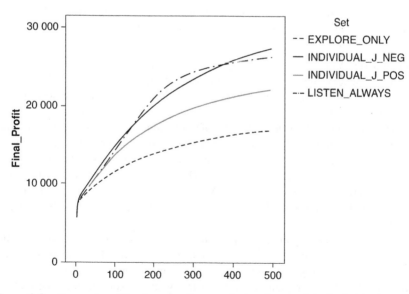

Figure 2.9   Dynamics of final profit of agents in 'explore_only', 'individual_J_pos', 'collective_J_pos' and 'listen_always' simulation settings (Boero et al. 2010, 6.5).

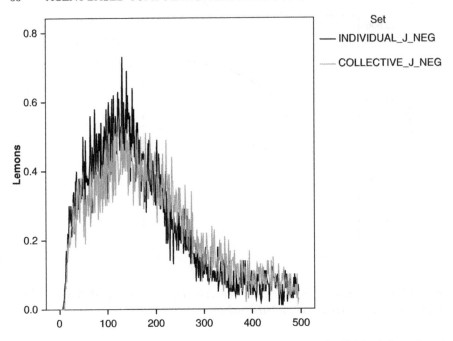

Figure 2.10   Dynamics of the average number of lemons in 'individual_J_neg' and 'collective_J_neg' simulation settings (Boero et al. 2010, 6.7).

reputation (i.e., for the 'collective_J_pos' and 'collective_J_neg' settings), where potentially false evaluations circulated more in the system. Reputation boosted the availability of information about other agents' behavior, replacing the need for personal experience, but at the expense of the reliability of information.

Then, we counted the average number of wrong hints followed by agents over time (called 'lemons') in these four settings (with and without reputation), and measured the average profit over time for hints. Doing so, we observed that reputation decreased lemons even more than personal experience (Figure 2.10). This therefore guaranteed more exploration capabilities to agents. Although profit grew steadily for all, it grew above all for cheaters (Figure 2.11; for other results on negative and positive attitudes towards partners, see Boero *et al.* 2010, 6.7, 6.8).

These results have significant implications for the impact of reputation in human societies and in particular on markets. First, they can provide an account of why agents, despite knowing that social communication channels often give false information, tend to follow reputation and gossip signals. It is curious to see that this also happens when the concrete added value of the information shared through these channels is really questionable. An example would be in financial markets, where institutional and structured information available to agents is plentiful and the added value of any new bit of information is mostly noise (e.g., Schindler 2007).

Our results suggest that from a macro level perspective, this circulation of information aids the explorative capabilities of the system. Secondly, when reputation

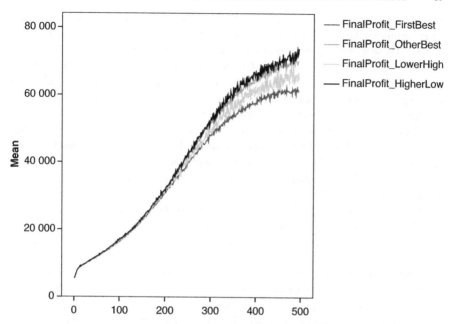

Figure 2.11   Dynamics of the average final profit of agents according to the type of information they transmitted in the 'individual_J_neg' simulation settings. 'FirstBest' means agents who communicated true hints about their best discovered security; 'OtherBest' means agents who communicated true hints about an average yield security; 'LowerHigh' means agents who communicated that the best discovered security yielded less than what it actually yielded; 'HigherLow' means agents who communicated that an average security yielded more than what it actually yielded (Boero et al. 2010, 6.7).

does not result in discrimination, social prejudices and stereotypes, it probably increases the social circles of agents by reducing the risk of interacting with unknown partners. In doing so, it can support cooperation better than direct experience-based partner selection. As a matter of fact, one of the causes of the evolution of humans as complex cognitive systems was probably the need to master heterogeneous and multiple social information coming from a large variety of networks (e.g., Subiaul et al. 2008).

2.6   The emergence of conventions

So far, we have reported examples of social dilemmas where there was a conflict between individual goals and collective benefits, such as in the Prisoner's Dilemma. The point is that social interaction is not always based on competition between agents in more or less strictly competitive games. Every day people interact in situations where the challenge is to converge towards the same or corresponding strategies, where multiple Nash equilibria are possible. In these cases, agents play 'coordination games'. These games are puzzles as it is difficult to understand the social mechanisms by which the equilibrium eventually becomes a robust social norm or institution.

Also in these cases, formal models and computer simulation can help, and growing social science research has dug into certain social mechanisms that account for the emergence of conventions, norms and institutions, such as path dependence, social conformity, routines and compliance (e.g., Conte and Castelfranchi 1995; Dosi *et al.* 1996; Durlauf and Young-Peyton 2001; Kenrick, Li and Burtner 2003; Tummolini *et al.* 2011). I have selected two simple examples that zero in on explanatory mechanisms and can illuminate the present debate on the evolutionary nature of social conventions and norms.

The first is Hodgson and Knudsen (2004), where the role of habit and conformity explained the emergence and maintenance of particular social conventions, such as a traffic convention concerning which side of the road to drive on. The results showed that in most cases human agents are effective in pursuing common ends together regardless of their capability of formulating rational expectations and complicated calculations about future scenarios, but because they can rely on habits that help to establish, reinforce and maintain a given social norm.

The second is Epstein (2001), who investigated another (related) social mechanism, which could account for the strength of social norms, that is, 'learning to be thoughtless'. The idea is that social norms, once established, help agents to reduce the cognitive costs of decisions through a self-reinforcing feedback between macro situation and micro decision.

In the first example, Hodgson and Knudsen (2004) followed Searle's idea that conventions are particular instances of institutional rules (Searle 1995). For instance, all countries have marriage rules that regulate this social contract between partners. However, it is a matter of convention, largely 'arbitrary', whether the rule is polygamy or monogamy. In this view, the 'arbitrariness' of these instances might be the product of a particular history, certain unplanned crucial social events or any other contingencies that characterized a particular country.

In this regard, the authors wanted to shed light on these 'arbitrary' mechanisms which determine the emergence of conventions. Moreover, they were referring to a well-established and venerable tradition (although neglected by most economists) that can be traced back to so-called 'old institutionalism'. Here, the idea was that conventions, norms and institutions were not simply the aggregate products of agents' forward-looking rational behavior. On the contrary, they were viewed as endogenous forces that molded people's preferences, strongly embedded in psychosociological factors (e.g., emulation, social approval, habit, and routines) and largely dependent on past-driven behavior, in the case of social norms also reinforced by ethical convictions.[10]

---

[10] It is worth mentioning here that Geoffrey Hodgson himself has spent most of his career so far to systematize and popularizer the approach of the 'old institutionalism' in economics (e.g., Hodgson 1998).

We need only to mention Thorstein Veblen and John R. Commons and their idea that the 'malleability' of individual preferences is pivotal to understanding that norm equilibrium is at the same time the product and consequence of individual action (e.g., Veblen 1899; Commons 1934). Habit (which may be also largely irrational from an economic point of view) is viewed as a means by which norms and institutions can be socially preserved over time.

The example of the impact of money as an economic institution, reported in Hodgson and Knudsen (2004), is particularly good. As argued by Veblen's pupil Wesley Mitchell, money, once established, changed the mentality, preferences and way of thinking of individuals for generations. At the same time, it self-reinforcing itself as a universal rule to compare and measure the value of everything in the economy and society (Mitchell 1937).[11] The Hodgson and Knudsen model tried to look at these important issues in a simple and abstract way.

The model was based on N agents ($N = 40$) randomly located in a 100×2 cell ring that had to decide whether to drive clockwise or counterclockwise around a ring to avoid collision. They could see a restricted portion of space (i.e., 10 cells ahead, see below for details), where they could count other agents in each lane and in each direction. Decisions were dependent on five heterogeneous parameters called: (1) *same-direction sensitivity*; (2) *opposite-direction sensitivity*; (3) *avoidance*; (4) *habit gene*; and (5) *habituation*. While the first three were fixed and randomly assigned at the beginning of the simulation according to normal distribution, the latter two changed over time.

Parameter (1) weighted the proportion of other agents ahead in their own lane going in the same direction as the agent, so measuring the agents' tendency towards conformism.

Parameter (2) weighted the proportion of other agents in the opposite lane going in the opposite direction of the agent, so measuring the tendency to avoid traffic. Parameter (3) weighted the number of very close agents forward, so measuring the agents' risk aversion. Parameter (4) expressed agents' gene towards habit, as agents were more or less addicted to habit. Parameter (5) expressed agents' more important habits (driving on the left or on the right), so that changing habit decreased with the number of similar choices made in the past (note that this parameter was set at zero for everyone at the beginning of the simulation).

The equation that explained the agents' behavior was as follows:

$$LREvaluation_n = w_{Sdirection} \times SSensitivity_n \times (2S_{L,n,t} - 1)$$
$$+ w_{Odirection} \times OSensitivity_n \times (2O_{L,n,t} - 1)$$
$$+ w_{Avoidance} \times Avoidance_n \times (C_{R,n,t} - C_{L,n,t})$$
$$+ w_{Habit} + Habitgene_n \times Habituation_{n,t}.$$

---

[11] It is worth mentioning here that before the old institutionalism, this same concept of money as an economic institution that changed the preferences and behavior of people, e.g., magnifying the application of rational calculation by individuals to many spheres of modern society, was found in Simmel (1907) and prior to that in Menger (1892).

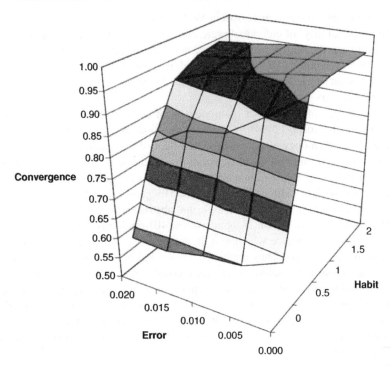

Figure 2.12   Convergence of the population on shared conventions for each level of habit and different error probabilities (Hodgson and Knudsen, 2004, p. 29). The higher the convergence value, the larger the diffusion of a given right/left convention. Convergence is calculated as the total number of periods in which an agent is on the left/right divided by the number of agents multiplied by the number of periods.

where w_x coefficients were fixed weights common to all agents, $S_{L,n}$ was the proportion of all agents going in the same direction as the agent, $O_{L,n}$ was the proportion of all agents going in the opposite direction, $C_{L,n}$ and $C_{R,n}$ were the number of very close agents in any direction (L, left; R, right). If $LREvaluation_n$ was greater than zero, then agents moved to the left. If this was false, agents moved to the right. An error probability was assumed. Finally, when two agents collided, they both died and new agents replaced them, by randomly assigned values.[12]

Results showed that the convergence of agents to a right/left convention is higher when the level of habit increases, independent of the level of error (Figure 2.12). As

---

[12] It is worth noting that authors came to this simplified version of the model after an exploration of many parameters that concerned various cognitive and behavioral aspects, such as the role of inertia in the decision. They then realized that these parameters were not decisive in influencing the system's behavior. In our view, this is an important methodological lesson to which we will return in Chapter 4: parsimonious models are more effective than complicated ones, especially when the former are the result of previous exploration on a large set of parameters.

COOPERATION, COORDINATION AND SOCIAL NORMS   73

Table 2.11   Degrees of convergence to a left/right convention (Hodgson and Knudsen 2004, p. 42). The value 1 means that all agents were on the left or right for the entire simulation run, while the value 0.5 means that there was no mean convergence.

Mean values	w_{Habit}					SD	w_{Habit}				
ε	0	0.5	1	1.5	2	ε	0	0.5	1	1.5	2
0.000	0.638	0.966	0.975	0.974	0.971	0.000	0.123	0.056	0.032	0.032	0.036
0.005	0.599	0.899	0.962	0.968	0.967	0.005	0.075	0.109	0.032	0.034	0.034
0.010	0.592	0.843	0.946	0.959	0.962	0.010	0.064	0.135	0.055	0.033	0.028
0.015	0.572	0.827	0.931	0.941	0.951	0.015	0.058	0.125	0.069	0.049	0.032
0.020	0.577	0.778	0.902	0.932	0.944	0.020	0.056	0.128	0.082	0.053	0.032

w_{Habit} increased, at least from 0 to 1, convergence around a convention was higher for all levels of error. Extensive statistical tests on a large parameter space, not reported here, confirmed the robustness of this finding (Hodgson and Knudsen 2004, p. 30).

For example, a dummy regression was estimated, which used w_{Habit} as the independent and convergence as the dependent variable. Results showed that habit increases convergence throughout the parameter space, with the linear effect of the former explaining 62% of the variation of the latter (Hodgson and Knudsen 2004, p. 31). Table 2.11 shows results averaged over 200 runs, each based on 20 000 periods, for a large combinations of error (ε) and habit weight (w_{Habit}). A t-test showed that for $w_{Habit} = 1$, higher convergence values were expected than for 0 or 0.5, whereas nothing crucially changed for higher values, such as 1.5 or 2.

It is worth noting that the uniqueness of habit in favoring convergence might be closely related to certain cognitive processes. To take this into account, a variety of simulations were performed with different decision horizons. Table 2.12 shows the results with horizons from agents' ignorance (= 0) to agents' omniscience (= 100). Results showed that the most favorable parameter space to the influence of habit on the emergence of a convention was the interval between 0 and 25 of the decision horizon. Although habit had a positive effect also for omniscient agents, the striking result is that habit complements for the lack of omniscience of agents.

Apart from the critical parameter of error, the authors found another important condition that under specific circumstances might alter the emergence of a convention, that is, the presence of a good portion of 'agile' agents. They were typically agents with a low level of habit gene, capable of avoiding traffic congestion and collisions by shifting from one lane to another. When a certain fraction of these avoided death, so as to rule out replacement and mutation, multiple equilibria were successfully established locally, with different social norms eventually co-existing over time. However, this stopped the system converging towards a unique convention.

For scholars interested in human affairs, this finding is far from trivial, as we know very well from historical and sociological accounts that in many social contexts, even a small number of smart and unscrupulous people can add noise to a social system and jeopardize social norms and institutions. But this is just one side of the coin.

Table 2.12   Degrees of convergence to a left/right convention with different decision horizons (Hodgson and Knudsen 2004, p. 45). The p-value is the value of the t-test comparing the mean for $w_{Habit} = 0$ and $w_{Habit} = 1$. 'Random' means a simulation scenario where authors assumed an initial random assignment of horizon values in the population (from 0 to 100). 'Mutating' means that authors also assumed a random assignment of horizon values when agents collided.

| Horizon | Degrees of convergence | | | |
	$w_{Habit} = 0$	$w_{Habit} = 1$	Habit effect	p-value effect
0	0.50	0.53	0.03	0.00
5	0.51	0.80	0.30	0.00
10	0.56	0.88	0.32	0.00
15	0.69	0.95	0.26	0.00
20	0.85	0.98	0.13	0.00
25	0.94	0.98	0.04	0.00
30	0.98	0.98	0.00	0.15
50	0.99	0.99	0.00	0.77
100	0.98	0.98	0.00	0.36
Random	0.97	0.98	0.01	0.00
Mutating	0.50	0.84	0.33	0.00

Indeed, let us suppose that we have to explain not the emergence of a given equilibrium from N competing norms, but norm changes in asymmetric situations, for example, when there is a norm equilibrium already established and asymmetric relations between N competing norms. Let us suppose that, as always happens in society, there are well-established power structures defending the pre-existing equilibrium (e.g., North 2005). 'Agile' people in this particular simulation scenario are now probably viewed under a different light, as important sources of norm change, particularly in periods of Durkheimian collective effervescence.

Epstein (2001) created a similar model to investigate the link between the strength of a social norm and decreased cognitive costs that individuals pay to decide what to do. This therefore suggests an evolutionary argument for the advantage of conformity (i.e., adhering to an entrenched norm without thinking about it, thereby investing time and energy to deal with other problems). Unlike before, Epstein did not assume any influence of habit or past decisions and agents used present information about other agents' behavior to predict future outcomes.

As before, the model consisted of a ring where N agents ($N = 191$) should decide between two conventions (e.g., whether to drive on the left or on the right) by relying on a sampling radius where they could observe what others were doing. Unlike before, where agents had fixed decision horizons, agent radius was heterogeneous and changed over time, so as to mimic the need of agents to find more serious investigations when a decision was uncertain.

More precisely, agents had an heterogeneous radius r where they calculated the relative frequency F of agents that adhered, respectively, to conventions L (drive on the left) or R (drive on the right). They simply conformed to the majority within their radius. To decide to which norm to adhere, they followed a fast and frugal approach as follows: if they found differences in sampling a larger radius, they increased their search; if they did not, they reduced the search. Finally, different levels of noise were assumed to mimic situations where the information about other behavior could be misinterpreted, according to which agents could adopt a norm randomly (see scenarios below).

Epstein created some simulation scenarios to understand the link between norms and individual computing. In the first, agents were initially assigned to a norm, a large radius with no noise present. As expected, the result was that individual computing is reduced and eliminated over time.

In the second, agents were randomly assigned to two norms, the radius was limited, and noise was still absent. The result showed that norms co-exist in different regions of the system's space. This means that agents conform locally but the system shows a globally diverse pattern. Moreover, agents at the boundary between the two regions are extensively computing, whereas those adhering to one of the two norms are not. Then, the noise parameter was set to 0.15, 0.30, 0.50, and to the maximum in various scenarios. These scenarios showed that the emergence of norms is characterized by punctuated equilibria (i.e., relatively long periods of norm equilibrium interrupted by rapid changes), the individual computing efforts are most intense at the boundaries between the norms and the agents endogenously converge towards an average radius' search around the value 2.0. Obviously, search values were unequally distributed, as the search was more intense for regions of system space where norms co-existed.

It was expected that noise would have a decisive influence on search. Extensive statistical tests showed that the steady-state mean search radius was [1.89, 2.03] when the noise value was 0.15, [2.89, 3.04] when the noise value was 0.30, [3.73, 3.81] when the noise value was 0.50 and [4.53, 4.63] when the noise was at a maximum. Therefore, individual computing did not attain its maximum when noise was at its maximum. This interesting finding was further investigated through a sensitivity parameter analysis, which considered the search radius and noise, and manipulated the tolerance parameter t, with different sampled values and large simulation runs. Findings showed that the agents' propensity to expand their radius is inversely related to tolerance. Even at the lowest level of tolerance, the average search radius did not attain its maximum and search was restricted even when noise was not (Figure 2.13).

These findings showed first, that norms, having emerged, feed back to agent decisions by reducing individual computing, Secondly, they showed that this holds to a certain extent also when a social system is characterized by high noise levels, for example, when individuals find it difficult to interpret behavior or norm evaluation by individuals is profoundly uncertain. Finally, they reproduce certain well-known stylized facts about the evolution of norms in social systems, such as punctuated

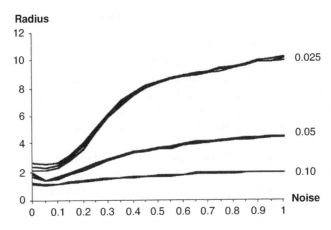

Figure 2.13   Steady state average radii and confidence intervals with various levels of noise and tolerances (Epstein 2001, p. 22).

equilibria and the dynamics of local conformity versus global diversity which characterize complex systems' behavior (e.g., Axelrod 1997).

To sum up, both examples provide intriguing and logical sociologically friendly explanations of the various reasons why our everyday life is populated by social norms that help us to coordinate our action towards collective benefit. Unlike the rational choice view which emphasizes forward-looking omniscient decisions, the results of the first example confirmed previous experimental findings on the strength of fast-and-frugal heuristics of human decision makers in complex social contexts (e.g., Gigerenzer and Selten 2001). This also suggests how much interest sociological models can gain from being founded on an experimentally grounded picture of individual action. The results of the second confirmed the intuition that norms are pillars of social order, in that they embody workable instructions which allow individuals to reduce decision costs (e.g., March 1994).

Moreover, both examples testified to the strength of a couple of well-known mechanisms in the studies of the institutional evolution, that is, path dependence (e.g., David 1985; Arthur 1994; North 2005) and punctuated equilibria (e.g., Timmermans, de Haan and Squazzoni 2008). As in the first case, the probability that a social system converges towards a unique normative equilibrium is strongly dependent on a particular set of initial conditions, as the passage of time implies increasing returns on good solutions locally found by agents.

That is, those who do not collide survive over time and so increase the chance that a particular solution spreads socially and intergenerationally, across space and time. If this is so, any prediction about equilibrium in social systems is extremely difficult and, more importantly, of a lower explanatory value than understanding particular attainance and maintenance mechanisms involved in due detail (e.g., Epstein and Hammond Ross 2002).

The same can be said for the punctuated forms of normative equilibria. It is worth noting that all mechanisms that are important to examine norms and institutions cannot be easily studied in empirical analyses, nor can they be thoroughly examined without computer simulation models.

Secondly, both examples underline the importance of selective pressures. Convergence to a given equilibrium is guaranteed by strong selective forces that push the system to eliminate bad local solutions. This can give us an idea about the importance of modeling macro—micro feedback as evolutionary mechanisms: when a norm emerges, those who survive are those who conform and so population changes over time by itself enforcing the norm.

Obviously, this approach does not rule out the idea that in social systems, structural and economic factors can also exert certain top-down influences, such as a drastic increase of food prices which might influence the emergence of a riot in relatively underdeveloped countries. It does not rule out the idea that macro—micro feedback could be mediated by agent cognition, that is, the capability of agents to purposively reflect about macro consequences of their action and about certain macro properties of the systems where they are embedded, so as to endorse or contrast established norms (e.g., Squazzoni 2008).

The point is that by looking at selective pressures, investigation can clarify long-term change, which is an underestimated dimension in sociology. So, norms are probably strong, robust and efficient especially when there is an effective selective environment that pressurizes agent behavior, for example, by marking a clear difference between what is good and what is bad.

Logically, when social contexts tend to be less selective of agent behavior, for example, because social order disbands and monitoring and social disapproval drastically weakens, agents probably find it difficult to understand what the norm is and what the advantage of complying with it is. Therefore, amoral behavior can proliferate, undermining collective benefits. In short, the weakness of the selective forces that often characterize the typical social environment that surrounds us, for example, the difficulty for us to read the features of the environment and to have clear facts about future effects on us and our peers, could explain a variety of social conditions where negative social outcomes, such as criminal organizations, urban violence, and financial crimes, tend to proliferate.

Thirdly, these examples help us to understand in more detail that the preferences of agents in many concrete social interactions cannot be taken for granted, as they are exogenous parameters of a model. Rather, if we assume that individual preferences are malleable and subject to social influence, these are probably the most important explanatory source in understanding why we have been capable of establishing and maintaining efficient social norms which preside over our collective good. At the same time, this perspective casts new light on the tautological argument of many economists that particular social norms have emerged because individuals had a clear and well-defined preference for them, thereby assuming that individuals had perfect knowledge and information to rationally define their preferences.

References

Aktipis, A. (2004) Know when to walk away: contingent movement and the evolution of cooperation. *Journal of Theoretical Biology*, 231, 249–260.

Arthur, W.B. (1994) *Increasing Returns and Path Dependence in the Economy*, University of Michigan Press, Ann Arbor.

Ashlock, D., Smucker, M.D., Stanley, E.A., and Tesfatsion, L. (1996) Preferential partner selection in an evolutionary study of prisoner's dilemma. *BioSystems*, 37, 99–125.

Axelrod, R. (1981) Emergence of cooperation among egoists. *American Political Science Review*, 75, 306–318.

Axelrod, R. (1984) *Evolution of Cooperation*, Basic Books, New York.

Axelrod, R. (1997) *The Complexity of Cooperation: Agent-Based Models of Competition and Collaboration*, Princeton University Press, Princeton.

Axelrod, R. (2011) Launching 'The Evolution of Cooperation'. *Journal of Theoretical Biology*, in press.

Axelrod, R. and Hamilton, W.D. (1981) The evolution of cooperation. *Science*, 211, 1390–1396.

Axelrod, R., Riolo, R.L., and Cohen, M.D. (2002) Beyond geography: cooperation with persistent links in the absence of clustered neighborhoods. *Personality and Social Psychology Review*, 6, 341–346.

Back, I.H. (2010) Commitment bias: mistaken partner selection or ancient wisdom? *Evolution and Human Behavior*, 31, 22–28.

Back, I. and Flache, A. (2006) The viability of cooperation based on interpersonal commitment. *Journal of Artificial Societies and Social Simulation*, 9(1), accessible at: http//jasss.soc.surrey.ac.uk/9/1/12.html.

Barabási, A.-L. (2002) *Linked: The New Science of Networks*, Perseus, Cambridge, MA.

Barrera, D. (2008) The social mechanisms of trust. *Sociologica*, 2, 2, accessibile at: http://www.sociologica.mulino.it/doi/10.2383/27728.

Beckman, C.M., Haunschild, P.R., and Phillips, D.J. (2004) Friends or strangers? Firm-specific uncertainty, market uncertainty, and network partner selection. *Organization Science*, 15(3), 259–275.

Bendor, J., Kramer, R.M., and Stout, S. (1991) When in doubt...: cooperation in a noisy prisoner's dilemma. *Journal of Conflict Resolution*, 35, 691–719.

Berg, J., Dickhaut, J., and McCabe, K.A. (1995) Trust, reciprocity and social history. *Games and Economic Behavior*, 10, 122–142.

Bienenstick, E.J. and McBride, M. (2004) Explication of the cultural transmission model. *American Sociological Review*, 69, 138–143.

Binmore, K. (1998) *Just Playing: Game Theory and the Social Contract II*, The MIT Press, Cambridge, MA.

Boero, R., Bravo, G., and Squazzoni, F. (2010) Trust and Partner Selection in Social Networks: An Experimentally Grounded Model, arXiv:1008.4705v1 [physics.soc-ph].

Boero, R., Bravo, G., Castellani, M., and Squazzoni, F. (2009a) Reputational cues in repeated trust games. *Journal of Socio-Economics*, 38, 871–877.

Boero, R., Bravo, G., Castellani, M., Laganà, F., and Squazzoni, F. (2009b) Pillars of trust: an experimental study on reputation and its effects. *Sociological Research Online*, **14**(5), accessible at: www.socresonline.org.uk/14/5/5.html.

Boero, R., Bravo, G., Castellani, M., and Squazzoni, F. (2010) Why bother with what others tell you? An experimental data-driven agent-based model. *Journal of Artificial Societies and Social Simulation*, **13**(3), accessible at: http://jasss.soc.surrey.ac.uk/13/3/6.html.

Bowles, S. (2008) Policies designed for self-interest citizens may undermine 'The Moral Sentiments': evidence from economic experiments. *Science*, **320**, 1605–1609.

Bowles, S. and Gintis, H. (2004) The evolution of strong reciprocity: cooperation in heterogeneous population. *Theoretical Population Biology*, **65**, 17–28.

Boyd, R., Gintis, H., and Bowles, S. (2010) Coordinated punishment of defectors sustains cooperation and can proliferate when rare. *Science*, **328**, 617–620.

Boyd, R., Gintis, H., Bowles, S., and Richerson, P.J. (2003) The Evolution of Altruistic Punishment. *PNAS*, **100**(6), 3531–3535.

Boyd, R. and Richerson, P.J. (2009) Culture and the evolution of human cooperation. *Philosophical Transactions of the Royal Society (B)*, **364**, 3281–3288.

Buskens, V. and Raub, W. (2002) Embedded trust: control and learning. *Advances in Group Processes*, **19**, 167–202.

Calvó-Armengol, A. (2001) On bargaining partner selection when communication is restricted. *International Journal of Game Theory*, **30**, 503–515.

Carpenter, J., Bowles, S., Gintis, H., and Hwang, S.-H. (2009) Strong reciprocity and team production. *Journal of Economic Behavior & Organization*, **71**(2), 221–232.

Chiang, Y.-S. (2008) A path toward fairness. Preferential association and the evolution of strategies in the ultimatum game. *Rationality and Society*, **20**(2), 173–201.

Cohen, M.D., Riolo, R.L., and Axelrod, R. (2001) The role of social structure in the maintenance of cooperative regimes. *Rationality and Society*, **13**, 5–32.

Commons, J.R. (1934) *Institutional Economics. Its Place in Political Economy. Volume I*, Transaction Publishers, New Brunswick, NJ [1989].

Condlin, R.J. (1992) Bargaining in the dark: the normative incoherence of lawyer dispute bargaining role. *Maryland Law Review*, **51**, 1–104.

Conte, R. and Castelfranchi, C. (1995) *Cognitive and Social Action*, UCL Press, London.

Conte, R. and Paolucci, M. (2002) *Reputation in Artificial Societies: Social Beliefs for Social Order*, Kluwer Academic Publishers, Dordrecht.

Conte, R., Edmonds, B., Scott, M., and Sawyer, K. (2001) Sociology and social theory in agent-based social simulation: a symposium. *Computational and Mathematical Organization Theory*, **7**, 183–205.

David, P. (1985) Clio and the economics of QWERTY. *The American Economic Review*, **75**(2), 332–337.

Dawkins, R. (1989) *The Selfish Gene*, 2nd revised edn, Oxford University Press, Oxford.

de Quervain, D.J.-F., Fischbacher, U., Treyer, V., *et al.* (2004) The neural basis of altruistic punishment. *Science*, **305**, 1254–1258.

de Waal, F. (2005) *Our Inner Ape*, Riverhead Books, New York.

de Vos, H., Smaniotto, R., and Elsas, D.A. (2001) Reciprocal altruism under conditions of partner selection. *Rationality and Society*, **13**(2), 139–183.

Dosi, G., Marengo, L., Bassanini, A., and Valente, M. (1996) Norms as emergent properties of adaptive learning: the case of economic routines. *Journal of Evolutionary Economics*, **9**(1), 5–26.

Dunbar, R.I.M. (1996) *Grooming, Gossip and the Evolution of Language*, Harvard University Press, Cambridge, MA.

Dunbar, R.I.M. (2004) Gossip in evolutionary perspective. *Review of General Psychology*, **8**, 100–110.

Durlauf, S. and Young-Peyton, H. (2001) *Social Dynamics*, The MIT Press, Cambridge, MA.

Dutta, B., Ghosal, S., and Ray, D. (2005) Farsighted network formation. *Journal of Economic Theory*, **122**, 143–164.

Edmonds, B. and Hales, D. (2003) Replication, replication, replication: some hard lessons from model alignment. *Journal of Artificial Societies and Social Simulation*, **6**(4), 11, accessible at: http://jasss.soc.surrey.ac.uk/6/4/11.html.

Epstein, J.M. (2001) Learning to be thoughtless: social norms and individual computation. *Computational Economics*, **18**, 9–24.

Epstein, J.M. and Hammond Ross, A. (2002) Non-explanatory equilibria: an extremely simple game with (mostly) unattainable fixed points. *Complexity*, **7**(4), 18–22.

Fehr, E. and Gätcher, S. (2000) Coordination and punishment. *American Economic Review*, **90**, 980–994.

Fehr, E. and Gätcher, S. (2002) Altruistic punishment in humans. *Nature*, **415**, 137–140.

Fodor, J. and Piattelli-Palmarini, M. (2010) *What Darwin Got Wrong*, Farrar, Straus and Giroux, New York.

Fudenberg, D. and Maskin, E. (1990) Evolution and cooperation in noisy repeated games. *American Economic Review*, **80**, 274–279.

Gigerenzer, G. and Selten, R. (eds) (2001) *Bounded Rationality – The Adaptive Toolbox*, The MIT Press, Cambridge, MA.

Gintis, H. (2000) Strong reciprocity and human sociality. *Journal of Theoretical Biology*, **206**, 169–179.

Gintis, H. (2009) *The Bounds of Reason. Game Theory and the Unification of the Behavioral Sciences*, Princeton University Press, Princeton.

Gintis, H., Bowles, S., Boyd, R., and Fehr, E. (eds) (2005) *Moral Sentiments and Material Interests: The Foundations of Cooperation in Economic Life*, The MIT Press, Cambridge, MA.

Gulati, R. (1995) Performance, aspirations and risky organizational change. *Administrative Science Quarterly*, **43**, 58–86.

Hales, D. (2000) Cooperation without space or memory: tags, groups and the prisoner's dilemma, in *Multi-Agent-Based Simulation* (eds S. Moss and P. Davidsson), Springer-Verlag, Berlin Heidelberg, pp. 157–166.

Hammond, R.A. and Axelrod, R. (2006) Evolution of contingent altruism when cooperation is expensive. *Theoretical Population Biology*, **69**(3), 333–338.

Hanson, D.P. (1991) Managing for ethics: some implications of research on the prisoner's dilemma game. *SAM Advanced Management Journal*, **56**, 16–20.

Haruvy, E., Roth, A., and Ünver, M. (2006) The dynamics of Law-Clerk matching: an experimental and computational investigation of proposals for reform of the market. *Journal of Economic Dynamics and Control*, **30**(3), 457–486.

Hauert, C., Traulsen, A., Brandt, H., *et al.* (2007) Via freedom to coercion: the emergence of costly punishment. *Science*, **316**, 1905–1907.

Hauk, E. (2001) Leaving the prison: permitting partner choice and refusal in prisoner's dilemma games. *Computational Economics*, **18**, 65–87.

Helbing, D. and Yu, W. (2008) Migration as a mechanism to promote cooperation. *Advances in Complex Systems*, **11**(4), 641–652.

Hodgson, G.M. (1998) The approach of institutional economics. *Journal of Economic Literature*, **36**(1), 166–192.

Hodgson, G.M., Knudsen, T. (2004) The complex evolution of a simple traffic convention: the functions and implications of habit. *Journal of Economic Behavior and Organization*, **54**, 19–47.

Jackson, M.O. and Watts, A. (2002) The evolution of social and economic networks. *Journal of Economic Theory*, **106**, 265–295.

Jackson, M.O. and Wolinksy, A. (1996) A strategic model of social and economic networks. *Journal of Economic Theory*, **71**, 44–74.

Joyce, D., Kennison, J., Densmore, O., *et al.* (2006) My way or the highway: a more naturalistic model of altruism tested in an iterative prisoners' dilemma. *Journal of Artificial Societies and Social Simulation*, **9**(4), accessible at: jasss.soc.surrey.ac.uk/9/2/4.html.

Kagel, J. and Roth, A. (2000) The dynamics of reorganization in matching markets: a laboratory experiment motivated by a natural experiment. *Quarterly Journal of Economics*, **115**, 201–235.

Kenrick, D.T., Li, N.P., and Burtner, J. (2003) Dynamical evolutionary psychology: individual decision rules and emergent social norms. *Psychological Review*, **110**(1), 3–28.

Kim, J.-W. (2010) A tag-based evolutionary prisoner's dilemma game on networks with different topologies. *Journal of Artificial Societies and Social Simulation*, **13**(3), accessible at: http://jasss.soc.surrey.ac.uk/13/3/2.html.

Kogut, B. (1989) The stability of joint ventures: reciprocity and competitive rivalry. *Journal of Industrial Economics*, **38**, 183–198.

Kollock, P. (1993) An eye for an eye leaves everyone blind: cooperation and accounting systems. *American Sociological Review*, **58**, 768–786.

Kollock, P. (1994) The emergence of exchange structures: an experimental study of uncertainty, commitment, and trust. *American Journal of Sociology*, **100**(2), 313–345.

Kollock, P. (1998) The anatomy of cooperation. *American Journal of Sociology*, **24**, 183–214.

Kuhn, S. (2007) Prisoner's Dilemma, in *Stanford Encyclopedia of Philosophy*, accessible at: http://plato.stanford.edu/entries/prisoner-dilemma/ [version October 22, 2007].

March, J.G. (1994) *A Primer on Decision Making: How Decisions Happen*, The Free Press, New York.

Mark, N. (2002) Cultural transmission, disproportionate prior exposure, and the evolution of cooperation. *American Sociological Review*, **67**, 323–344.

Mark, N. (2004) Reply to Bienenstick and McBrige. *American Sociological Review*, **69**, 144–149.

Menger, C. (1892) On the origin of money. *Economic Journal*, **2**(2), 239–255.

Mitchell, W. (1937) *The Backward Art of Spending Money*, Transaction Publishers, New Brunswick, NJ [1999].

Molm, L.D., Takahashi, N., and Peterson, G. (2000) Risk and trust in social exchange: an experimental test of a classical proposition. *American Journal of Sociology*, **105**(5), 1396–1427.

Nemeth, A. and Takács, K. (2007) The evolution of altruism in spatially structured populations. *Journal of Artificial Societies and Social Simulation*, **10**(3), accessible at: http://jasss.soc.surrey.ac.uk/10/3/4.html.

North, D.C. (2005) *Understanding the Process of Economic Change*, Princeton University Press, Princeton.

Nowak, M.A. and May, R.M. (1992) Evolutionary games and spatial chaos. *Nature*, **359**, 4877–4881.

Nowak, M.A. and Sigmund, K. (1992) Tit for tat in heterogeneous populations. *Nature*, **355**, 250–253.

Nowak, M.A. and Sigmund, K. (1993) A strategy of win-stay, lose-shift that outperforms TIT-FOR-TAT in the prisoner's dilemma game. *Nature*, **364**, 56–58.

Nowak, M.A. and Sigmund, K. (2005) Evolution of indirect reciprocity. *Nature*, **437**, 1291–1298.

Ohtsuki, H., Hauert, C., Lieberman, E., and Nowak, M.A. (2006) A simple rule for the evolution of cooperation on graphs and social networks. *Nature*, **441**, 502–505.

Ortmann, A., Fitzgerald, J., and Boeing, C. (2000) Trust, reciprocity, and social history: a reexamination. *Experimental Economics*, **3**, 81–100.

Ostrom, E. (2000) Collective action and the evolution of social norms. *Journal of Economic Perspectives*, **14**(3), 137–158.

Ostrom, E., Walker, J., and Gardner, R. (1992) Covenants with and without a sword: self-governance is possible. *American Political Science Review*, **86**(2), 404–417.

Piazza, J. and Bering, J.M. (2008) Concerns about reputation via gossip promote generous allocations in an economic game. *Evolution and Human Behavior*, **29**, 172–178

Podolny, J. (2001) Networks as the pipes and prisms of the market. *American Journal of Sociology*, **107**, 33–60.

Riolo, R.L., Cohen, M.D., and Axelrod, R. (2001) Evolution of cooperation without reciprocity. *Nature*, **414**, 441–443.

Santos, F.C., Pacheco, J.M., and Lenaerts, T. (2006) Cooperation prevails when individuals adjust their social ties. *PLOS Computational Biology*, **2**(10), 1284–1291.

Schindler, M. (2007) *Rumors in Financial Markets. Insights into Behavioral Finance*, John Wiley & Sons, Ltd, Chichester.

Searle, J. (1995) *The Construction of Social Reality*, The Free Press, New York.

Sigmund, K. (2010) *The Calculus of Selfishness*, Princeton University Press, Princeton.

Simmel, G. (1907) *The Philosophy of Money*, Routledge, London [1990, second edition].

Slonim, R. and Garbarino, E. (2008) Increases in trust and altruism from partner selection: experimental evidence. *Experimental Economics*, **11**, 134–153.

Sommerfeld, R.D., Krambeck, H-J, Semmann, D., and Milinski, M. (2007) Gossip as an alternative for direct observation in games of indirect reciprocity. *PNAS*, **104**(44), 17435–17440.

Squazzoni, F. (2008) The micro-macro link in social simulation. *Sociologica*, **2**(1), doi: 10.2383/26578, accessible at: http://www.sociologica.mulino.it/journal/article/index/Article/Journal:ARTICLE:179.

Squazzoni, F. (2010) The impact of agent-based models in the social sciences after 15 years of incursions. *History of Economic Ideas*, XVIII(2), 197–233.

Subiaul, F., Vonk, J., Okamoto-Barth, S., and Barth, J. (2008) Do chimpanzees learn reputation by observation? Evidence from direct and indirect experience with generous and selfish agents. *Animal Cognition*, **11**(4), 611–623.

Swedberg, R. (2001) Sociology and game theory: contemporary and historical perspectives. *Theory and Society*, **30**, 301–335.

Timmermans, J., de Haan, H., and Squazzoni, F. (2008) Computational and mathematical approaches to societal transitions. *Computational and Mathematical Organization Theory*, **14**, 391–414.

Tummolini, L., Andrighetto, G., Castelfranchi, C., and Conte, R. (2011) A convention or (tacit) agreement betwixt us, in Dagstuhl Seminar Proceedings 09121, Normative Multi-Agent Systems, accessible at: http://drops.dagstuhl.de/opus/volltexte/2009/1919.

Veblen, T. (1899) *The Theory of the Leisure Class*, Prometheus Books, New York, [2010].

Watts, D. (1999) *Small World: The Dynamics of Networks Between Order and Randomness*, Princeton University Press, Princeton.

Welser, H.T., Gleave, E., and Vaughan, D.S. (2007) Cultural evolution, disproportionate prior exposure and the problem of cooperation. *Rationality and Society*, **19**(2), 171–202.

White, H.C. (2004) *Markets from Networks: Socioeconomic Models of Production*, Princeton University Press, Princeton.

Wiessner, P. (2005) Norm enforcement among Ju/'hoansi Bushmen. a case of strong reciprocity? *Human Nature*, **16**(2), 115–145.

Yagamashi, T., Cook, K.S., and Watabe, M. (1998) Uncertainty, trust, and commitment formation in the United States and Japan. *American Journal of Sociology*, **104** (1), 165–194.

3

Social influence

This chapter reviews work on the relevance of social influence on social patterns and dynamics, such as residential segregation and collective opinion. We are all influenced by others in many different ways, such as conformity, persuasion and peer pressure, in many different contexts such as the family, friendship, co-worker relationships, or the mass media. This has been widely recognized, especially in social psychology (e.g., Moscovici 1985; Zimbardo and Leippe 1991; Paicheler 1998; Markovski and Thye 2001; Pratkanis 2007). Taking into account these aspects is one of the most important advantages of social interaction modeling. It is difficult to understand the role played by social influence in large scale social systems without modeling.

In the previous chapter, most examples looked at examining social order and norms, emphasizing the explanatory value of social structures on pro-social behavior. Here, the *explanandum* is the emergence of social patterns which have 'structuring' or 'configurational' properties (Macy and Willer 2002; Cederman 2005; Miller and Page 2007), and the key *explanans* role is played above all by agent behavior.

Here, examples allow us to look at the many complex facets of the micro–macro link, by focusing on micro behavior and details of macro outcomes. Complex social outcomes can be explained in terms of agent behavior and interaction by translating micro–macro link issues into concrete model assumptions. As a result, agent-based computational sociologists can contribute to 'secularize' the struggle between micro and macro supporters in our discipline and to defend a pragmatic and model-oriented approach (Squazzoni 2008). This is because ABMs allow us to approach social interaction modeling as a problem of abstraction and scales (i.e., local vs. global) more than a problem of ontology and categorical levels (i.e., 'individual' and 'social') (Petri 2012).

In this respect, Thomas Schelling (1971, 1978) and Mark Granovetter (1978) showed how the explanation of a social outcome is much more informative when it can address how individual behavior generates social patterns rather than assuming that they are determined by other macro variables or are simple aggregates of

Agent-Based Computational Sociology, First Edition. Flaminio Squazzoni.
© 2012 John Wiley & Sons, Ltd. Published 2012 by John Wiley & Sons, Ltd.

individual characteristics. The explicit modeling of agent interaction allows us to map micro–macro links so that what seems to be at first sight strange and counter-intuitive collective behavior can be explained in terms of interaction and aggregation.

As mentioned in Chapter 1, the importance of micro details and the nonlinearity of aggregation processes make a statistical approximation of the macro behavior of a system from averaged micro behavior impossible. These are cases where the law of large numbers does not apply, because of the complex set of interactions involved at the micro level. The point is that ABM is the only means to treat and investigate these systems formally (Miller and Page 2007).

Granovetter and Soong summarized the novelty of these models compared with standard statistical models as follows:

> These models have three distinct advantages over most current models: (1) their treatment of dynamics is explicit and central (i.e. they do not deal in comparative statistics), (2) they make no assumption of linear relations among variables, and (3) they are driven not by correlations but by well-defined causal mechanisms. We see models of this kind as part of a broader movement in sociology toward explicit, concrete, dynamic analysis and away from the general linear model, which, assuming that the size of causes must determine the size of consequences, prepares us poorly for the many surprises that social life has in store (Granovetter and Soong 1988, p. 103).

Readers more familiar with complex systems theory will see how much these sociological arguments owe to complexity thinking (e.g., Squazzoni and Boero 2005; Miller and Page 2007; Castellani and Hafferty 2009).

The rest of the chapter is structured as follows: Section 3.1 focuses on segregation dynamics, by now a classical topic in ABM research. Segregation may be defined as 'the non-random allocation of people who belong to different groups in social positions and the associated social and physical distances between groups [. . .]. Segregation is created and maintained through the interdependent actions of individuals' (Bruch and Mare 2009, pp. 270 and 272).

Here, I specifically focus on residential segregation, where the challenge is to link processes at the individual, neighborhood and macro/urban/city-wide level of observation and analysis (Bruch and Mare 2009, p. 278). In most cases, such a link is difficult to establish, observe and analyze without advanced computational modeling techniques. In this respect, some initial explorations which combine ABMs and Geographic Information Systems (GIS) were undertaken that showed innovative ways of examining social interaction in realistic spatial neighborhood and city structures (e.g., Gimblett 2002; Gimblett and Skov-Petersen 2008).

Recently, this was also done to specifically study Schelling-like residential segregation (e.g., Crooks 2010; Omer 2010). The important point here is that, from Schelling's contribution to more recent examples, this field exemplifies the challenge of understanding unintended macro consequences of individual behavior (e.g.,

Boudon 1982; Elster 2007). It also shows the real advantage of formalized models rather than descriptive accounts and models of endogenous micro processes rather than macro-oriented theoretical constructs. As we will see, residential segregation has also attracted a lot of attention as it is viewed as the major cause of serious social problems and so has important policy implications.

Section 3.2 then illustrates a general typology of social influence mechanisms called 'threshold behavior'. From Granovetter (1978) who was largely influenced by the Schelling segregation model, this field has evolved with interesting applications for innovation and opinion dynamics.

In many cases, these models have expunged most of the complexity of Schelling's approach, so that social interaction can be examined with computer simulation based on graph and equation-based models. Some critics would not consider these ABMs, as the most complex features of social interaction are abstracted away. However, we have included them here as they are particularly significant at the explanatory level and are a sound and promising source of inspiration for more complex and sophisticated models. In this respect, our attention will be addressed particularly towards opinion dynamics, as this is a prominent field in ABM research which emphasizes how certain social mechanisms might account for the change of collective opinion.

Section 3.3 deals with the role of social influence in explaining culture dynamics. Here, the main puzzle is the interplay between local uniformity and global polarization. There is evidence that although individuals are subjected to homophily and conformity pressures, there is polarization of cultures, generalization of extremist cultures and the survival of minorities.

From different angles, Nowak, Szamrej and Latané (1990), Axelrod (1997) and Mark (1998) have delved into certain social mechanisms that might account for such a hiatus between micro and macro evidence. Again, it is worth restating that discrepancy is difficult to approach without modeling and simulation.

Finally, I have focused on a more subtle and complex type of social influence, namely social reflexivity. For this we mean the capacity of agents to recognize, infer and reason about characteristics of their social environment and to use these interpretations to contextualize their behavior (Boero, Castellani and Squazzoni 2004a, p. 57). Largely inspired by Gidden's (1986) view on human agency, these examples allow us to look at a more complex link between macro features and micro behavior than other examples, even from the previous chapter.

Indeed, in most models the feedback between macro features and micro behavior is mediated by environmental modification. In natural sciences, it is common to look at macro–micro feedback via stigmergy that is, a basic indirect coordination mechanism that implies environmental modifications made by a given agent at time t_0 which might stimulate a given action by other agents at time t_1. In other words, agents influence each other via environment modifications and in so doing they create self-organization patterns (e.g., subsequent actions tend to reinforce and build on each other) (e.g., Bonabeau, Dorigo and Theraulaz 1999).

It is reasonable to suppose that social agents might influence each other not only through local direct interaction and stigmergy, but also via cognition (e.g., Conte 1999; Conte et al. 2001). Not only do individuals constantly respond and adapt to environmental changes, they are complicit in determining such changes. They also routinely monitor each other, the setting of their interaction and the system features where they are embedded and use relevant information derived from this to base their behavior. They might therefore explicitly endorse or contrast other people's goals, as well as dispute, modify or contrast certain features of these social systems (e.g., Conte and Castelfranchi 1996; Conte 1999; Conte *et al.* 2001).

Obviously, to understand these important aspects of human cognition in social interaction, a higher level of model complexity at the micro level has to be taken into account. This has been questioned from two different perspectives. First, there is no clear empirical or experimental evidence that human beings generally follow complicated cognitive procedures to decide what to do, as they mostly follow simple heuristics and intuitive behavior patterns (Gigerenzer and Selten 2001; Buchanan 2007; Rosewell and Ormerod 2009). Moreover, as suggested by Sawyer (2005), ABM research definitively indicates that social and organizational patterns might emerge and constrain behavior at the micro level even when agents have no internal cognitive representations at all (see also Goldstone and Janssen 2005).

Secondly, the sophistication of the cognitive dimension of agent behavior makes it difficult to save the primary focus of real sociological models, that is, understanding macro patterns, while assuring a model's transparency, replication and finding generalization (e.g., Squazzoni 2007). As Coleman (1990) stated, given that sociological models have to pay attention to situation, interaction and outcome, 'one must keep the action component as simple as possible by abstracting away all elements not considered crucial'. Along the same lines, Goldthorpe (2007) emphasized that in sociology the diversity of the cognitive or motivational aspects of action and the nuances of its subjective meaning do not deserve analytic attention (see also Hedström 2005).

On the other hand (as we will see later in a simple example), it is not true that taking into account richer individual behavior and social influence mechanisms implies necessarily building very complicated cognitive architecture (most of them experimentally untested or untestable) behind agent behavior. However, my understanding is that it is reasonable to approach this issue from a pragmatic and purely instrumental viewpoint. This means that this point should not be approached in terms of binary or all-or-nothing decisions or as an ontological crusade where we drastically support one of the two views.

My opinion is that this is a trade-off decision between simplification and 'complexification', the equilibrium of which has to be concretely found according to the explanatory purpose of the model in question (Gilbert 2005; Squazzoni 2007). When a model has a given empirical target, it will tend more towards complexity. When it has a more general theoretical purpose, it will tend to be simpler.

3.1 Segregation dynamics

One of the most important reasons why humans are unique outliers is that, since the era of foraging societies, we have developed complex social structures where genetically unrelated individuals have co-resided. This implies that bilateral kin associations and brother–sister affiliations proliferated, both sex dispersal facilitated frequent and friendly intergroup relationships, as well as migration and low group genetic relatedness of co-residential social bands were more likely to occur. This was confirmed by a recent empirical survey on 32 hunter-gatherer societies (Hill *et al.*, 2011).

The point here is that, as Georg Simmel brilliantly argued about social differentiation and the stranger, social relationships among co-existing individuals continuously develop within a continuum of nearness and distance, which is mostly irrespective of relatedness (Simmel 1950). Therefore, for extensive co-residing as in modern cities, individuals have also developed subtle, complex and sometimes partially unconscious and unintended ways of dissociating from and discriminating against others. Indeed, one of the most pervasive properties of social organization is that individuals tend to cluster around people with similar social characteristics, such as ethnicity, sex, languages and wealth, thereby discriminating others in various ways (Bruch and Mare 2009). This is what Thomas Schelling's famous segregation model helps us to understand.

Schelling's model is the most popular ABM and one of the most celebrated models in social sciences in general. There are at least four reasons for this. First, the model is general, simple and logical. It is therefore easy to understand, check, manipulate and extend. Secondly, it looks at an important empirical puzzle, such as residential discrimination by ethnicity. This has been a long lasting pattern of many large cities notably in the US from the late 1960s to today. This puzzle has important social and public policy implications, as residential segregation affects public good provision, undermines social integration and has other negative social consequences (see below). At the same time, it does so by providing a counter-intuitive explanation which suggests that residential segregation is an outcome of agent interaction more than an intended purpose of nasty and racist people. Therefore, there is a long-standing crucial empirical puzzle and a real explanation.

Thirdly, it gives an example of one of the most striking social science puzzles ever, that is, the challenge of understanding unintended macro consequences of individual behavior and shows the real advantage of looking at this with formalized models rather than descriptive accounts. Finally, being so simple and general, it has generated variants and extensions that have been subsequently examined by many others, so testifying to the advantage of formalization to achieve finding cumulativeness collectively.

As we will see, there are two types of extensions: (a) tests of the original findings against a variety of different (quantitative and qualitative) parameter values to verify the validity domain of the explanation (e.g., Epstein and Axtell's and Pancs and Vriend's examples below), and (b) extensions of the explanatory findings to a variety of other phenomena related to segregation (e.g., Auchincloss *et al.*'s example below).

Originally conceived for educational purposes (Aydinonat 2005), and first elaborated by placing black and white pieces on a chessboard, the first version of the model was one-dimensional and published in Schelling (1969). Subsequently, a two-dimensional version was added in Schelling (1971, 1978; for a reconstruction of different versions, see Pancs and Vriend 2007).

As reported by Casti (1994, p. 213), the original two-dimensional version was based on a rectangular grid of 16*13 cells, which represented an idealized urban space. In this space, cells represented a homesite that could be occupied by one of the 138 households, black or white, with about a quarter of the cells being empty (Casti 1994, p. 213). The assumptions were that agents (households) of two groups (black or white) preferred to have a certain percentage of their neighbors of the same group (50% or more), had a local vision (a Moore neighborhood composed of eight agents directly surrounding their location), could detect the composition of their neighbors and were motivated to move to the nearest available location where the percentage of like neighbors was acceptable, that is, within the given threshold preference.

By allowing interaction, a typical tipping mechanism eventually occurred: as the group in a minority position entered a given neighborhood in sufficient numbers, it caused the earlier majority group to begin evacuating for other neighborhoods. More specifically, households that reached their tipping point and moved out of the neighborhood, reduced the number of households of the group they belonged to in the neighborhood, leaving whoever was left a little closer to its tipping point. This implied that subsequent entrants who took the place of those who left were predominantly of the minority, and that the process ultimately and irreversibly changed the composition of neighborhoods.

Schelling explained this domino effect due to the 'interdependence of decisions' as follows:

> We can foresee the possibility of a spiral or domino effect, or unravelling process. There will be some interdependence of decisions. Anyone who moves out reduces [...] the number of whites remaining [...]. Assuming some pressing black demand for housing, perhaps an increasing demand as the number of prospective black neighbour grows, and a diminishing white demand to move into a neighbourhood as the black percentages rises, each white who reaches his tipping point and departs brings the remaining whites a little closer to their tipping points (Schelling 1972, p. 161).

Figure 3.1 shows a typical simulation outcome of the NetLogo version of Schelling's model, while Figure 3.2 shows the segregation dynamics under different conditions. I set the threshold preference function, respectively, at 25, 33 and 50%. In other words, we assumed that agents did not dislike diversity as they wanted to live with no more than 1/4, 1/3 or 1/2 of like neighbors.

First, as is shown in Figure 3.2, it is worth noting that segregation patterns do not linearly correspond to household preferences, as a relatively small change in individual preferences led to a large change in the macro outcome. More precisely, while a threshold preference for 25% of like neighbors was sufficient to generate 56% of like neighbors in each neighborhood, a 33% threshold generated 75% of like neighbors (a 50% threshold increased the similarity value to 86%). Secondly

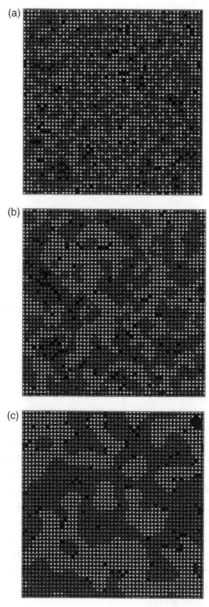

Figure 3.1   Residential patterns in the NetLogo segregation model with households' threshold preferences of alike neighbors at 25% (a), 33% (b) and 50% (c) (Wilensky 1999).

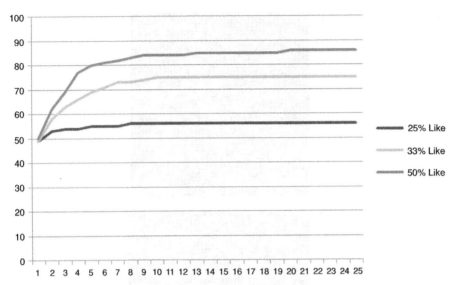

Figure 3.2   Similarity index dynamics in the NetLogo version, with preferences of like neighbors at 25, 33 and 50% (Wilensky 1999).

and contextually, results show that segregation does not require nasty, racist agents to occur, simply an almost fair preference for at least 1/3 of like neighbors, that is, households firmly accepted being a minority in their neighborhood.

As mentioned above, this model has created a prolific stream of research with extensions, tests, empirical applications and theoretical generalizations. For instance, Epstein and Axtell (1996, pp. 165–170) explored various parameter changes to examine the robustness and the generalization of the original findings. They introduced a Von Neumann neighborhood (four agents orthogonally surrounding each location), a 50*50 lattice with 2000 households, 20% of the sites vacant, more tolerant thresholds in individual preferences (preferences from 50 to 25% of households of the same group with the same neighbor, as in our simulation shown before), different movement rules (households did not move to the nearest satisfactory sites, as in the original version, but on an acceptable site at random), and a finite lifetime for households, so that the settlement patterns changed perpetually. Their results confirmed that even a small preference for like neighbors is enough to tip a society into a segregated pattern (see also Clark and Fossett 2008).

Other variants were explored by Pancs and Vriend (2007), who introduced agents with intentional preferences toward integration and deliberate refusal of segregation. They showed that even when all agents have a strict preference for perfect integration, segregation still occurs because of the threshold shape of household preferences (see also Zangh 2004). Laurie and Jaggi (2003) found that the enlargement of a household's idea of targeted neighborhoods could promote a richer range of segregation/integration patterns.

However, this was tempered by Fossett and Waren (2005) who tested Laurie and Jaggi's model with empirical evidence based on ethnic demography. Singh, Vainchtein and Weiss (2011) tested different group sizes and in-group threshold functions. In these cases, an agent's happiness linearly increased according to the number of like agents in their neighborhood and decreased linearly when neighborhoods were dominated by other types of agents. These results were sensitive to aggregation patterns of happiness thresholds. Moreover, when agents preferred to live in integrated neighborhoods, the two groups arranged themselves in a tessellated-like structure.

Fagiolo, Valente and Vriend (2007) generalized the original findings still further by examining certain more realistic network structures than the lattice-based spatial topology of the original model. They found that segregation persists in various types of networks, such as regular, small-world, and scale-free networks. They confirmed that mild proximity preferences may suffice to generate segregation independent of the network structure.

Yin (2009) suggested an empirically calibrated version of the model to examine the interplay of ethnic and economic segregation in the city of Buffalo. Using empirical data on neighborhood composition and housing prices from 1970 to 2000 and integrating ABM and GIS techniques to model the study area in spatial detail, she built a model of the area around Delaware Park, the recreational heart of Buffalo. Simulation results showed that neighborhood economic and racial composition were interrelated in the city and determined the empirically observed segregation patterns.

It is worth noting that Schelling's findings have also recently been validated experimentally. Benito et al. (2011) translated the original model into an experimental game, where subjects played first with sequential stay/move choices and then with simultaneous stay/move choices. The sequential experiment also confirmed a segregative equilibrium outcome. The same result was achieved with simultaneous choices, such as subject heterogeneity which generated a series of focal points in the first round of the experiment, afterwards used by subjects to generate a segregative equilibrium.

An interesting extension was suggested by Gilbert (2002), who introduced 'second-order emergent properties' into the original model. While Schelling's version tried to understand unintended macro consequences from micro behavior subjected to spatial proximity influence, Gilbert focused on whether macro consequences could in turn influence micro behavior, by further exacerbating segregation outcomes. 'Second-order emergent properties' meant macro–micro feedback which influenced agent behavior (e.g., Conte and Castelfranchi 1996; Gilbert 1996; Conte et al. 2001).

In Gilbert's case, this feedback was mediated by agent cognition, whereas in other cases it may have been channeled by evolutionary selection pressures (e.g., only best behavior survives and is replicated over time, as in most evolutionary game-theory inspired models) or modifications of the social structure (e.g., who interacts with whom is determined by previous interaction outcomes so that the social structure diachronically influences agent behavior).

More specifically, Gilbert focused on the agents' capability of detecting 'the presence of emergent features and act accordingly'. Therefore, unlike evolutionary game-theory inspired ABMs, in this case the macro–micro feedback was endogenously internalized by the cognitive capability of agents to generate 'mental representations' of the evolved macro structures (Hales 1998). We will also return to this with other examples in Section 3.4.

First, Gilbert replicated the standard version of the model. Space was characterized by a grid of 500×500 square patches where 1500 agents were distributed, with a majority of green and a minority of red squares. Then, he introduced a typical macro-level effect that could influence household preferences, that is, the crime rate. He assumed that the cost of a home in each possible neighborhood depended in part on the local crime rate which depended on the ratio of agents localized there (e.g., the redder it was the higher the crime rate).

He also assumed that instead of choosing new locations at random, agents could only move to areas where they could afford to buy or to rent. This added a macro constraint, that is, a relationship between the value of new and the old locations. The simulation result was a well-structured clustering of agents, with poor reds confined to the poorest neighborhoods and richer greens aggregated around desirable areas.

He then added the agents' capability of detecting the presence of emergent features and acting accordingly. More specifically, agents could label patches as either red or green according to patch past history and could recognize which patch was best for them. For example, we could make the analogy of the emergence of a good or bad 'image' of particular neighbors and the effect that a neighborhood's attractiveness has on residential decisions.

The simulation outcomes were closely clustered, that is, a macro dynamic similar to that which Schelling attained in his standard model. Therefore, Gilbert's findings confirmed Schelling's. They showed that cognitively, more sophisticated agents, capable of taking into account a wider and more complex range of reasons to decide when, where and for what to move, might lead to further segregation rather than reduce it.

In a recent and disputed article (see Chapter 4), Bruch and Mare (2006) investigated how much Schelling's findings were biased by the typical threshold shape of individual preferences assumed by the author. Their starting point was that surveys and vignette data showed that individuals tend to respond continuously to variations in the racial makeup of their neighborhoods. On the contrary, in the original version, Schelling assumed an individual indifference about a subset of neighborhoods, for example, all neighborhoods 0–49% of one's own group were considered equally undesirable and all neighborhoods of at least 50% of one's own group equally desirable.

These authors assumed that households could experience a small increase in desirability of their location for each given percentage increase in the proportion of own-group households in their neighborhood. Then, they tested a preference function where preferences varied continuously with the proportion of own-group neighbors. Their results showed that linear function preferences could soften residential segregation. As a consequence, they argued that race preferences alone could not account for the segregation patterns observed in many American cities and that an explanation of residential segregation should take into account other factors, perhaps more related to threshold preferences such as income, housing prices, or the availability of mortgages.

As we will see in detail in Chapter 4, confidence in these findings was eroded by Van de Rijt, Siegel and Macy (2009). By replicating Bruch and Mare's version, they pointed out rules that determined how agents moved when unsatisfied. They also explored other modifications related to Pancs and Vriend (2007) and Zangh (2004). These results showed that in a multicultural population with integrative preferences, threshold preferences at a micro level might help to prevent tipping on condition that agents made mistakes and moved to neighborhoods that did not correspond to their preferences. This was as if they did not have complete information about the real composition of the new targeted neighborhood.

Their findings help us to understand the specific links of individual preferences and social outcome involved in segregation. Once agents have a clear preference toward diversity, move to undesirable neighborhoods or promptly react to their neighborhood's changes, segregation is likely to occur. On the contrary, once agents have a clear preference toward ethnicity, react promptly to their neighborhood's changes and rarely make mistakes in selecting their new neighborhood, integration is more likely.

An intriguing extension has been recently suggested by Auchincloss et al. (2011), who showed that residential segregation might play a role in determining the diffusion of obesity and related illnesses in low-income families. This extension is interesting as it shows that Schelling's findings could be generalized to account for a variety of other interesting empirical puzzles. This inspiration is close to Schelling's original idea, when he outlined that:

> some segregation is a corollary of other modes of segregation: residence is correlated with job location and transport. If blacks exclude whites from their church, or whites exclude blacks, the segregation is organized, and it may be reciprocal or one-sided. If blacks just happen to be Baptists and white Methodists, the two colors will be segregated Sunday morning whether they intend to be or not. If blacks join a black church because they are more comfortable among their own color, and whites a white church for the same reason, undirected individual choice can lead to segregation. And if the church bulletin board is where people advertise rooms for rent, blacks will rent rooms from blacks and whites from whites because of a communication system that is correlated with churches that are correlated with color (Schelling 1971, p. 143).

They started from a well-recognized empirical pattern: in many urban areas in the US, minority and low-income neighborhoods have less chance to purchase healthy food compared with high-income neighborhoods. Consequently they are more likely to be obese and have related illnesses. On the contrary, high-income households spend more on food and travel farther to purchase healthy food. This causes inequality in diet, which is not solely determined by preferences (as low income households would have a clear preference for junk food) or economic reasons (healthy food is more expensive), but by a complexity of factors, including residential segregation.

The model was based on a toroidal space of 50×50 cells where two types of agents, namely households and food stores, were localized. Households had two attributes, income and food preference. Stores were assigned a type of food (more or less healthy) and an average price. Healthy food was more expensive. Households ranked stores according to different criteria such as price of food, distance, their own food habit, and preference for healthy food. According to these parameters, households selected where to shop. Stores were allowed to move following opportunities, close, or occupy a vacant location.

These authors created different simulation scenarios, where they manipulated relevant parameters such as segregation (i.e., by testing no segregation, segregation by income and/or for healthy food stores), food price and preferences (e.g., assuming that low-income households could have preferences for unhealthy or healthy food). They found that in the absence of other factors, residential segregation alone could increase the income differential in diet. It did not matter whether low-income households had clear preferences for healthy food. Favorable preferences and favorable prices for healthy food were the only conditions to eliminate the diet differential and rule out the segregation effect. These findings have clear policy implications as they suggest combining incentives toward preferences for healthy food and targeted intervention to support healthy food stores in low-income neighborhoods.

This is just one example of research on social and public policy implications of residential segregation inspired by Schelling's model, particularly in the US. For instance, Alesina, Baqir and Easterly (1999) documented that in cities where ethnic groups were residentially segregated and politicians had strong ethnic references, the amount of public spending for public goods provision in those neighborhoods was low. Reardon and Bischoff (2011) reported a strong correlation between income and residential segregation in metropolitan areas in the US between 1970 and 2000. Andersson, Östh and Malmberg (2010) showed that a US-like segregation has recently occurred also in Sweden and that this has affected school segregation. Nechyba (2003) showed the negative impact of segregation on the quality of schools and consequently on the labor market. For example, it is likely that when referral networks are spatially segregated by ethnicity, disadvantaged groups rely more on insider referrals and consequently lose any mobility chances and are trapped in low-quality jobs (e.g., Elliott 2001).

In conclusion, the most important lesson from these studies is that if individual preferences and perceived differences between groups refer just to one characteristic, such as ethnicity, religion or political position and decision is binary, segregation is unavoidable and social integration is impossible. The difficult question is that, as reported by a recent empirical survey in the US, there is the widespread tendency of people to isolate themselves from others who differ on salient aspects which define their social identity. These could be religion, political ideology, and family behavior, although they are difficult to assess precisely (Gelman et al. 2011).

Pancs and Vriend (2007, p. 23) suggested that a difference could be made if people take into account multidimensional characteristics when forming an opinion about others. In this case, individuals might have more chance to find something in common with others. Nevertheless, if the social identity of people is defined as before, the co-location of individuals cannot change preferences toward more friendly positions and so social integration is impossible. For social integration, other conditions should enter the picture. More tolerance for other groups is not enough, as many variants of Schelling's model have definitively demonstrated.

The reader will have noticed how much these insights can say something interesting about the current debate on multiculturalism and the failure of social integration policies. So far, all policies pursued by Western countries to promote social cohesion have been focused on individual citizen preferences, in order to strengthen tolerance towards diversity. Now, there is widespread recognition that these policies have failed and that we are 'sleepwalking our way to segregation', as reported by a chairman of the Commission for Racial Equality in the UK (Fagiolo, Valente and Vriend 2007, p. 317).

Given the evidence of the previous studies, we should focus more on promoting constructive interaction between different people and favoring a multidimensional perception of respective identities, rather than insisting on individual preferences or simple co-location. Segregation seems a conditioned reflex to protect in-group cohesion that is difficult to eradicate. This is particularly so in largely differentiated and globalized contemporary societies where the tension between 'us' and 'them' always finds new targets.

3.2   Threshold behavior and opinions

The idea behind the concept of threshold behavior is that, because many people's decisions are inherently costly, requiring information, time and a variety of resources, individuals tend to display inertia in switching states. But once a given personal preference threshold is reached, their decision is extremely sensitive to the action of even a single individual with whom they are in contact with (e.g., a neighbor), so that this infinitesimal action can tip him/her from one state to another (Watts 2002, p. 5767). If a single case is projected onto a large population of agents, a paradigmatic example of complexity is found: small details in time and space might determine macroscopic behavior at the macro level (e.g., Miller and Page 2007). The challenge is to understand first what these details are, and secondly, under what circumstances they can make a real difference.

Mark Granovetter's model of collective behavior has followed Schelling's footsteps by thoroughly investigating this threshold-based tipping point mechanism (Granovetter 1978). He applied this idea to many social situations in which agents were asked to take a binary choice. It is worth mentioning that although simple, these choice models are frequent in reality, as complex decision-making processes, such as signing a treaty on climate change or a declaration of war, often result in this kind of decision (Watts and Dodds 2009).

Unlike Schelling and his focus on spatial proximity relationships, Granovetter explicitly introduced the assumption that individual behavior depends in part on the composition of the whole system of individuals who have already made a choice. Therefore, the focus shifts from local to global influences on individual behavior and social interaction is despatialized. At the same time, most of the complex aspects of modeling social interaction which were implicated in Schelling's example are bypassed so that computer simulation can be used to complement equation-based models.

Granovetter used the example of a hypothetical crowd poised on the brink of a riot, where all agents were uncertain about the costs and benefits of rioting. A simple version of the model was based on 100 agents called to take a binary choice (e.g., to join or not to join a riot) following an individual threshold, that is, the proportion of the group he/she would have to see join before he/she would have done so. The threshold was distributed from 0 to 100. Agents were heterogeneously distributed between 'radicals' (low threshold and high benefit of rioting), 'instigators' (people who rioted even when no one else did) and 'conservatives' ((high threshold and low benefit of rioting).

To simplify, this meant that agent $x = threshold\ 0$ will decide to riot regardless of what others decide, the *agent* $y = threshold\ 1$ will follow x, *agent* $z = threshold\ 2$ will follow y and so on until the hundredth agent. Agent x, the so-called 'instigator', will cause a riot. This was a linear link between micro behavior and macro outcomes called the 'domino' or 'bandwagon' effect. The proportion of outcomes was linearly related to the proportion of causes towards attaining the equilibrium (100 agents who rioted).

Now, suppose we remove *agent* $y = threshold\ 1$. The consequence will be to nip the riot in the bud, that is, a completely different outcome at a macro level from a small difference at the micro.

Granovetter then assumed an average threshold distribution in the population and introduced the tendency of agents to weigh other people's decisions differently depending on friendship. This is to introduce social influence on rational individual action, which is an important constituent of the social structure. He assumed that the influence of the friend's decision counted twice that of strangers. Suppose that, in a population of 100 agents, agent $w = threshold\ 50$ faced a situation of 48 rioters and 52 nonrioters. In this case, agent w will decide not to riot. Now assume that agent $w = threshold\ 50$ was a node of a friendship network of 20 agents, 15 of which have already decided to riot. According to this, now agent w will not 'see' the group as composed of 48 rioters and 52 nonrioters but by $[(15^*2) + (33^*1)]$ rioters and $[(5^*2) + (47^*1)]$ nonrioters, that is, by 63 rioters out of 120, with a threshold on 0.525, higher than 0.50. The result will be that agent w will decide to join the riot.

Therefore, with social influences, social outcomes are not easily derived from the individual attributes of the population. Specific properties of the social structure can explain why certain macro outcomes might occur even if this does not reflect the preferences of all or the majority of individuals involved. In these situations, the effects of social structure may overwhelm those of individual preferences and this implies that the equilibria at a macro level are unstable with no chance to predict macro behavior through a deterministic solution. This evidence emphasizes the importance of understanding the 'situation-specific' aggregation processes.

As a paradigmatic example of an entire typology of social influence mechanisms, Granovetter's model has influenced a variety of tipping point models in many fields, such as contagion (e.g., Dodds and Watts 2004), social movements (e.g., Hedström 1994), crime (e.g., Picker 1997), voting (e.g., Mayer and Brown 1998), civil wars (e.g., Cederman 2003), retirement (e.g., Epstein 2006) and youth unemployment (e.g., Hedström 2005; Åberg and Hedström 2011). Now it could be viewed as a prominent case of a wide category of models that examine 'influence-response' mechanisms in social interaction (see the review in Watts and Dodds 2009).

For instance, Watts (2002) and Watts, Dodds and Newman (2002) extended Granovetter's original model to account for the impact of different types of social structures on collective outcomes. Watts (2002) investigated random networks, where individuals were influenced by a small subset of immediate neighbors at random. They found that the type of connectivity, that is, who interacted with whom and how each agent was connected to all others, mattered more than individual preferences. This in turn determined 'global cascades' where a given equilibrium was finally selected for potentially infinite population size. He found that such an equilibrium definitively generalized when a connected network of 'activated' individuals could easily reach the entire population, thereby spreading a particular behavior.

Watts, Dodds and Newman (2002) investigated the impact of networks of group-affiliated individuals and found that group-based networks were more sensitive than random networks for global cascades. Their simulation showed that, when a social structure was clustered around diverse groups, the population was more vulnerable to social influence by cohesive groups even when it was extremely resilient to social contagion. Their conclusion was that threshold-based social influence in group-based networks spreads in ways that are qualitatively distinct from the case of all-to-all and random networks.

One of the most developed fields in this area is opinion dynamics and particularly the study of extremism propagation (e.g., Galam and Moscovici 1991; Deffuant et al. 2000, 2002; Hegselmann and Krause 2002; Weisbuch et al. 2002; Weisbuch, Deffuant and Amblard 2005). The puzzle is to explain why we see extremist and marginal opinions sometimes prevail in society and become the norm. This holds for dramatic periods of our history, for example the rise to power of the Nazis, but also for less dramatic issues, such as the diffusion of minority fads.

These issues have been investigated in empirical research (e.g., Moscovici, Lage and Naffrechoux 1969; Nemeth and Wachtler 1973; Moscovici 1985).

The idea is to use abstract models to examine under which conditions an extremist opinion may spread at the general level. By understanding the conditions for the emergence of extremism on a simulated large-scale social system, a more precise analysis of extremism is also empirically possible.

These studies start from the idea that individuals have various opinions and take into account only other people's opinions which are not too far from their own. Another idea is that extremists are more convinced of the truth of their opinion and so are more influential than others who have less confidence in their own opinion (e.g., Deffuant *et al.* 2000; Weisbuch *et al.* 2002). Unlike Granovetter's example, here agents do not take a binary choice, but opinions are distributed between two extremes and a threshold function determines whatever agents ignore opinions which are far from it (e.g., Hegselmann and Krause 2002).

One of the most influential contributions in this field was by Deffuant *et al.* (2002), who created a very stylized model to understand when extremism could occur or a moderate majority could resist extremist influence. They considered a population of N agents characterized by two variables, a given opinion x and a given uncertainty u. Both x and u were heterogeneous and changed over time according to agent interaction.

Two assumptions were of paramount importance. First, authors assumed that the higher the agent's confidence in his/her opinion, the higher was his/her influence on other opinions. Secondly, opinions were drawn from a uniform distribution between -1 and $+1$, where 0 was the value of the moderate position and -1 and $+1$ those of extremist opinions. The authors assumed that agents with opinions closer to the two extremes (-1 and $+1$), the so-called extremists, were more confident about their opinion so that extremism and confidence were strongly correlated.

Social influence was modeled as follows: once randomly paired, agents influenced each other only if the distance between their respective opinions was below a given (heterogeneous) threshold; if so, agents' opinions became more similar and more confident agents influenced others more.

Their simulations produced various dynamical regimes, with parameter zones in which extremists had a small influence and zones in which the majority of the population was radicalized. More specifically, they found (a) 'central convergence', and (b) 'single' and (c) 'bipolarization' patterns. The mechanism (a) meant that the population stayed generally on moderate positions with small clusters of extremists who attracted only other agents closer to their extreme positions without becoming the majority. Mechanism (b) meant that the population converged to one of the two extreme opinions, while (c) meant that the population split into two big co-existing extremist clusters.

They found that *central convergence* was likely for an initial small uncertainty of moderates, as extremists had an influence only on other agents close to their opinions but not in general. Figure 3.3 shows central convergence when the uncertainty parameter u was low ($u = 0.4$), with 20% of extremists ($p_e = 0.2$) and $N = 200$. The darker zone close to the two extremes indicates that the influence was due to extremists. The large lighter zone indicated that the extremists' influence was negligible, while there were two intermediary points between these two areas which indicated that the extremists' influence was contrary to the global opinion trend. Figure 3.4 shows the emergence of *bipolarization* when uncertainty increased (e.g., $u = 1.6$, but also with lower values of u, such as 0.8, the outcome was the same).

More specifically, the dynamics were as follows: initially, the moderate agents clustered around the center and the influence of extremists was negligible. Then a competition between the respective influences arose, as uncertainty globally decreased and reached values for which agents had only one extreme to be influenced by, so that extremists' influence increased (i.e., no concomitant competition between

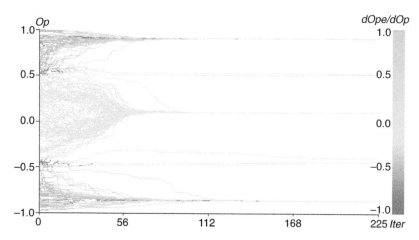

Figure 3.3   Influence of extremists when moderate uncertainty is small: the 'central convergence' (Deffuant et al. 2002, 5.6). The x-axis shows the number of iterations of the simulation and the y-axis the opinions, while the shades show uncertainty.

two extremists over each agent). Finally, the extremists eventually won and split the population into two almost equal parts. Figure 3.5 shows *single extreme convergence* when the percentage of extremists over the population was decreased ($p_e = 0.1$), as the above competition was won by the central clustering process.

Here, we can distinguish population trajectories in three stages. First (see the darker zone around − 1.0 at the bottom), agents which were in the bottom half of the cluster were attracted by the strongest influence of extremists. Secondly (see the

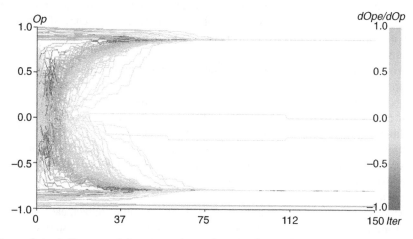

Figure 3.4   Influence of the extremists when moderates' uncertainty is high: the 'bipolarization' (Deffuant et al. 2002, 5.12).

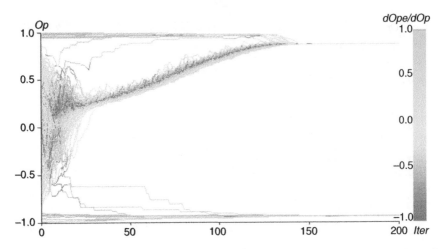

Figure 3.5   Influence of extremists when their percentage is low and moderates' uncertainty is high: the 'single extreme convergence' (Deffuant et al. 2002, 5.15).

darker strips between 0 and 1, and between 0 and 0.5), agents which were in the top half of the cluster were caught in the middle of the extremist and majority influences. Thirdly (see the light threads between 0.5 and 1 in the upper part), as soon as agents were attracted by extremists, the influence of these became stronger and they returned to the center of the cluster, also attracting further agents and eventually turning into a majority.

In conclusion, their results showed that when uncertainty decreases, so extremists become more and more confident of the truth of their opinion, the pattern was a multiplicity of small clusters, surrounding extremists. This outcome is reversed when extremists have more contact with a larger population of moderates. This indicates that, in historical periods of high uncertainty, the influence of extremists over moderates can dramatically increase, so radical minorities might become a majority.

Amblard and Deffuant (2004) extended this model by examining the influence of certain types of social networks on extremist propagation mechanisms (see also Weisbuch, Deffuant and Amblard 2005). The idea was that in the real world, individuals do not have only random encounters, as they are embedded in social structures that condition who interacts with whom. By assuming small-world networks (e.g., Watts 1999) with variable connectivity and randomness of connections and by thoroughly exploring the parameter space for the uncertainty of moderates and the proportion of extremists, they found that the population drift to extremes occurred only beyond a critical level.

More specifically, they found that when agents had little contact, each extremist could influence its own neighborhood so that several extremist clusters emerged, extremism was polarized and co-existed at the population level. When connectivity was increased around a critical parameter value, extremists attracted only a very small part of the population. This was because extremists were excluded from the central majority, while in general as connectivity increased, the population converged to one of two extremes.

Following this, Deffuant (2006) compared different types of uncertainty models and networks (e.g., fully connected, random network, lattice topology). He found that extremism more probably took place when moderates were clustered and isolated from others. This was because extremists were influential without being influenced in turn. Secondly, he found that moderates were dominant in networks where individuals were all close to each other. In short, he showed that one of the most important secrets of extremists' survival and success was to remain different from the mass of moderates (see also Gargiulo and Mazzoni 2008).

These findings were then extended by Mckeown and Sheely (2006), who added the influence of the mass media on pre-existing social networks. They found that bipolarization was likely when agents were more confident in their opinion and mass media communication was common or where there was moderate willingness to change opinion and more mass media communication. On the contrary, single extreme convergence was found when there was moderate willingness to change opinion and less mass media communication.

Finally, Deffuant, Huet and Amblard (2005) generalized this approach to understand the diffusion of innovation. They assumed that agents who gave a high social value to particular innovations tended to look for information to evaluate expected individual payoff of adoption more precisely. They neither considered nor transmitted information if the social value assigned by them to innovation was low.

Their results showed that under these conditions a certain innovation with high social value and low expected individual payoff was more likely to succeed than that with low social value and high individual benefit. Moreover, they found that under certain circumstances, a minority of extremists could have a crucial role in propagating innovation by polarizing its social value.

Obviously, one may argue that these are excessively simplified and abstract models and that empirical analysis should be taken into account more carefully. However, the importance of these examples is that they allow us to appreciate modeling to find cumulativeness and constructive inter-subjective collaboration and explain crucial reality puzzles. Indeed, besides the value of these studies to understand the conditions under which well-confident fanatics and extremists might outperform moderates in society, they also contribute in allowing us to understand possible implications of dramatic polarization of politics in contemporary democracies.

3.3   Culture dynamics and diversity

Why, if people are becoming ever more similar in tastes, beliefs, attitudes and behavior under common social influences, do these differences simply not disappear altogether? Why does this not happen above all in the present social environment, where globalization and increasing face-to-face/at a distance, synchrony/asynchrony interactions might amplify social influence and increase common selective pressures against behavior? This counterfactual question has been the subject of investigation in several psychosociological studies and ABM research. It is of paramount importance as it allows us to understand the crucial role played by social interaction in determining qualitative differences between micro evidence and macro outcomes.

In an influential contribution both in social psychology and ABM research, Bibb Latané suggested a very simple and abstract mathematical model to measure social impact on individual behavior (Latané 1981). He defined social impact as any influence on individual feelings, thoughts and behavior by real, implied or imaginary action by others. He stated that social impact could be viewed as a multiplicative function of the strength, immediacy and number of other agents involved and that it may follow a power function, so that the marginal effect of Nth other agents was less than that of the $(n - 1)$th.

When influence came from outside a social group, he stated that the impact of others could be divided so that the result was an inverse power function of the strength, immediacy and number of other agents standing together. He used this model to approach a variety of situations, such as embarrassment in public performance, news events on conversation, social inhibition of emergency response, chivalry in elevators, and tipping in restaurants. His analytic findings suggested that, in spite of social impact, there was a chance that a given population may not converge towards unique collective attitude, opinion or behavior.

The interesting point for us is that he soon recognized that his model had two great limitations. First, it did not take into account social interaction, as it statically measured the magnitude of the impact but did not concretely model the influence process at the micro level. Secondly, being too abstract for mathematical tractability, it was impossible to account for large group sizes or complicated sequences of agent interactions (Nowak, Szamrej and Latané 1990).

To fill this gap, Latané developed an ABM aimed at understanding how the well-documented malleability of individual opinions under social influence did not create complete uniformity of attitudes, beliefs, opinions or behavior at a collective level (Nowak, Szamrej and Latané 1990; Latané and Nowak 1997; Latané 2000). In doing so, he complemented Schelling's investigation on micro and macro loosening and also overlapped with opinion dynamics. Moreover, he touched upon serious policy implications, as summarized by Nowak, Szamrej and Latané (1990):

> The mystery of public opinion becomes particularly salient before every election, as pollsters try to follow the shifting preferences of the electorates. In part, these preferences reflect common reactions to events and images shared through the mass media and diverse concerns arising out of economic and social circumstances. In part, however, they reflect a process of group interaction as people discuss their beliefs and impressions with relatives, friends, neighbours, co-workers, and others. Presumably, if social scientists could understand this process of social interaction, they could be in a better position to predict public opinion (Nowak, Szamrej and Latané 1990, p. 363).

The model consisted of a population of N agents ($N = 1600$) which had the following four attributes: (1) a [0,1] flip-flop individual attitude, belief, opinion or behavior; (2) the ability to persuade others with opposing beliefs to change their opinion (in the form of a randomly assigned value in a $\{0\ldots100\}$ range and randomly reassigned after each attitude change); (3) the ability to provide support to others with similar beliefs (as before); and (4) a given position in the social structure, in terms of a given agent's location within a lattice of 40×40 neighboring cells.

Taken together, these parameters affected the degree to which each agent was influenced by and influenced others. More specifically, the authors assumed that agents changed their attitude whenever the impact from a group with a different opinion was greater than the impact of their supporting group.

Their simulation showed that under different combinations of the initial distribution of the two groups, the population never converged totally towards one single dominant outcome. The partial polarization of attitudes, so that agents moved towards the majority but did not achieve uniformity of opinion, was explained in terms of the flip-flop nonlinear nature of attitude and the formation and continued existence of locally coherent clusters of similar agents. These were always conditioned by small variations in persuasiveness, supportiveness and local structure effects, so that areas that included strong minority representations could be sheltered from the overall majority. Some further development of the model showed that when resisting the initial selection, minority followers achieved higher values of supportiveness over time and a tendency to cluster around the most supportive agents, thereby surviving at the margins of the population (Latané and Nowak 1997).

This model has motivated extensions and applications in a variety of fields, such as political attitudes and voting behavior (e.g., Regenwetter, Falmagne and Grofman 1999; Kottonnau and Pahl-Worstl 2004), assimilation and contrast in social judgement (e.g., Jager and Amblard 2005), cultural influences in organizations (e.g., Harrison and Carroll 2002), and leadership (e.g., Holyst, Kacperski and Schweitzer 2001).

In an influential contribution, Robert Axelrod (1997) examined in detail local convergence/global polarization dynamics, by focusing on culture dynamics. The model consisted of a population of N agents ($N = 100$) located in a geographical space which consisted of a 10×10 grid, with no movement and fixed (north, east, south and west) neighborhood interaction.

The author assumed that each agent had a particular culture. He defined culture as a 'set of individual attributes that are subject to social influence' (Axelrod 1997, p. 204). He also assumed that it consisted of a set of five features, such as language, religion, style of dress and so forth, each taking on any one of 10 traits. Therefore, the higher the percentage of features with identical traits between two agents, the higher their respective cultural similarity. The probability of interaction was proportional to the cultural similarity two neighbors had. Not only were agents who were similar to each other more likely to interact, but they also became more similar.

Interaction consisted of selecting at random a given feature of an agent on which its neighbor differed (if one) and changing the corresponding trait of the former to that of the latter. This eventually changed the cultural similarity of the two agents.

For instance, assume that two agents were neighbors with the following respectively cultural traits: 82 330 and 67 730. As they shared the same traits for 2/5 of their cultural features (i.e., 82 330 and 67730), they were 40% likely to interact. Suppose they were paired to interact and that the 82 330 agent was picked first. The social influence rule stated that the first agent picked will be influenced by the second by acquiring the first different trait of the latter counting from the left along the number string. Therefore, the 82 330 agent will become a 62 330 agent and the respective similarity between the two paired agents will increase to 3/5 of their features (i.e., 67 730 and 62 330).

He showed that, if we look at the case of site A at the beginning of the simulation and over time[Figure 3.6(a)–(d)], from an initial similarity of 40% (dark gray boundaries), the emergence of distinct cultural regions arose after 20 000 events that included four or five sites, to then get bigger by 40 000 events. It ended up with three completely stable regions, as adjacent sites could not interact anymore having no features in common. Therefore, these initial results indicated that, in spite of strong pressure towards cultural integration, similarity did not completely rule out the persistence of regional diversity. Moreover, we can also see that culture dynamics were path-dependent.

Subsequently, Axelrod manipulated certain crucial parameters, such as the numbers of traits and features, to investigate the emergence of stable cultural regions in the system. With 10 traits and 5 features, the average number of cultural regions was 3.2. By increasing the number of features, outcomes were counter-intuitive due to the growing likelihood of a population convergence towards a unique culture. The opposite was true when traits were increased and features remained small. Indeed, when there were few features and many traits, two neighbors were likely to share no features and thus were unable to interact.

Other manipulations of the range of interaction and the size of the environment showed that the bigger the neighborhood and the environment, the fewer stable regions there were. The first finding was reasonable to expect, as large distance–scale interactions are likely to favor cultural convergence. The second however was unexpected. Moreover, Axelrod found that the number of stable regions started to decrease only above a certain environment size (e.g., above 12×12 sites). Further simulations showed that this was the case because the correlations between neighborhoods meant that a larger environment took much longer to reach stability, local boundaries were more likely to dissolve and larger regions were more likely to absorb smaller ones.

To sum up, the simulation showed both intuitive and counter-intuitive findings. It was expected that cultural diversity would increase with the number of possible traits that each culture could take and decrease with the range of interaction. It was unexpected that diversity would decrease when culture had more cultural features and the environment was larger.

This paradox of diversity between group cultures while individuals faced common selective pressures toward similarity has motivated many subsequent model extensions, modifications and replications.

Kennedy (1998) modified and generalized Axelrod's model to take into account social influence based on relative neighbor performance. Klemm *et al.* (2003a)

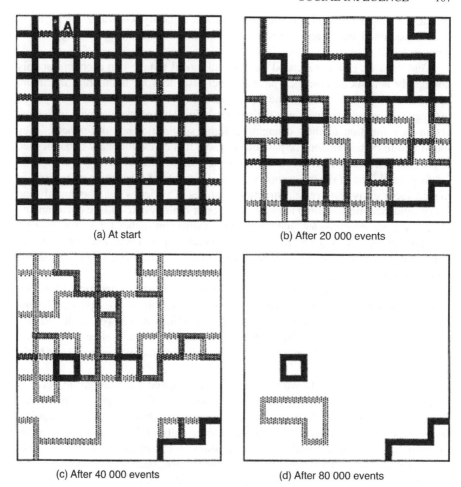

(a) At start   (b) After 20 000 events

(c) After 40 000 events   (d) After 80 000 events

Figure 3.6   Culture similarity patterns (Axelrod 1997, p. 210). Note that cultural similarity between adjacent sites is coded as: black = ≤ 20%, dark gray = 40%, gray = 60%, light gray = 80%, and white in the case of perfect similarity (= 100%).

included noise in trait changes and found that there was a particular threshold below which noise determined a mono-cultural equilibrium, while above it pushed population into diverse cultural regions. Klemm *et al.* (2003b, 2003c) examined the impact of dimensionality and various network topologies and found that differences here could create different cultural equilibria at a macro level.

Greig (2002) showed that the expansion of communications between agents increased the rate of cultural change and the level of cultural homogeneity, but reduced how much cultural attributes predominated after interaction. Shibanai, Satoko and Ishiguro (2001) examined the distribution of global information feedback in facilitating an earlier convergence and maintenance of cultural diversity, so that mass media, for instance, could provide support for a minority. González-Avella *et al.* (2007) examined direct and indirect mass media influence in producing cultural homogeneity.

Centola *et al.* (2007) extended the original model to take into account not only homophily and social influence pressures but also network homophily in culture interaction. As in Boero, Bravo and Squazzoni's model on partner selection reported in Chapter 2, here the network was not arbitrarily fixed but co-evolved with individual action as a function of their changing cultural similarities and differences. They found that in certain regions of parameter space, this co-evolutionary dynamics led to patterns of cultural diversity that were stable with cultural drift.

In general, one of the most important developments of this stream of research is to shift focus away from certain structural features of societies (e.g., homophily and social influence mechanisms) to characteristics of biology-like culture environment. Here, there are evolutionary chances to exploit different niches for various usually correlated groups. As noted by Bravo (2010), this also gives a more realistic picture of what really happens in societies. Indeed, social life is characterized by in-/out-group boundaries between agents and groups.

A first example of this is Lustick (2000) who, inspired by constructivist theory, modified the similarity-triggered adaptation of cultural traits in Axelrod's model and assumed that agents could have a repertory of identities which were activated as a function of the environment. He found that tipping and cascade effects were much more likely when a small number of strongly confident identities were present in the population.

A second example is Bravo (2010), who investigated the relationship between space boundaries and cultural groups by following a biology-inspired evolutionary approach. Starting from the idea that any co-existence between cultures required boundaries, he showed that these could guarantee cultural diversity in the long run, on condition that (a) the social environment allows for a sufficient number of niches to be exploited by different groups and (b) group boundaries are at least partially impermeable. If boundaries between groups are permeable, the selection process tends to lead to a single culture. If at least some impermeability is assumed, in-/out-group mechanisms might defend group cohesion and protect cultural diversity.

Finally, it is worth noting that similarity pressures not only allow heterogeneous agents to converge towards homogenous patterns at the macro level, but also the opposite, that is, homogeneous agents might produce differentiation. This can be understood by referring to a simple model by Noah Mark (1998), who examined the emergence of social differentiation from a population of homogenous agents.

Mark showed that no assumption about individual differences was necessary to generate social differentiation. Following Carley's (1991) constructivist theory on information and knowledge, here similarity between agents was not motivated by social influence but by knowledge sharing: being boundedly rational, individuals tend to become similar as they tend to interact more frequently and share information with others who have a common knowledge background. This is because a common background is needed to interact (e.g., a common language, some common beliefs) and it is only by interacting in a social process of communication that individuals can create information and knowledge.

The model was based on a population of N agents ($N = 6$, 50, 100 in different simulation tests) with an initial homogenous distribution of knowledge and no social structure embeddedness. Knowledge was modeled as a set of facts, that is, an array of numbers which each agent may or may not own. The author assumed that the probability that an agent A initiated interaction with an agent B was equal to the number of facts they had in common, divided by the sum of the numbers of facts A shared with each agent in the system. He assumed that agents could have multiple interactions at the same time. Once paired, agents created and shared new facts. Moreover, agents had also limited memory, so that they forgot information and needed social interaction to recall it.

By letting agents interact, the author measured social differentiation at a system level as the degree to which interaction occurred within distinct sets of individuals. As a result, the system was undifferentiated when interaction was equally likely between all agents so that agents knew exactly the same information. He used system size (i.e., the number of agents) and agent memory (the length of rounds in which agents did not forget an individual piece of information) as independent variables, and cultural homogeneity (i.e., a measure of shared knowledge in the system) as the dependent variable.

Mark's simulation findings showed that system size positively affected differenti- ation, while agent memory extensions decreased it, as the size of connected groups of agents increased. Therefore, if the size system increased and the agents' capability of storing knowledge remained stable, social differentiation proliferated. This implies, for instance, that social inequality and discrimination, rather than being dependent on other macro structural factors, could be dependent upon a similar self-organized dif- ferentiation pattern, as relevant information and assets tend to flow within networks of connected people who share knowledge and this tends to perpetuate differentiation.

It is worth noting that these findings provide a simpler explanation of social differentiation than functionalistic approaches which use the relevance of compli- cated and largely unobservable macro factors or the intentional action of dominant elites (e.g., Parsons 1966; Alexander and Colomy 1990). Another remarkable point especially for micro–macro issues, is that Mark's model incorporated a kind of Coleman-like micro–macro–micro diachronic feedback, as agent knowledge deter- mined who interacted with whom. In addition, who interacted with whom determined agent knowledge and consequently who interacted with whom, and so forth.

3.4 Social reflexivity

What happens when agents are conscious that other agents matter 'warts and all' and therefore could intentionally take into account, exploit or contrast this through their action? What happens if agents are assumed to be social reflexive agents, that is, capable of inferring properties of the social contexts where they are embedded in and act accordingly?

The fact that individuals constantly react and adapt to changes in their environment and that in different ways are complicit in determining such changes in turn is without doubt. Many examples have looked precisely at this interplay of individual behavior and environment. The idea that humans actively construct their environment is exemplified by the well-known self-fulfilling prophecy mechanisms introduced by Robert Merton (1968, p. 477):

> The self-fulfilling prophecy is, in the beginning, a *false* definition of the situation evoking a new behaviour which makes the original false conception come 'true'. This specious validity of the self-fulfilling prophecy perpetuates a reign of error. For the prophet will cite the actual course of events as proof that he was right from the very beginning.

It is probable that in situations where individuals are sensitive to other behavior and subjected to social influence, for example, because of uncertainty, ambiguity and/or interdependence of behavior, this type of mechanism might determine the intrinsic unpredictability of social outcomes.

This was what Georg Soros insisted on in his largely neglected theory of financial markets, which was aimed at providing an alternative view of the rationality of markets compared with neoclassical theory which was based on market disequilibrium, instability and unpredictability. He formulated the idea that once expectations and predictions about other behavior and possible effects of their and other decisions at the aggregate level are taken into account by individuals, the consequence is that individual knowledge is less important and potential biases and self-fulfilling prophecies enter the picture (e.g., Soros 2008). In his view, this was the main source of unpredictability of complex socioeconomic systems and the real qualitative difference between understanding natural and social systems.

He wrote that:

> Reflexivity is confined to social phenomena – more specifically, those situations in which participants cannot base their decisions on knowledge – and it creates difficulties for the social sciences from which the natural sciences are exempt. Reflexivity can be interpreted as a circularity, or two-way feedback loop, between the participants' views and the actual state of affairs. People base their decisions not on the actual situation that confronts them but on their perception or interpretation of that situation. Their decisions make an impact on the situation (the manipulative function), and changes in the situation are liable to chance their perceptions (the cognitive function) (Soros 2008, p. 8).

By specifying the features of social action, Max Weber was the first to outline the differences between 'mutually oriented action' and 'the similar actions of many persons', by providing the well-known example of an umbrella being put up by people under rain.

> Social action is not identical with the similar actions of many persons [. . .]. Thus, if at the beginning of a shower a number of people on the street put up their umbrellas at the same time, this would not ordinarily be a case of action mutually oriented to that of each other, but rather of all reacting in the same way to the like need of protection from the rain (Weber 1978, p. 23).

This means that a social interaction effect exists if and only if, the behavior of others influences an individual's focal action (Hedström 2005, p. 46). These subtle differences reveal a variety of possible social interaction effects which should be distinguished from mere environmental effects and focus on certain cognitive aspects of human action, such as beliefs and reflexivity.

Other authors have developed this further. George Herbert Mead (1932) viewed reflexivity as a pillar for the emergence of self-consciousness. On the contrary, in his well-known theory of structuration, Anthony Giddens (1986) insisted on the largely unconscious effect of reflexivity and argued that agents 'in circumstances of interaction' were mutually involved in 'reflexive monitoring of action' that 'typically, and again routinely, incorporated the monitoring of the setting of such interaction' (Giddens 1986, p. 4). He stated that reflexivity was not to be intended merely as ' "self-consciousness" but as the monitored character of the ongoing flow of social life' and was 'grounded in the continuous monitoring of action which human beings display and expect others to display' (Giddens 1986, p. 5).

Although not so easily tractable with simplified models, we have tried to take into account this perspective in a couple of contributions. It is worth recalling here that another important example was made by Gilbert's (2002) extension of Schelling's segregation model, where second-order properties were introduced that exactly follow this idea of reflexivity.

Our first model exemplifies the cognitive side of reflexivity and the idea of building complex models to look at subtle facets of human decisions in organizational contexts, such as businesses. In this case, the model was tuned to fine-grained empirical evidence on the nexus of factors taken into account by decision makers in small and medium enterprises localized in specific geographical districts. The second one exemplifies how parts of these aspects could be investigated in more abstract and simplified ways without 'complexificating' the micro level too much.

Inspired by a large amount of empirical evidence, particularly through a multitude of case studies conducted in Italy, we modeled a district of hundreds of interacting agents which were aimed at co-organizing production under given market and technology constraints (Boero, Castellani and Squazzoni 2004a, 2004b).

Many scholars in this field have looked at the difference of behavioral attitudes between firms embedded in districts and those which were not (e.g., Becattini 2003; Lazzaretti 2003, 2008; Rullani 2003). Unfortunately, they did not find a way to measure theoretical intuitions with empirical evidence. We therefore developed a model aimed at looking at these issues. We suggested that industrial district dynamics were both aggregate effects of inter-firm interactions and features of the district agents' 'state of mind'. Therefore, we argued that firms could behave in a more or less 'districtualized' way, that is, in more selfish/individualistic or committed/social ways and we examined the implications of this for the market and technology adaptation of the district system as a whole.

The model was based on a population of N firms/agents ($N = 400$) which had the task of co-organizing production of goods in parallel and distributed production chains to meet increasing exogenous market pressures. Production partnership, technological learning, and economic performance were all dependent upon local information and adaptation. Indeed, one of the most striking peculiarities of these systems is that there is no master mind or general manager who coordinates production, but a multitude of small and medium enterprises specialized in different activities that informally and continuously coordinate each other along production chains. This is achieved by sharing customers' orders, production details, information, output capacity, and investment.

The economic performance of each firm was dependent upon its position in available technological trajectories. The structural part of the model, that is, production constraints, technological innovation and market pressures, was similar to Squazzoni and Boero (2002). Firms had to decide whether to explore technological innovation by taking risk investment or exploit/improve already available technological options. They were embedded in spatial proximity relationships that gave them access to information about technological options.

Firms were routinely controlling different sources of information to decide what to do in their critical strategic business areas, namely partner selection, technology and market environment, organization and economic efficiency. The idea was that firms were capable of inferring a good/bad situation in these critical areas from available information and that bad situations on a specific area pushed them to change existing business strategies in that particular area. For instance, by comparing their own level of technological learning level with that of their neighbors, they inferred that they were behind them, they then focused on technology and invested in that area. Vice versa, when they observed that their profit over time was decreasing, they focused on partner selection and changed partners.

We assumed that firms had boundedly computational capabilities, in terms of time, attention and memory. In short, they wanted to do a lot, control everything, improve the current situation using available information, but they could not do so perfectly. By following March (1994), we assumed first that they could not control, manage and face the entire set of information about technology, market and production partnerships with the same level of attention, and second, that there was a trade-off between extent and detail of the information achievable.

Finally, we assumed that firms could have four behavioral attitudes, more or less 'districtualized'. Attitudes had specific and detailed counterparts in the recipes that firms applied to carry on their business. On the extreme of 'un-districtualization', there were firms 0. They were *self-centered*, not committed to partners, focused on their economic performance and did not share profit with partners for coordinated technology investment. Firms 1 were *responsible production managers*, not strictly focused on individual economic performance but searching for stable production partnerships. They shared a percentage of profit for coordinated technology investment with partners.

Firms 2 were *cluster-thinkers*, interested in enlarging partnerships across production chains and in sharing partners and information with others and they shared at least 20% of profit with others to support technology investment. At the extreme of 'districtualization', there were firms 3, called *district-thinkers*. They were influenced by information about the district as a whole, shared information with everyone, kept stable partners until a given amount of resources was available to do so and shared most profits with partners if needed. Obviously, we assumed conditions under which agents could break partnerships, no matter what type of attitude they had, for example, when profits decreased below a certain threshold.

Boero, Castellani and Squazzoni (2004a) assumed that all firms started self-centered and defined specific conditions under which they could change attitudes. Basically, if economic performance was increasing and production partnerships satisfactory, agents tended to trust in others more, being more confident about the district environment and then moved towards more 'districtualized' attitudes.

However, changes were reversible. It is worth noting that we assumed two technological shocks (around round 500 and 1000 of the simulation), where new and more innovative technologies entered the picture and market pressure grew drastically. This meant that the market selected only the highest quality products, that is, products produced with the most innovative available technology. These were phases where drastic attitude changes were expected and more self-centered attitudes were more likely to take place. Boero, Castellani and Squazzoni (2004b) focused specifically on the two more extreme behavioral attitudes.

Results showed that the firms which survived most in the market were the more 'districtualized' firms, whereas self-centered firms were more likely to be victims of market selection, being drastically outperformed by others (Figure 3.7). Moreover, it is worth noting that firms reacted to technological shocks by increasing their relationship contexts and by sharing information with a larger sample of other firms (Figure 3.8).

Another finding was that behavioral attitude 1 (i.e., responsible production manager) performed poorly by causing advantage loss of more self-centered attitudes without giving any advantage that other more 'districtualized' attitudes provided. We also tested different combinations of attitudes, for example, all 0 (self-centered), half 0 and half 1 (self-centered and responsible production managers) and so on, and found that the firms were more capable of surviving market selection when behavioral attitudes were heterogeneously distributed over the population.

These results corroborated previous results about the link between behavioral strategies and technology adaptation (e.g., Squazzoni and Boero 2002). In segmented production systems, one of the most important points is the coordination of technological learning among firms. When you have to collaborate with others to produce a given good, being a brilliant but lonely technological outlier counts less than having

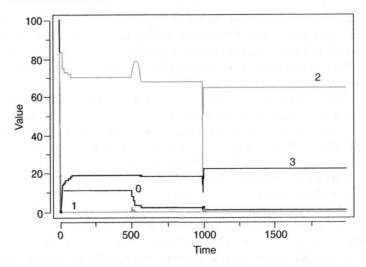

Figure 3.7   Firms surviving market selection over time for different behavioral attitudes (Boero, Castellani and Squazzoni 2004a, p. 63). 0 stands for self-centered firms, 1 for responsible production managers, 2 for cluster-thinking firms, and 3 for district-thinkers.

good-level technologically homogenous partners. This is even more true when time-to-market is a crucial competitive advantage, as in many industrial districts. If so, a long-term oriented and positive collaborative attitude towards other partners is more important than short-term optimal economic performance.

These results confirmed previous empirical findings that suggest that one of the secrets of the long-standing success of industrial districts, particularly in Italy

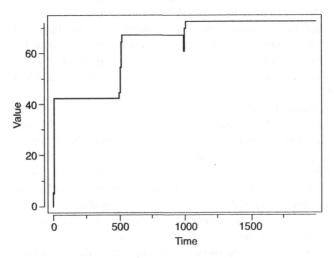

Figure 3.8   Average dimension of information/profit sharing neighborhood relation-ships (Boero, Castellani and Squazzoni 2004a, p. 64).

in the manufacturing industry, could be precisely their profound heterogeneity. Empirical and theoretical literature has correctly suggested that industrial districts are a kind of paradigm of the idea of a continuous mix of competition and collaboration, as these types of behavior seem particularly suitable for decentralized, distributed and parallel systems operating in changing environments (e.g., You and Wilkinson 1994; Porter 1998).

Obviously, by including detailed empirical knowledge, our model was quite complicated and so difficult to replicate, extend or generalize. In a second example, we built a simplified and abstract model to look at the impact of cognitive sophistication of agent behavior under a similar type of social interdependence, that is, where the co-location of others is a feature of the social setting which is perceived by agents (Boero, Castellani and Squazzoni 2008). We will summarize this model as an example of how to approach cognitive sophistication of agent behavior in a very different way compared with the previous example.

Inspired by the well-known 'heatbugs' prototype now run in all the most popular ABM platforms, such as NetLogo and Repast, the model consisted of a population of N agents ($N = 101$) located in a toroidal 80×80 two-dimensional finite space of cells. They were randomly assigned a heterogeneous happiness function at the beginning of the simulation, which was linked to the temperature they liked. They had a space of vision of the eight neighboring cells. They could stay or move step-by-step across the cells to fit their own ideal temperature. They could only move towards empty cells. The fit between the ideal temperature of each agent and the current temperature in each cell was calculated by an attainment discrepancy value (e.g., Mezias 1988; Murphy, Mezias and Chen 2001) as follows: the more this value tended to 0, the more the agent was happy as it found a perfect environmental fit ($=$ correspondence between the ideal and the current temperature).

The point was that, by moving across space, agents produced heat and left it on the cell where they had been. Heat diffused synchronously across neighboring cells, equally in all directions, proportionally to the heat differential between cells and evaporated proportionally to the amount of heat produced. An evaporation rate, constant over the environment, determined how heat faded. Heat spread in space according to a fixed value from 0 to 1 and was constantly updated.

This model mimics an optimization and coordination problem very close to most social dilemmas we find in reality. Agents interacted so that the decision of each agent brought about an immediate change in the space of possibilities of other correlated agents and more loosely of all others. While each agent tried to maximize its happiness function, this possibility was dependent upon other action under a complex web of mutual influence.

We simulated different scenarios where agents used various behavioral heuristics, more or less cognitively sophisticated (summarized in Table 3.1). The first two scenarios were used as a baseline for comparisons. In scenarios 3 to 6, we tested different heuristics which were assigned to the entire population at the beginning of the simulation and were fixed over time. The heuristics were concerned with the stopping/movement decision and varied in cognitive sophistication. For instance, $H2$ was smart and simple as it stated that agents were trying to move towards the cells

Table 3.1   Simulation scenarios and rules of agent behavior in Boero, Castellani and Squazzoni's (2008) model.

	Scenarios	Behavior
1	Not moving	Agents did not move
2	Random	Agents moved randomly
3	*H1*	If cell temperature was lower than the ideal, agents moved to the neighbor with the highest temperature; if not, they switched to neighbors with the lowest temperature
4	*H2*	If attainment discrepancy was different to 0, agents moved to the neighbor with the temperature closer to their ideal one
5	*H3*	If attainment discrepancy was different to 0, agents moved randomly across the cells until their attainment discrepancy value was $\leq$ that of time t_{-1}; then they stopped where they were
6	*H4*	If the temperature was higher than their ideal and they had other neighbors, agents moved away from neighboring agents in the opposite direction to avoid others causing a further increase of the temperature; vice versa, if the temperature was lower than their ideal and they had other neighbors, agents remained in the same cells to exploit an expected further increase in temperature. If agents did not have any neighbors, they moved randomly
6	*H4*	If the temperature was higher than their ideal and they had other neighbors, agents moved away from neighboring agents in the opposite direction to avoid others causing a further increase of the temperature; vice versa, if the temperature was lower than their ideal and they had other neighbors, agents remained in the same cells to exploit an expected further increase in temperature. If agents did not have any neighbors, they moved randomly
7	Social agents (*H1, 2, 3,* and *4*)	Agents had randomly assigned one of the previous heuristics and randomly changed them when their attainment discrepancy was 10% $\geq$ of the average attainment discrepancy at the population level
8	Social agents (groups)	As setting 7, but now agents were divided in half into 'greens' and 'blues' and were capable of detecting the color of their neighbors. In the presence of a majority of neighbors of their own group, their attainment discrepancy decreased; vice versa, it increased for a given value

where the temperature was closer to their ideal. *H3* was more sophisticated as it took into account a more subtle search process for happiness (i.e., agents moved randomly across the cells until their attainment discrepancy value improved). *H4* was even more sophisticated as it tried to exploit the presence of others to improve agent fitness. In the *H4* case, agents were capable of forecasting an increase of temperature caused by other neighbors and exploited this by staying there, in case they needed heat, or by opposing this by leaving, in case they needed cold. Therefore, there was a deliberate recognition of the co-location of others as a set of constraints/possibilities to be taken into account.

A difference was made in scenario 7, where agent heterogeneity and the impact of certain macro features on individual behavior were added. Now agents were equipped with a complete heuristic toolbox with all four heuristics previously tested. They had a randomly assigned heuristic and were capable of comparing their attainment discrepancy with that of the average population. When the mismatch between other agents' average happiness and their happiness was higher than a given threshold (i.e., $10\% \geq$), agents changed heuristics randomly and so had the chance to sequentially test the fitness of each heuristic. Here, agents' happiness at an individual level was a comparative notion and was influenced by the current situation of all others.

In the last scenario, we introduced agents belonging to social groups, so that happiness now was influenced locally by other similar neighbors. More specifically, agents were now capable of detecting the color of their neighbors. We assumed that in the presence of a majority of neighbors of their own group, the agents' attainment discrepancy decreased. Otherwise it increased a given value. Finally, it is worth noting that we assumed an error effect in all scenarios so that agents had a 20% probability to move randomly towards an empty cell in each round.

We ran over 100 simulations with different values for the random numbers generator. We then measured average and maximum unhappiness, average and maximum values of attainment discrepancy over time, the percentage of agents not moving over time, mapped the macro dynamics with space visualization techniques and built an inequality index that measured the distance between average unhappiness and maximum happiness. More specifically, the inequality index was 0 when unhappiness was equally distributed across the population. It followed the following formula:

$$i_s^t = \frac{MU_s^t - AU_s^t}{AU_s^t}$$

where *s* was the scenario, *t* the time, *MU* the value of maximum unhappiness and *AU* the average unhappiness.

As shown in Table 3.2, our simulation results indicated first that *H2*, the simplest heuristic, was the best to achieve highest average happiness and the lowest pick of unhappiness, but not to reduce inequality and/or guarantee system stability. On these latter aspects, *H3* and *H4* did better, but they in turn implied higher values of average unhappiness and higher picks of unhappiness. The figures drastically changed with

Table 3.2   Results in representative simulation snapshots. It is worth noting that we run simulations until a relatively stable state was reached by the system. While in the last scenario, a steady equilibrium state was reached at step 17 200, when all agents were stopped in a given cell, in all the other scenarios the system never reached a steady equilibrium state.

	Step 300	Step 700	Step 1500	Step 5000	Step 15 000	Step 17 200
H1						
Av. unhappiness	2850	2500	2200	2140	1890	
Max. unhappiness	15 000	12 000	10 000	11 350	9200	
Inequality	4.26	3.8	3.54	4.30	3.87	
% Stopped	0	0	0	0	0	
H2						
Av. unhappiness	2865	2000	1590	1305	1270	
Max. unhappiness	18 000	11 500	9500	6240	7710	
Inequality	5.28	4.75	4.97	3.78	5.07	
% Stopped	0	0	0	0	0	
H3						
Av. unhappiness	10 580	10 330	9950	10 250	10 250	
Max. unhappiness	23650	20 100	21 380	21 550	21 300	
Inequality	1.23	0.95	1.15	1.1	1.08	
% Stopped	38	40	46	42	35	
H4						
Av. unhappiness	10 740	10 240	10 270	9815	10 122	
Max. unhappiness	23 000	24 440	22 700	21 000	22 500	
Inequality	1.14	1.39	1.21	1.14	1.22	
% Stopped	13	14	15	18	9	
H1+4						
Av. unhappiness	3700	3500	2300	1970	2150	
Max. unhappiness	14 500	15 000	14 500	12 000	9000	
Inequality	2.92	3.29	5.3	5.09	3.19	
% Stopped	10	6	5	10	9	
Groups						
Av. unhappiness	1463	200	−760	−3550	−4600	−4650
Max. unhappiness	20 000	21 000	15 000	6000	8820	0
Inequality	12.67	104	20.74	2.69	2.92	1
% Stopped	58	67	69	86	99	100

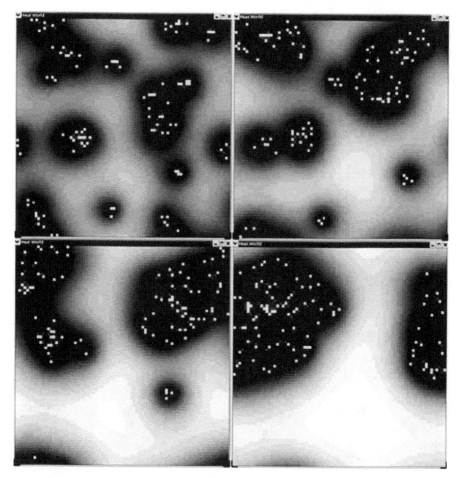

Figure 3.9   Simulation scenario with H2. *From top left to top right, and from bottom left to bottom right, spatial patterns at 300–700, and 1500–5000 simulation rounds (Boero, Castellani and Squazzoni 2008, p. 162).*

social groups, where not only the system achieved the highest values of happiness and the lowest inequality, but reached a steady state around 17 200 rounds.

Interesting differences between scenarios were also evident when we observed the spatial patterns. In Figures 3.9, 3.10 and 3.11, we have included some representative snapshots of agent distribution patterns over time. Note that the white zone indicates space without agents, the halo represents a zone of temperature concentration, while bright points represent agents.

If we compare *H2* with *H4*, it is interesting to note the very different spatial distribution of agents. *H2* determined a clear-cut difference between agents clustered in a single spatial region and zones of temperature concentration around the cluster.

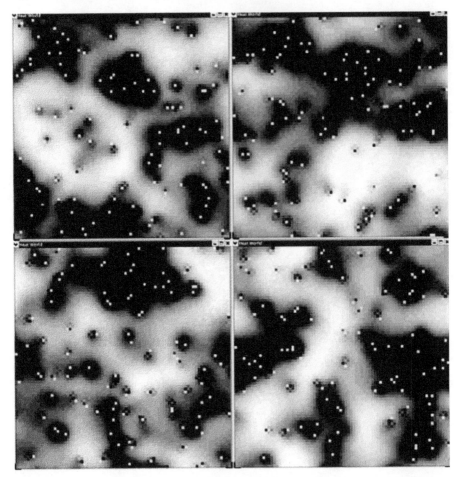

Figure 3.10   Simulation scenario with H4. *From top left to top right, and from bottom left to bottom right, spatial patterns at 300–700, and 1500–5000 simulation rounds (Boero, Castellani and Squazzoni 2008, p. 164).*

Agents never stopped but stayed within the region. *H4* determined a spatial jeopardization of agents with less clear-cut differences between portions of space occupied by agents and zones of temperature concentration. Only a few agents stopped, while the majority continued to move across space.

Crucial differences were achieved when social groups were added. We reconstructed the history of this simulation as follows. About round 700, the distribution pattern was characterized by two regions, that is, the wider one located in the top of the system, while the second was located more horizontally in the bottom (see Figure 3.11). Each region was composed of agents belonging to both groups and there was a chain figuration between agents. Agents warmed each other up without melting

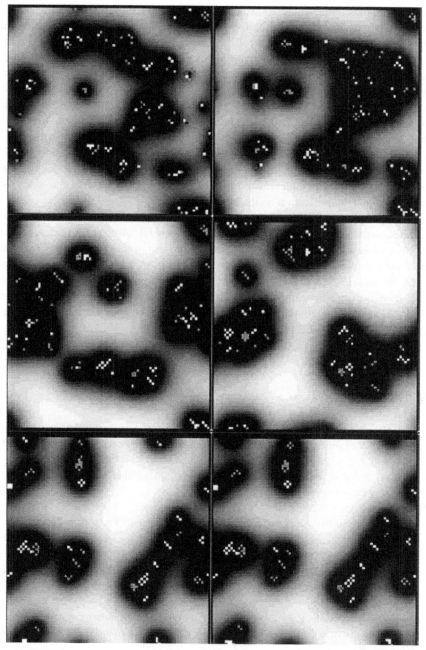

Figure 3.11   Simulation scenario with social groups. *From top left to top right, from middle left to middle right, and from bottom left to bottom right, spatial patterns at 300–700, 1500–5000, and 15 000–17,200 simulation rounds (Boero, Castellani and Squazzoni 2008, p. 167).*

themselves and around round 5000 they eventually stabilized with just one agent still on the move. About round 17 200, the system crystallized into a steady equilibrium state with each agent stopped in a cell.

These results showed first that although smart and simple rules of thumb might be efficient for agents (e.g., the case of *H2*), they might ignore collective welfare and cause large instability in a system. Secondly, this example shows that certain cognitive sophisticated properties of social action might also be examined by simplification and abstraction. Unlike the previous example, where we aimed to achieve empirical adherence at the expense of transparency and generalization, here various macro–micro feedback mechanisms were investigated in a simple model. Taken together, these two examples fully illustrate the two extremes of modeling, with empirical detail and complexification of model parameters on the one side, and abstraction and simplification on the other.

As argued before, we can say that there is no ontological preference or a best way between simplification and complexification in general, although a preference for simplification and reduction is always reasonable in formalized science. However, there is an important lesson to which we will return in the next chapter. The high flexibility and richness of ABM could tempt us to build quite complicated and 'realistic' models even when simpler and abstract models would explain more (Hedström 2005). Also, we might think that complicated factors should *per se* mean complicated models, which is not true.

References

Åberg, Y. and Hedström, P. (2011) Youth unemployment: a self-reinforcing process? in *Analytical Sociology and Social Mechanisms* (ed. P. Demeulenaere), Cambridge University Press, Cambridge, pp. 201–226.

Alesina, A., Baqir, R., and Easterly, W. (1999) Public goods and ethnic divisions. *Quarterly Journal of Economics*, **114**(4), 243–1284.

Alexander, J.C. and Colomy, P. (eds) (1990) *Differentiation Theory and Social Change: Comparative and Historical Perspectives*, Columbia University Press, New York.

Amblard, F. and Deffuant, G. (2004) The role of network topology on extremism propagation with the relative agreement. *Physica A*, **343**, 725–738.

Andersson, E., Östh, J., and Malmberg, B. (2010) Ethnic segregation and performance inequality in the Swedish school system: a regional perspective. *Environment and Planning A*, **42**, 2674–2686.

Auchincloss, A.H., Riolo, R.L., Brown, D.G., *et al.* (2011) An agent-based model of income inequalities in diet in the context of residential segregation. *American Journal of Preventive Medicine*, **40**(3), 303–311.

Axelrod, R. (1997) The dissemination of culture: a model with local convergence and global polarization. *The Journal of Conflict Resolution*, **41**(2), 203–266.

Aydinonat, N.E. (2005) An interview with Thomas C. Schelling: interpretation of game theory and the checkerboard model. *Economics Bulletin*, **2**(2), 1–7.

Becattini, G. (2003) From the industrial district to the districtualization of production activity: some considerations, in *The Technological Evolution of Industrial Districts* (eds F. Belussi, G. Gottardi, and E. Rullani), Kluwer Academic, Dordrecth, pp. 3–18.

Benito, J.M., Branãs-Garza, P., Hernández, P., and Sanchis, J.A. (2011) Sequential versus simultaneous Schelling models: experimental evidence. *Journal of Conflict Resolution*, **55**(1), 60–84.

Boero, R., Castellani, M., and Squazzoni, F. (2004a) Cognitive identity and social reflexivity of the industrial district firms. Going beyond the 'Complexity Effect' with agent-based simulations, in *Agent-Based Social Systems: Theories and Applications* (eds G. Lindemann *et al.*) Springer-Verlag, Berlin Heidelberg, pp. 48–69.

Boero, R., Castellani, M., and Squazzoni, F. (2004b) Micro behavioural attitudes and macro technological adaptation in industrial districts: an agent-based prototype. *Journal of Artificial Societies and Social Simulation*, **7**(2), accessible at: http://jasss. soc.surrey.ac.uk/7/2/1.html.

Boero, R., Castellani, M., and Squazzoni, F. (2008) Individual behavior and macro social properties. An agent-based model. *Computational and Mathematical Organization Theory*, **14**, 156–174.

Bonabeau, E., Dorigo, M., and Theraulaz, G. (1999) *Swarm Intelligence: From Natural to Artificial Systems*, Oxford University Press, New York.

Boudon, R. (1982) *The Unintended Consequences of Social Action*. St Martin's Press, New York.

Bravo, G. (2010) Cultural Commons and Cultural Evolution. arXiv:1002.1196v1 [q-bio.PE]

Bruch, E. and Mare, R.D. (2006) Neighborhood choice and neighborhood change. *American Journal of Sociology*, **112**, 667–709.

Bruch, E. and Mare, R.D. (2009) Segregation dynamics, in *The Oxford Handbook of Analytical Sociolgy* (eds P. Bearman and P. Hedström), Oxford University Press, Oxford, pp. 269–314.

Buchanan, M. (2007) *The Social Atom. Why the Rich Get Richer, Cheaters Get Caught, and Your Neighbor Usually Looks Like You*, Bloomsbury, New York.

Carley, K. (1991) A theory of group stability. *American Sociological Review* **56**, 331–354.

Castellani, B. and Hafferty, F.W. (2009) *Sociology and Complexity Science. A New Field of Inquiry*, Springer-Verlag, Berlin Heidelberg.

Casti, J. (1994) *Complexification: Explaining a Paradoxical World through the Science of Surprise*, John Wiley & Sons, Ltd, New York.

Cederman, L.-E. (2003) Modeling the size of wars: from billiard balls to sandpiles. *American Political Science Review*, **97**, 135–150.

Cederman, L.-E. (2005) Computational models of social forms: advancing generative process theory. *American Journal of Sociology*, **110**(4), 864–893.

Centola, D., González-Avella, J.C., Eguíluz, V.M., and San Miguel, M. (2007) Homophily, cultural drift, and the co-evolution of cultural groups. *Journal of Conflict Resolution* **51**(6), 905–929.

Clark, W.A.V. and Fossett, M. (2008) Understanding the social context of the Schelling segregation model. *PNAS*, **105**(11), 4109–4114.

Coleman, J.S. (1990) *Foundations of Social Theory*, The Belknap Press of Harvard University Press, Cambridge, MA.

Conte, R. (1999) Social intelligence among autonomous agents. *Computational Mathematical Organization Theory*, **5**(3), 203–228.

Conte, R. and Castelfranchi, C. (1996) Simulating multi-agent interdependences: a two-way approach to the micro-macro link, in *Social Science Microsimulation* (eds K.G. Troitzsch, U. Mueller, N. Gilbert, and J. Doran), Springer-Verlag, Berlin, pp. 394–415.

Conte, R., Edmonds, B., Scott, M., and Sawyer, K. (2001) Sociology and social theory in agent-based social simulation: a symposium. *Computational and Mathematical Organization Theory*, **7**, 183–205.

Crooks, A.T. (2010) Constructing and implementing an agent-based model of residential segregation through vector GIS. *International Journal of Geographical Information Science*, **24**(5), 661–675.

Deffuant, G. (2006) Comparing extremism propagation patterns in continuous opinion models. *Journal of Artificial Societies and Social Simulation*, **9**(3), http://jasss.soc.surrey.ac.uk/9/3/8.html.

Deffuant, G., Huet, S., and Amblard, F. (2005) An individual-based model of innovation diffusion mixing social value and individual benefit. *American Journal of Sociology*, **4**, 1041–1069.

Deffuant, G., Amblard, F., Weisbuch, G., and Faure, T. (2002) How can extremism prevail? A study based on the relative agreement interaction model. *Journal of Artificial Societies and Social Simulation*, **5**(4), accessible at: http://jasss.soc.surrey.ac.uk/5/4/1.html.

Deffuant, G., Neau, D., Amblard, F., and Weisbuch, G. (2000) Mixing beliefs among interacting agents. *Advances in Complex Systems*, **3**(1–4), 87–98.

Dodds, P.S., and Watts, D.L. (2004) Universal behavior in a generalized model of contagion. *Physical Review Letters*, **92**, 13–24.

Elliott, J.R. (2001) Referral hiring and ethnically homogeneous jobs: how prevalent is the connection and for whom? *Social Science Research*, **30**, 401–425.

Elster, J. (2007) *Explaining Social Behavior: More Nuts and Bolts for the Social Sciences*, Cambridge University Press, New York.

Epstein, J.M. (2006) *Generative Social Science. Studies in Agent-Based Computational Modeling*, Princeton University Press, Princeton.

Epstein, J.M. and Axtell, R. (1996) *Growing Artificial Societies. Social Science from the Bottom Up*, The MIT Press, Cambridge, MA.

Fagiolo, G., Valente, M., and Vriend, N.J. (2007) Segregation in networks. *Journal of Economic Behavior & Organization*, **64**, 316–366.

Fossett, M. and Waren, A. (2005) Overlooked implications of ethnic preferences for residential segregation in agent-based models. *Urban Studies*, **42**(11), 1893–1917.

Galam, S. and Moscovici, S. (1991) Towards a theory of collective phenomena: consensus and attitude changes in groups. *European Journal of Social Psychology*, **21**(1), 49–74.

Gargiulo, F. and Mazzoni, A. (2008) Can extremism guarantee pluralism? *Journal of Artificial Societies and Social Simulation*, **11**(4), accessible at: http://jasss.soc.surrey.ac.uk/11/4/9.html.

Gelman, A., McCormick, T., Teitler, J., and Zheng, T. (2011) Segregation in social networks based on acquaintanceship and trust. *American Journal of Sociology*, **116**(4), 1234–1283.

Giddens, A. (1986) *Constitution of Society: Outline of the Theory of Structuration*, University of California Press, Berkeley and Los Angeles.

Gigerenzer, G. and Selten, R. (eds) (2001) *Bounded Rationality – The Adaptive Toolbox*, The MIT Press, Cambridge, MA.

Gilbert, N. (1996) Holism, individualism and emergent properties. An approach from the perspective of simulation, in *Modelling and Simulation in the Social Sciences from the Philosophy Point of View* (eds R. Hegselmann, U. Mueller, and K.G. Troitzsch), Kluwer Academic Publishers, Dordrecht, pp. 1–27.

Gilbert, N. (2002) Varieties of emergence, in *Social Agents: Ecology, Exchange, and Evolution. Agent 2002 Conference* (ed. D. Sallach), University of Chicago and Argonne National Laboratory, Chicago, pp. 41–56.

Gilbert, N. (2005) When does social simulation need cognitive models?, in *Cognition and Multi-Agent Interaction: From Cognitive Modeling to Social Simulation* (ed. R. Sun), Cambridge University Press, Cambridge. MA, pp. 428–432.

Gimblett, R. (2002) *Integrating Geographic Information Systems and Agent-Based Modeling Techniques for Simulating Social and Ecological Processes*, Oxford University Press, Oxford.

Gimblett, R. and Skov-Petersen, H. (eds) (2008) *Monitoring, Simulation, and Management of Visitor Landscapes*, University of Arizona Press, Tucson.

Goldstone, R.L. and Janssen, M.A. (2005) Computational models of collective behaviour. *Trends in Cognitive Sciences*, **9**(9), 424–430.

Goldthorpe, J.H. (2007) *On Sociology. Volume One: Critique and Program*, Stanford University Press, Stanford.

González-Avella, J., Cosenza, M.G., Klemm, K., *et al.* (2007) Information feedback and mass media effects in cultural dynamics. *Journal of Artificial Societies and Social Simulation* **10**(3), 9, accessible at: http://jasss.soc.surrey.ac.uk/10/3/9.html.

Granovetter, M. (1978) Threshold models of collective behavior. *American Journal of Sociology*, **83**(6), 1420–1443.

Granovetter, M. and Soong, R. (1988) Threshold models of collective behavior: Chinese restaurants, residential segregation, and the spiral of silence. *Sociological Methodology*, **18**, 69–104.

Greig, J.M. (2002) The end of geography? Globalization, communications, and culture in the international system. *Journal of Conflict Resolution*, **46**(2), 225–243.

Hales, D. (1998) Stereotyping, groups and cultural evolution: a case of 'Second-Order Emergence'?, in *Multi-Agent Systems and Agent-Based Simulation. First International Workshop, MABS '98. Proceedings* (eds J.S. Sichman *et al.*), Springer-Verlag, Berlin Heidelberg, pp. 140–155.

Harrison, J.R. and Carroll, G.R (2002) The dynamics of cultural influence networks. *Computational and Mathematical Organization Theory*, **8**(5), 5–30.

Hedström, P. (1994) Contagious collectivities: on the spatial diffusion of Swedish trade unions, 1890–1940. *American Journal of Sociology*, **99**(5), 1157–1179.

Hedström, P. (2005) *Dissecting the Social. On the Principles of Analytical Sociology*, Cambridge University Press, Cambridge, MA.

Hegselmann, R. and Krause, U. (2002) Opinion dynamics and bounded confidence. Models, analysis, and simulation. *Journal of Artificial Societies and Social Simulation*, **5**(3), accessible at: http://jasss.soc.surrey.ac.uk/5/3/2.html.

Hill, K.R., Walker, R.S., Božičević, M., *et al.* (2011) Co-residence patterns in hunter-gatherer societies show unique human social structure. *Science*, **311**, 1286–1989.

Holyst, J.A., Kacperski, K., and Schweitzer, F. (2001) Social impact models of opinion dynamics. *Annual Reviews of Computational Physics*, **9**, 253–273.

Jager, W. and Amblard, F. (2005) Uniformity, bipolarization and pluriformity captured as generic stylized behavior with an agent-based simulation model of attitude change. *Computational and Mathematical Organization Theory*, **10**, 295–303.

Kennedy, J. (1998) Thinking is social: experiments with the adaptive culture model. *Journal of Conflict Resolution*, **42**(1), 56–76.

Klemm, K., Eguíluz, V.M., Toral, R., and San Miguel, M. (2003a) Global culture: a noise-induced transition in finite systems. *Physical Review E*, **67**, 045101.

Klemm, K., Eguíluz, V.M., Toral, R., and San Miguel, M. (2003b) Role of dimensionality in Axelrod's model for the dissemination of culture. *Physica A*, **327**, 1–5.

Klemm, K., Eguíluz, V.M., Toral, R., and San Miguel, M. (2003c) Nonequilibrium transitions in complex networks: A model of social interaction. *Physical Review E*, **67**(2), 026120.

Kottonnau, J. and Pahl-Wostl, C. (2004) Simulating political attitudes and voting behaviour. *Journal of Artificial Societies and Social Simulation*, **7**(4), accessible at: http://jasss.soc.surrey.ac.uk/7/4/6.html.

Latané, B. (1981) The psychology of social impact. *American Psychologist*, **36**, 343–365.

Latané, B. (2000) Pressures to uniformity and the evolution of cultural norms. Modeling dynamics social impact, in *Computational Modeling of Behavior in Organizations. The Third Scientific Discipline* (eds C. Hulin and D. Ilgen), American Psychological Association, Washington, DC, pp. 189–215.

Latané, B. and Nowak, A. (1997) Self-organizing social systems: necessary and sufficient conditions for the emergence of clustering, consolidation, and continuing diversity, in *Progress in Communication Sciences* (eds G.A. Barnett and F.J. Boster), Ablex Publishing Company, Norwood, NJ, pp. 43–74.

Laurie, A.J. and Jaggi, N.K. (2003) Role of vision in neighbourhood racial segregation: a variant of the Schelling segregation model. *Urban Studies*, **40**, 2687–2704.

Lazzaretti, L. (2003) City of art as a high culture local system and cultural districtualization processes: the cluster of art restoration in Florence. *International Journal of Urban and Regional Research*, **27**(3), 635–648.

Lazzaretti, L. (2008) The cultural districtualization model, in *Creative Cities, Cultural Clusters and Local Economic Development* (eds P. Cooke and L. Lazzaretti), Edward Elgar, Cheltenham, pp. 93–120.

Lustick, I.S. (2000) Agent-based modelling of collective identity: testing constructivist theory. *Journal of Artificial Societies and Social Simulation*, **3**(1), accessible at: http://jasss.soc.surrey.ac.uk/3/1/1.html.

Macy, M., and Willer, R. (2002) From factors to actors: computational sociology and agent-based modeling. *Annual Review of Sociology*, **28**, 143–166.

March, J.G. (1994) *A Primer on Decision Making: How Decisions Happen*, The Free Press, New York.

Mark, N. (1998) Beyond individual preferences: social differentiation from first principles. *American Sociological Review*, **63**, 309–330.

Markovski, B. and Thye, S.R. (2001) Social influence on paranormal beliefs. *Sociological Perspectives*, **44**(1), 21–44.

Mayer, D., and Brown, T. (1998) The statistical mechanics of voting. *Physical Review Letters*, **81**, 1718–1721.

Mckeown, G. and Sheely, N. (2006) Mass media and polarisation processes in the bounded confidence model of opinion dynamics. *Journal of Artificial Societies and Social Simulation*, **9**(1), accessible at: http://jasss.soc.surrey.ac.uk/9/1/11.html.

Mead, G.H. (1932) *The Philosophy of the Present*, University of Chicago Press, Chicago.

Mezias, S.J. (1988) Aspiration level effects: an empirical investigation. *Journal of Economic Behavior and Organization*, **10**, 389–400.

Merton, R.K. (1968) *Social Theory and Social Structure*, The Free Press, New York.

Miller, J.H. and Page, S.E. (2007) *Complex Adaptive System. An Introduction to Computational Models of Social Life*, Princeton University Press, Princeton.

Moscovici, S. (1985) Social influence and conformity. *Handbook of Social Psychology*, **2**, 347–412.

Moscovici, S., Lage, E., and Naffrechoux, M. (1969) Influence of a consistent minority on the responses of a majority in a color perception task. *Sociometry*, **32**, 365–380.

Murphy, P.R., Mezias, S., and Chen, Y.R. (2001) Adapting apirations to feedback: the role of success and failure, in *Organizational Cognition. Computation and Interpretation* (eds T.K. Lant and Z. Shapira), Lawrence Erlbaum Associates, London, pp. 125–146.

Nechyba, T.J., (2003) School finance, spatial income segregation and the nature of communities. *Journal of Urban Economics*, **54**(1), 61–88.

Nemeth, C. and Wachtler, J. (1973) Consistency and modification of judgment. *Journal of Experimental Social Psychology*, **9**, 65–79.

Nowak, A., Szamrej, J., and Latané, B. (1990) From private attitude to public opinion: a dynamic theory of social impact. *Psychological Review*, **97**(3), 362–376.

Omer, I. (2010) High-resolution geographic data and urban modeling: the case of residential segregation, in *Geospatial Analysis and Modelling of Urban Structure and Dynamics* (eds B. Jiang and X. Yao), Springer-Verlag, Berlin Heidelberg, pp. 15–29.

Paicheler, G. (1998) *The Psychology of Social Influence*, Cambridge University Press, Cambridge, MA.

Pancs, R., and Vriend, N.J. (2007) Schelling's spatial proximity model of segregation revisited. *Journal of Public Economics*, **92**(1–2), 1–24.

Parsons, T. (1966) *Societies. Evolutionary and Comparative Perspectives*, Prentice-Hall, Englewood Cliffs, NJ.

Petri, Y. (2012) Micro, macro and mechanisms, in *The Oxford Handbook of Philosophy of the Social Sciences* (ed. H. Kincaid), Oxford University Press, New York (in press).

Picker, R. (1997) Simple games in a complex world: a generative approach to the adoption of norms. *University of Chicago Law Review*, **64**, 1225–1288.

Porter, M.E. (1998) *On Competition*, Harvard Business Review Books, Boston.

Pratkanis, A. (2007) *The Science of Social Influence. Advances and Future Progresses*, Psychology Press, London.

Reardon, S.F. and Bischoff, K. (2011) Income inequality and income segregation. *American Journal of Sociology*, **116**(4), 1092–1153.

Regenwetter, M., Falmagne, J.C., and Grofman, B. (1999) A stochastic model of preference change and its application to 1992 presidential election panel data. *Psychological Review*, **106**, 362–384.

Rosewell, B. and Ormerod, P. (2009) Validation and verification of agent-based models in the social sciences, in *Epistemological Aspects of Computer Simulation in the Social Sciences* (ed. F. Squazzoni), Springer-Verlag, Berlin Heidelberg, pp. 130–140.

Rullani, E. (2003) The industrial district (ID) as a cognitive system, in *The Technological Evolution of Industrial Districts* (eds F. Belussi, G. Gottardi, and E. Rullani), Kluwer, Amsterdam, pp. 63–88.

Sawyer, R.K. (2005) *Social Emergence: Societies as Complex Systems*, Cambridge University Press, Cambridge, MA.

Schelling, T.C. (1969) Models of segregation. *American Economic Review*, **59**, 488–493.

Schelling, T. (1971) Dynamic models of segregation. *Journal of Mathematical Sociology*, **1**, 143–186.

Schelling, T. (1972) A process of residential segregation: neighborhood tipping, in *Racial Discrimination in Economic Life* (ed. A. Pascal), D.C. Heath, Lexington, pp. 157–184.

Shibanai, Y., Satoko, Y., and Ishiguro, I. (2001) Effects of effects of global information feedback on diversity extensions to Axelrod's adaptive culture model. *Journal of Conflict Resolution*, **45**(1), 80–96.

Simmel, G. (1950) *The Sociology of Georg Simmel*, compiled and translated by Kurt Wolff, Free Press, Glencoe, IL.

Singh, A., Vainchtein, D., and Weiss, H. (2011) Limit sets for natural extensions of Schelling's segregation model. *Communications in Nonlinear Science and Numerical Simulation*, **16**(7), 2822–2831.

Soros, G. (2008) *The Crash of 2008 and What It Means*, Perseus Books, New York.

Squazzoni, F. (2007) Does cognition (really and always) matter? The *Vexata Quaestio* of the micro-foundations of agent-based models from a sociological viewpoint, in *Interdisciplinary Approaches to the Simulation of Social Phenomena. Proceedings of the Fourth Conference of the European Social Simulation Association* (ed. F. Amblard), IRIT Editions, Toulouse, pp. 543–556, accessible at: http://essa2007.free.fr/ESSA2007Proceedings.pdf.

Squazzoni, F. (2008) The micro-macro link in social simulation. *Sociologica*, **2**(1), doi: 10.2383/26578, accessible at: http://www.sociologica.mulino.it/journal/article/index/Article/Journal:ARTICLE:179.

Squazzoni, F. and Boero, R. (2002) Economic performance, inter-firm relations and local institutional engineering in a computational prototype of industrial districts. *Journal of Artificial Societies and Social Simulation*, **5**(1), accessible at: http://jasss.soc.surrey.ac.uk/5/1/1.html.

Squazzoni, F. and Boero, R. (2005) Towards an agent-based computational sociology: good reasons to strengthen cross-fertilization between complexity and sociology, in *Advances in Sociology Research. Volume II* (ed. L.M. Stoneham), Nova Science Publishers, New York, pp. 103–133.

Van de Rijt, A., Siegel, D., and Macy, M. (2009) Neighborhood chance and neighborhood change: a comment on Bruch and Mare. *American Journal of Sociology*, **114**, 1166–1180.

Watts, D. (1999) *Small World: The Dynamics of Networks Between Order and Randomness*, Princeton University Press, Princeton.

Watts, D. (2002) A simple model of global cascades on random networks. *PNAS*, **99**(9), 5766–5771.

Watts, D. and Dodds, P. (2009) Threshold models of social influence, in *The Oxford Handbook of Analytical Sociology* (eds P. Hedström and P. Bearman), Oxford University Press, Oxford, pp. 475–497.

Watts, D., Dodds, P., and Newman, M.E.J. (2002) Identity and search in social networks. *Science*, **296**(5571), 1302–1305.

Weber, M. (1978) *Economy and Society: An Outline of Interpretative Sociology*, University of California Press, Berkeley.

Weisbuch, G., Deffuant, G., and Amblard, F. (2005) Persuasion dynamics. *Physica A*, **353**, 555–575.

Weisbuch, G., Deffuant, G., Amblard, F., and Nadal, J.-P. (2002) Meet, discuss and segregate! *Complexity*, **7**, 55–63.

Wilensky, U. (1999) NetLogo. Accessible at: http://ccl.northwestern.edu/netlogo/. Center for Connected Learning and Computer-Based Modeling, Northwestern University, Evanston, IL.

Yin, L. (2009) The dynamics of residential segregation in Buffalo: an agent-based simulation. *Urban Studies*, **46**(13), 2749–2770.

You, J. II and Wilkinson, F. (1994) Competition and cooperation: toward understanding industrial districts. *Review of Political Economy*, **6**(3), 259–278.

Zangh, J. (2004) Residential segregation in an all-integrationist world. *Journal of Economic Behavior and Organization*, **54**, 533–550.

Zimbardo, P.G. and Leippe, M.R. (1991) *The Psychology of Attitude Change and Social Influence*, 3rd edn, McGraw-Hill, New York.

4

The methodology

This chapter focuses on methodology. In the previous chapters, my message has been that explanation is the most important aspect for agent-based computational sociology. Here, we look at methodological standards and how they can promote collaboration and generalization. Methodology is important to promote logical rigor in theory building, achieve testable results and promote cumulativeness. Indeed, *ad hoc* research without reference to well-established methodological standard is not credible, contributes little and is difficult to communicate.

As stated by Martensson and Martensson (2007), research is 'credible' when it is consistent, rigorous and transparent. This means that theoretical statements are internally valid and results are reliable and linked to existing knowledge. It is 'contributory' when it is original, relevant and can be generalized. This means the ability of a model to look at current puzzles and do so by guaranteeing cumulative research paths, both empirically and theoretically. It is 'communicable' when it is accessible, and 'consumable' by others, even non-specialists or practitioners.

To achieve most of these important aspects, a methodological standard is necessary. Methodology is a constructive framework that provides a socially shared system of principles, rules and practices which defines how research should be performed (and eventually taught). This definition applies to agent-based computational sociology as to any other field. However, being a recent development, ABM research has premises and consequences which need to be seriously considered as it sometimes falls outside familiar social science methods.

Furthermore, the points discussed here will clarify whether agent-based computational sociology is methodologically closer to experimental and empirical research than to theoretical and philosophical speculation.

Obviously, achieving such a methodological standard is outside our scope here. My aim is simply to sketch a common framework, identify good practices, focus on critical problems and outline future development. Thankfully, the ABM community has started to pay more attention to methodology and certain best practices have been discovered. Some of these come from standard social science, whilst others are more ABM-specific. This chapter aims at providing a coherent picture.

Looking at methodological issues retrospectively, there has recently been a shift from extension/exploration to elaboration/consolidation. The first wave of ABMs in the 1990s included applications of this new method to interesting social science puzzles. For example, scholars applied ABMs to cooperation, social norms, opinion dynamics, urban studies, market dynamics, political behavior and social conflict. At that time, the uniqueness of this type of research and certain differences between ABMs and more traditional research methods were emphasized.

From 2000, ABM scientists have increasingly tried to improve methodology in order to consolidate their research. Attention shifted from ABM uniqueness to integration and cross-fertilization with other methods, such as qualitative, quantitative, and experimental research. In my opinion, this new perspective was not a withdrawal from the original pretension of innovation. Rather, it is a necessary step to help explain empirical puzzles, make cutting-edge research and institutionalize agent-based computational sociology. This is also necessary so that agent-based computational sociology is a reference for trans-disciplinary innovation.

My purpose here is to support this new perspective and suggest reasons for combining ABMs with other methods. My view is that agent-based computational sociology needs to recompose the fragmentation of our discipline, rather than to add further parochialism. This can be achieved more easily if different methods and communities collaborate with each other.

The first aim of this chapter is to present the ABM method as a coherent sequence of best practices which ideally should be followed. This method clarifies what the specificity of agent-based computational sociology is. However, we also need to show the advantages of integration with other methods. At the same time, the analysis of these steps can help us to underline present weaknesses and needs for the future.

It must be said that these issues imply reference to intricate epistemological debate, for example, the link of theory and reality, which deserves a vast amount of philosophical considerations. Here, I will only touch on this topic, although certain aspects have already been discussed in Chapter 1.

After presenting the methodological sequence, I will focus on two important issues, that is, replication and multi-level empirical validation. Recently, these points have become of great interest, as improvements in replication and validation have made better science and promoted the recognition of ABM research in more established communities.

In Chapter 1, it was argued that one of the most important advantages of ABMs is that they allow peers to check, reproduce, manipulate and extend models, which is crucial to produce testable findings and favor cumulativeness. Here, I have focused on the methodological counterpart of this point.

First, I will look at all facets of replication, particularly its relationship to verification and validation. Replication is *the process of how a model is independently scrutinized by peers by re-running it*. It is at the core of both empirical and experimental science. As stated by Axelrod (1997), it is 'one of the hallmarks of cumulative sciences'. It is what makes agent-based computational sociology similar to experimental sciences, even if it is in a special sense as ABM scientists conduct experiments with virtual societies.

To illustrate this point, I will review two recent replication *querelles* where peers have independently replicated each other's models, found respective mistakes and/or limitations and incrementally developed new insights. These *querelles* allow us to understand that replication has not only a check and test function; it is also a means to improve our understanding of the issues at stake.

I expect different reactions from these cases. Some readers could see them as examples of model failures and consequently as proof of the immaturity of this type of research. One could argue that ABMs are hardly transparent and too complex so that modelers often do not have perfect control of their own 'creatures'. Moreover, the fact that journal reviewers do not have the time to seriously replicate models due to their own knowledge gap and the unavailability of original sources or low-quality description by authors, supports this argument. As Gintis (2009) argued by referring to economics, this would explain the lower status of ABM research compared with analytic science for theory building.

If there is no doubt that replication is far from being a simple undertaking, this is also true for experimental and empirical research. Indeed, the difficulty for reviewers to evaluate coherence and validity is the same in any field. For instance, in neurosciences or molecular biology, reviewers cannot re-run experiments originally reported by the submission authors. This leads me to believe that agent-based computational sociology is in any case an important step forward compared with present methodological practices in sociology, which is very weak in experimental methods.

I expect that other readers will appreciate the advantage of ABMs in making replication possible once and for all. Unlike qualitative sociological research, here, intersubjective tests to find generalization are potentially and often actually possible. In my view, this is what is important. Given that we have not developed a cumulative body of knowledge by incrementalism in our discipline yet, I see more advantages than disadvantages.

However, it must be acknowledged that methodological development of ABM research is needed to make models more transparent, manageable, testable and replicable. Certain some colleagues have suggested adopting standards to document, archive, and make available models (e.g., Janssen *et al.* 2008; Polhill *et al.* 2008). Recently, important steps forward have been undertaken in this direction. An example is the establishment of the *Open ABM Consortium*,[1] where there is a repository of models with technical instructions voluntarily posted by authors to favor replication and where replication studies are reported.

Recently, there has been growing attention towards more rigorous methodological requirements by journals which publish ABM articles. For instance, requests to submit to the open archive or to upload models and well-documented codes in supplementary

---

[1] The *Open ABM Consortium* aims to improve how scientists and practitioners develop, share and use ABMs. It includes an online archive to maintain and make available source code, description and instructions of models. It also includes replication studies. It is accessible at: http://www.openabm.org/about.

material information are seen as compulsory requirements to have an article accepted or even submitted. These measures can help to improve methodological standards.

Standardization and good practices will probably proliferate in the future, which will help overall recognition of ABM research. However, it is worth outlining again that this is a common problem, even in more mature and developed fields. The fact that ABM scientists have recognized this and have started to work seriously in this direction, testifies to a good state of affairs rather than being a proof of weakness.

Another point to remember is that sociology is basically an empirical science and methodologically coherent ABM research is incomplete without reference to empirical evidence. This is why I will focus on empirical validation and more specifically on what I call 'multi-level empirical validation'. For this I mean *the process by means relevant model parameters are informed by and simulation findings are evaluated against empirical data*. In my view, the challenge for ABM research in sociology is not only to replicate empirical macro regularities from model assumptions (i.e., what is usually meant for empirical validation), but if possible, also to do so by empirically specifying relevant model parameters (i.e., what is usually meant for empirical calibration).

I will amalgamate these two concepts to emphasize the fact that empirical specification is often decisive in discriminating between alternative theoretical explanations (Squazzoni and Boero 2005). This is mostly the case of social phenomena, where we do not have all-embracing theories about micro level processes.

To integrate theory and data, ABM needs to work with other research methods. I will provide a list of useful methods to gather data for ABMs, such as experimental, stakeholder, qualitative and quantitative research. I will also provide examples of ABMs based on empirical data. This will also help us to emphasize challenges and implications of this cross-methodological integration.

4.1   The method

Following the earlier chapters, the reader will now have understood that ABMs imply a specific approach to sociological investigation. This can be summarized by the idea of seeing social phenomena as the result of social interaction. Quantitative sociologists usually study social phenomena (e.g., unemployment) by establishing possible correlations between dependent and independent variables which look at macro factors (e.g., family income or education). Qualitative sociologists prefer to investigate subjective experience of people (e.g., the effect of unemployment on confidence and identity).

On the contrary, ABM sociologists focus on social phenomena as the aggregate result of social interaction. Following the example of unemployment, the research question of an ABM sociologist would be as follows: given specific macro circumstances (e.g., a particular market structure), how does interaction between heterogeneous individuals pursuing various strategies to get into the market and influencing each other, cause the unemployment patterns that we observe in reality?

This approach allows us to identify those micro-founded generative mechanisms which might account for social patterns. This has been explained in Chapter 1. Here, we want to identify the methodological counterpart of this argument. Let us enter into detail on this point. ABM investigations are usually undertaken through a sequence of steps as follows: (1) the definition of the research question, (2) specification of the model building blocks, (3) model implementation, execution and verification, (4) simulation output analysis, (5) (multi-level) validation, (6) reporting and publication, and (7) replication.

It is worth outlining first that these distinctions are not always clear-cut in practice, as certain steps might influence each other. Secondly, not all these steps are always undertaken. For instance, step 5 is not always at hand (see below). Step 7 concerns contributions which attract wider attention more than average contributions. Therefore, replication is not always pursued as needed. Moreover, the sequence may implicate certain changes. For example, step 7 can be instrumental for steps 3 and 5. Finally, steps may be subsequently undertaken by independent scholars or teams (see Section 4.2). These features, however, do not disqualify the ideal typical value of the sequence I have made. So, let us describe these steps in detail.

The definition of a research question includes fixing the model *explananda* and circumscribing the target. These operations have both a descriptive and an analytical part. The descriptive part can be done by following the literature or by observation. However, as argued by Goldthorpe (2007), a good research question can be probably found more easily when we start from observation and a good description of empirical regularities. This can be done both from direct data and 'stylized facts', that is, broad-scale, stylized statistical regularities. The idea of 'stylized facts' was first introduced by Kaldor (1961) to study economic growth differently from the abstract neoclassical perspective. This would compensate for the lack or defect of statistical data in economics. Approaching research questions from 'stylized facts' means starting investigation from identifying 'broad tendencies' of empirical facts. This helps us to look at crucial puzzles, even in the absence of specific data.

Obviously, this is not sufficient. The descriptive part should be accompanied by an analytical one. Goldthorpe (2007, p. 207) suggested that:

> Social regularities, once relatively surely established by descriptive methods, are then to be regarded as the basic *explananda* of sociological analysis: sociological problems are ones that call all in one way or another be expressed in terms of social regularities – their formation, continuity, interrelation, change, disruption, and so on. When, therefore, analysis becomes causal, social regularities represent the effects for which causes have to be discovered. And this task, contrary to what proponents of the idea of causation as robust dependence would seem to have supposed, cannot be purely statistical one but requires a crucial subject-matter input.

This means that modeling has the prerequisite of 'hypothesizing generative processes at the level of action that have explanatory adequacy and that are of a theoretically grounded kind' (Goldthorpe 2007, p. 40). Indeed, to pass from the descriptive to the analytical, ABM investigation requires research questions to be first framed and then posed in terms of expected macro consequences of agent behavior in social interaction.

It is worth noting that this framework does not restrict the scope of sociologists. Indeed, most sociological puzzles can be fruitfully framed in terms of social interaction problems. For example, if we want to study ethnic discrimination in labor markets, it is probable that we have to focus on interaction between employers as they influence each other in selecting workforce and their decisions are signals for others (Abdou and Gilbert 2009). If we want to study the recent growth of 'binge drinking' among young people in the UK, it is necessary to look at social interaction as people imitate each other in small groups and 'binge drinking' spreads across social networks (Ormerod and Wiltshire 2009). As previously described, focusing on interaction is even more crucial to understand how seemingly rational behavior aggregates to produce suboptimal, unpredictable outcomes.

My point here is that there is a specific approach of agent-based computational sociologists. Economists are insuperable in simplifying a variety of 'what-others-suppose' complex issues (also social and political ones) as aggregate implications of agent self-interest and rationality. In the same vein, agent-based computational sociologists should specialize in interpreting social reality in terms of agent interaction in social structures, that is, social interaction. This is an inspiration that has united all ABM scientists mentioned in this book. I suggest this as the *conditio sine qua non* of agent-based computational sociology.

Once the first step is fixed, the next is modeling, that is, translating a rough and paper-and-pencil model into a computerized one. The challenge here is to define model building blocks and identify parameters, that is, building a modeled system which approximates the target in varying degrees of detail.

Canonical operations are as follows: defining the structural part of the model (e.g., agent attributes, interaction structure, and features of the environment), the behavioral part (e.g., rules of agent behavior), time (e.g., discrete, events, sequences), the flow of agent activities into the model and aggregate measures. The computerization of a model involves both substantive and more abstract and computing-related technical issues. For example, it includes how to design agent behavior, but also how to reproduce parallelism of agent decisions and optimize and manage the flow of computing activities, not to mention the preliminary choice of programming languages and simulation platforms (e.g., Gilbert 2008).

Once translated into a computational version, the next step is the execution of the model under various parameter conditions. Execution is instrumental for internal tests and verification. Verification is the process of inquiry into the correctness of the model implementation (Gilbert and Troitzsch 2005; David 2009). Sometimes it is confused with validation. The difference is that while verification concerns the process of how each computational model procedure is checked that it does what it was planned to do, validation involves checking the correctness of the link between simulation output and model target, that is, between *explananda* and *explanandum* (Gilbert and Troitzsch 2005; Ormerod and Rosewell 2009). Therefore, while verification implicates inquiry into the adequacy of the computational artifact for the modeler's intention, validation implicates focusing on the explanatory capacity of the artifact for the model target. In some cases, independent replication is fundamental both for verification and validation. I will focus in more detail both on replication and validation below.

The analysis of simulation output involves various data analysis techniques, from traditional statistical techniques used for sensitivity analysis (e.g., across-run variability, sensitivity to initial conditions) to visualization techniques which allow the observer to map emerging dynamics in space and time during simulation. ABMs are complex models which involve agent interaction in nonlinear ways in specific structures and include various variables and parameters. Therefore, various types of data might be decisive to assure confidence in their results. The examples reported previously have showed the heterogeneity of output commonly used by modelers to understand model behavior.

Given this, the aim of any modeler is not just to understand what is going on in his/her model. Simulation results should be considered 'valid' for their explanatory value against the target of interest. This calls for the problem of the relationship between theory and observation to be resolved. This is where validation enters the picture.

Given that ABMs can have a nomothetic or idiographic purpose (e.g., Gilbert and Ahrweiler 2009) and that models compete, are confronted and/or are collectively and incrementally developed, I distinguish between three types of validation, that is, *internal*, *cross-* and *empirical* validation. Again, while it is difficult to make clear-cut distinctions between these types, it is reasonable to do so for the sake of understanding.

Internal validation means *the process by which the coherence between* explananda *and* explanandum *is scrutinized*, possibly also by peers. The coherence between theoretical assumptions and explanatory consequences can be logically tested by examining a model under different parameter conditions. Given that ABMs look at complex systems with many variables and parameters, it is only by simulating, running and testing the model that one can be confident of the explanatory coherence of model results. This is far from trivial as it is this confidence that allows us to state that 'if x (e.g., agent behavior), then y (e.g., a given outcome), because of z (i.e., the explanatory mechanism)', that is, to explain something (e.g., Hedström 2005). It is worth noting that I talk of 'internal' validation as a reference to empirical data is not required, if not indirectly (e.g., empirical literature). This is the difference between 'internal' and 'empirical' validation (see below).

For *cross-validation*, I mean the process by which the explanatory power of models which look at the same or a similar issue is tested comparatively according to a given criterion, for example, simplification or empirical adherence. This can help to corroborate, generalize or circumscribe the validity domain of results.

Ormerod and Rosewell (2009) suggested a good example of this. They referred to the case of business cycle models and emphasized the added value of simplicity as an evaluation criterion to discriminate between explanations. They recognized that this field included various models, which differed in scope and scale but produced more or less the same stylized facts.

A first example was Ormerod (2002), who started from evidence that most business cycle fluctuations were determined by the corporate sector and assumed heterogeneous and boundedly rational firms. Firms followed simple rules to decide their output and to form their own market sentiment. His model generated empirically grounded evidence, such as autocorrelation and the power spectrum of real US output growth in the twentieth century.

Dosi, Fagiolo and Roventini (2006) developed a similar business cycle model but with more complicated and richer features, for example, two types of firms (e.g., R&D technology and consumer goods producers), firm entry and exit, technological change, consumptions, and so on. They increased the richness of the structural component of the model (e.g., market features), but kept simple behavioral rules, such as in the previous case. Their results were consistent with stylized facts such as fat-tailed firm growth rate distributions, productivity dispersion, and right skewed firm size distribution. Some results overlapped with the previous example, others were additional insights.

Finally, Wright (2005) simplified behavioral assumptions even more, starting from purely stochastic, zero-intelligence behaviors, and obtained both overlapping and additional insights compared with previous examples. The point is that while these models looked at different stylized facts, closer inspection showed many similarities. In particular, these models had a common capacity of achieving a more complete understanding of business cycles than mainstream approaches.

After this, the question was to define a criterion to evaluate these models. Ormerod and Rosewell (2009, pp. 137–138) suggested that explanatory performance of models should be measured according to the simplification of their assumptions on human behavior, as this was widely supported by experimental evidence:

> Deciding which of these models is more valid (we assume that they are equally verified) is not straightforward. They each produce results which are consistent with what is observed and do so with agent decision rules which are easy to describe and explain. The elements of the reality which are explained are in each case more comprehensive than the standard model but add different levels of explanation. [...] One criterion that might be used to determine performance is simplicity of behaviour, on the principle that if simple agent rules can produce good description, this is better than having complicated ones. Another way of expressing this is to ensure that agents are only required to have the minimum necessary ability to process information or to learn [...]. The idea that agents act, in general, in a way far removed from the precepts of rational choice economics is now supported by an impressive body of evidence [...]. It is models which assign, implicitly or explicitly, a high level of cognition to agents which need special justification rather than those which do not.

More extensive and systematic work on cross-validation in ABM research is needed that makes evaluation and cumulativeness stable features of this type of research.

Empirical validation means *the process by which model results are confronted and corroborated with empirical data.* Here, I extend this definition to that of *multi-level empirical validation,* which is *the process by which relevant model parameters are informed by and simulation findings are evaluated against empirical data.* As we will see below, this extension is important. Although this definition combines two intuitively distinct components, such as empirical calibration of parameters and empirical validation of simulation results, it defends the idea that the challenge in sociology is not only to replicate/generate observed statistical regularities at the macro level, but also to accomplish this starting from empirically well-specified micro assumptions. We will look in detail at this point later.

Finally, *documenting and publication* are crucial steps to communicate model results. They are also pivotal for replication, as this depends largely upon the quality of documenting and transparency of models. Recently, pressure from top journals and replication issues (see below) have brought this point into the spotlight. Standards to document and publish ABM studies are now available (e.g., Bauer, Müller and Odell 2001; Grimm *et al.* 2006; Polhill *et al.* 2008; Grimm *et al.* 2010; Polhill 2010). This means that anyone interested in a model should have the chance to (a) easily access model codes and instructions, (b) easily understand model features, following model documents and code comments, and (c) easily replicate model results.

A good example of this approach is Polhill *et al.* (2008, see also some updates in Polhill 2010), who suggested following the ODD ('Overview, Design Concepts and Details') protocol to document models. They provided three examples from ecological literature. The ODD protocol is designed to make model description readable and complete for anyone and, although not directly following object-oriented programming, can be easily completed with UML class diagrams and fully describes any ABM. Its advantage is that it stipulates a structure to describe them logically and includes guidelines to provide all relevant information.

It is structured around three elements, namely 'overview', 'design concepts' and 'details' (Grimm *et al.* 2006, 2010). *Overview* consists of 'purpose', where what is to be done and can be done with the model is fully explained. In 'entities, state variables and scales', the model structure is reported (including model entities, types of agents and variables), possibly by using UML class diagrams. In 'process overview and scheduling' all the model processes and how they have been scheduled are documented.

Design concepts describe the general concepts underlying model design so that all important design decisions can be easily understood by anyone. It includes 'basic principles' and 'learning'. The first describes theories, hypotheses and modeling approaches which underpin the model design, the second reports on agent decision making adaptation. It also includes 'objectives', where agent fitness and decision rules are reported. Moreover, it lists certain standard concepts used in most simulations, such as stochasticity (if present and the reason for it) and collectives (if agents are grouped and how and why).

Finally, *details* is aimed at enabling model reimplementation. This consists of 'initialization', where initial simulation values are reported and reference to any data used is included. There are 'input data', where access to online archives for data used and even the original random number seed are included. Finally, there are 'sub-models', where all the 'process overview and scheduling' processes are fully explained, for example, how parameter values were chosen or how sub-models were tested and calibrated.

Documentation is usually accompanied by the model's full publication in the online journal supplementary material section, in personal author web sites, or even better, in some online repository of models such as *Open ABM Consortium*, mentioned above. There is increasing recognition that standardization for model documentation and publication is crucial to improve ABM methodology (e.g., Richiardi *et al.* 2006; Janssen *et al.* 2008).

Having said this, let us now focus on two relevant points, replication and multi-level validation, which are linked to documentation and publication. I would like to focus on them as they are fundamental to improve ABM research in sociology and have been recently subject to intense discussion.

4.2   Replication

Replication is the *process by means a given model is independently scrutinized by peers by re-running it*. The possibility that a model can be re-implemented, re-run, tested, manipulated, modified and extended by peers is the key advantage of formalization. This guarantees that original findings can be tested, so that *ad hoc* explanations can be distinguished from general ones. If the results of a model can be repeatedly generated, this means that they are not an exceptional case. This is a *conditio sine qua non* for knowledge cumulativeness in science (Wilensky and Rand 2007, 3.1). This is a general statement which should also apply to agent-based computational sociology.

Replication is fundamental for *verification*, *internal validation* and *alignment* or *cross-validation*. It is difficult to distinguish in practice these aspects, but they should be distinguished here for the sake of clarity.

As we have already said, verification is the process of inquiry into the correctness of the model's implementation (Gilbert and Troitzsch 2005; David 2009). Usually, it is performed by modelers themselves or by their peers. It is of great help especially when a model is replicated in other simulation languages or platforms. This allows us to check the correctness of the original model behavior under different technical circumstances. This can reveal mistakes in the original implementation or hidden processes previously neglected by the original modelers.

It seems intuitive that models do what modelers have planned them to do. However, this is not always the case with complex models such as ABMs. Given that various qualitative and quantitative parameters and nonlinear interaction are involved in these models, it is probable that peers might independently identify processes that original modelers were unaware of.

This is important, for example, as a recent online survey on a sample of 2000 scientists showed that the skills of computational scientists on programming are largely inappropriate. For instance, only 47% of scientists involved in the survey had a good understanding of software testing. Very few followed best practices, such as using a version-control system, tracking sources, writing testable software, seriously testing it and making it freely available for replication (Merali 2010). The results of this survey showed that the codes of many models were likely to be riddled with tiny errors that possibly did not cause execution problems but could affect results. This is why independent verification by replication is necessary to increase confidence in simulation findings.

But this is not all. Indeed, verification is instrumental for internal validation. By replicating a model, peers could raise important issues about technical aspects, evaluate the influence of certain design choices on results and reveal excessive dependency of explanatory results from particular model specifications. In addition, they could circumscribe the domain of explanation argued by modelers.

More constructively, replication can also motivate theoretical intuition and allow us to extend findings in various directions. For example, it could prove that original findings explained more features of a particular domain than previously expected or they could even explain interrelated phenomena, whose connection was not seen by the original authors. It could allow us to test findings more thoroughly against a large variation of important parameters or it could even help to add new features to the model which specify the impact of crucial parameters better. An example of this can be found in the residential segregation literature illustrated previously, where replication allowed peers to extend the explanatory power of Schelling's original model.

Furthermore, replication is important for *alignment* or *cross-validation*, which is *the process by which N models are evaluated which produce equivalent results under equivalent conditions*. As argued by Axtell *et al.* (1996):

> Alignment is essential to support two hallmarks of cumulative disciplinary research: critical experiment and subsumption. If we cannot determine whether or not two models produce equivalent results in equivalent conditions, we cannot reject one model in favour of another that fits data better; nor are we able to say that one model is a special case of another more general one – as we do when saying Einstein's treatment of gravity subsumes Newton's.

The idea that by replication, peers could help us to incorporate previous models into new ones and so develop more general knowledge is important. Indeed, it makes it possible to proceed through collective incrementalism which is instrumental for scientific progress.

Some call this 'TAPAS' (e.g., Frenken 2006). TAPAS stands for 'take a previous model and add something'. It is a collective strategy to consolidate good models, save time and energy by avoiding doing the same thing twice and assuring cumulative knowledge by model extension and incremental development. Although largely devalued by mainstream economists, who followed this strategy to build the complicated scaffold of standard economic models, this is a reasonable collective strategy that can have great value especially if combined with empirical evidence (see below).

Finally, each replication has its own degree of success. Axtell *et al.* (1996) argued that there are three decreasing levels of replication: (1) 'numerical identity', when results of two models are reproduced precisely; (2) 'distributional equivalence', when results are statistically indistinguishable from each other; and (3) 'relational equivalence', when qualitative relationships between model parameters can be successfully reproduced. The large number of numerical and qualitative parameters, stochasticity and nonlinearity involved in this type of models make isomorphism between original and replication sometimes difficult to achieve. Nevertheless, it is reasonable to consider these levels as guidelines to evaluate replication success.

Obviously, all these points are possible only if peers can replicate models. This is not always the case, especially when original authors did not fully report model features or did not publish codes or full technical descriptions. This has mostly been true in the past. Now, under the pressure of the community and relevant journals, the trend is to guarantee that peers have everything needed to replicate models. This has further increased the quality of ABM research and its recognition, as suggested above.

In this respect, Ormerod and Rosewell made a parallel between what is happening now to ABMs and the history of econometrics, which is interesting to report in full here:

> The ability to perform regressions, except of the simplest kind, was severely limited until the 1970s by access to computer power. There was then a proliferation of articles on applied econometrics, which turned into a torrent during the 1980s with the development of the personal computer. Initially, published papers carried the results but no data. Even the descriptions of data sources were often cursory if not cryptic. Replicating someone else's results was a time consuming task, which often failed [. . .]. Gradually, a better code of practice in describing data sources evolved, followed by an increasing insistence by the leading journals that the actual data used in the regressions (including all the transformations used) be made available to other researchers, initially in the paper itself and now via the web. So econometrics has seen a gradual evolution of better replication practice, enabled by successive wave of technology [. . .]. A similar sort of process will presumably take place with ABMs (Ormerod and Rosewell 2009, pp. 132–133).

All these discussions testify to the fact that sensitivity towards methodological issues has recently increased in the ABM community (e.g., Axtell *et al.* 1996; Rouchier *et al.* 2008). Examples now abound. Let us now look at some of these.

One of the most influential contributions was by Edmonds and Hales (2003) who replicated Riolo, Cohen and Axelrod's model (2001). Here, a model was built to examine the influence of tags (i.e., arbitrary observable cues or markings about others) on cooperation between rational agents. The original results showed that cooperation emerges via tags without assuming any reciprocity between agents. Edmonds and Hales performed many statistical tests on simulation parameters, tried alternative implementations when ambiguity was found in the original model, as in the selection procedure for reproduction. They examined the dependency of results from critical parameters, such as the donation rate, cost of donating and tolerance against differences in tags. They found significant differences in cooperation rates and dynamics between the original and replicated versions. They suggested that unreplicated simulation models should not be taken on faith and that, as with other kinds of experimental/empirical research, simulations need to be independently replicated.

They also suggested some interesting tips to detect mistakes and understand the crucial impact of parameters. They suggested using particular statistical tests over long-term averages to check the alignment of simulations, turn off features of the original model in the case of misalignment until alignment is achieved and then re-adding them progressively. This can help us to understand which feature is the critical one which determines the observed differences. They suggested implementing the same model in different simulation languages and platforms, if possible programmed by different people (Edmonds and Hales 2003, 10.1).

Rouchier (2003) replicated Duffy's model on speculation (Duffy 2001), which was in turn based on experimental findings of previous work by Kiyotaki and Wright (1989). Relying only on information documented in the article, she was capable of closely replicating the previous model. However, she found significant differences in respective results due to the author's inaccuracy in precisely reporting agent behavior algorithms assumed in the model and scarce exploration of important parameters, such as population size and interaction time. Again, one of the main lessons was that scholars should fully exploit the advantages of computer simulation for extensive model exploration, for example, running large population size and long-time simulations in different parameter conditions.

This was also found by Galan and Izquierdo (2005) who replicated Axelrod's influential model on the evolution of social norms (Axelrod 1986). The aim of the original article was to examine the power of meta-norms (i.e., punishment against norm violators) to enforce norms in a population of rational self-interested agents. They obtained different results by running the model for longer and modifying the values of certain parameters. They provided relevant insights into the need for running large-scale/long-term simulations that included stochastic components. The idea was to study 'not only how the system *can* behave but also how it *usually* behaves'. They also combined simulations with mathematical analysis which helped to verify model behavior.

Wilensky and Rand (2007) replicated Hammond and Axelrod's (2006) model on ethnocentrism. The original article showed that the tendency of humans to favor in-group members could support cooperation even when this was costly. Wilensky and Rand showed that the replication of original results was possible only by adding further conditions.

Izquierdo, Izquierdo and Gotts (2008) replicated Macy and Flache's (2002) work on the reinforcement learning dynamics in typical social dilemmas. They provided further insights, illustrated certain advances and discussed the robustness of the original results to occasional mistakes made by agents in choosing their action. In addition, they showed that outcomes were strongly dependent on the speed of agent learning and that even small quantities of randomness could dramatically influence outcomes. Therefore, replication helped to circumscribe the generalization of previous findings. The same was true for the replication of Mark's model on disproportionate prior exposure by Welser, Gleave and Vaughan (2007) described in detail in Chapter 2.

Janssen (2009) replicated the well-known Anasazi model mentioned in Chapter 1 (Dean *et al.* 2000), which is an example of trans-disciplinary investigation on a crucial historical puzzle through ABMs (i.e., why did the Anasazi disappear from the Long House Valley in Arizona, after long-term residence there?). Janssen's replication confirmed the general intuition of the original modelers about the irrelevance of environmental factors to explain the sudden abandonment of the valley by the Anasazi community. However, he also showed that two parameters that adjusted the carrying capacity of the valley and the demographics of agent population played a crucial role to fit the empirical data. In this case, replication revealed the previously largely underestimated importance of certain parameters.

Radax and Rengs (2010) replicated Epstein's demographic Prisoner's Dilemma model (Epstein 1998), by introducing a method to systematically generate a large number of model replications and testing for their equivalence to the original model. Although a number of their replicated versions qualitatively resembled the original results, replication allowed them to emphasize the previously neglected or hidden influence of certain design choices by the modeler, such as the updating method, the timing of events and the randomization of the activation order.

Given the methodological importance of this point, let us focus on two illustrative replication *querelles* which involved a group of agent-based sociologists. Indeed, these allowed understanding and new insights which were revealed by independent replication. In particular, they showed how modeling can foster collaboration. I have focused on them also because of their serious sociological content: the first one dealt with residential segregation, the second one with trust and social relationships.

4.2.1   The querelle about segregation

The subject of this recent *querelle* was reported in Chapter 3. The origin was an article published in the *American Journal of Sociology* by Elizabeth Bruch and Robert D. Mare (Bruch and Mare 2006), which received a considerable number of awards. The article was aimed at presenting an empirical revision of Schelling's canonical model. The authors' starting point was that surveys and vignette data reported that individuals tend to respond continuously to variations in the racial make-up of their neighborhoods rather than to follow threshold preferences. Accordingly, they replicated Schelling's version and manipulated the shape of the preferences. Their finding was that linear function preferences, allowing households to adapt to neighborhood composition and more promptly continuously change, could avoid residential segregation. The most striking conclusion was that Schelling's original findings, rather than being a generally expected outcome of the interdependence of household decisions every time and everywhere, occurred only under special circumstances.

They also investigated the role played by chance, relaxing the assumption that households knew exactly the features of new target neighborhoods to move to. They found that also chance, if combined with sensitivity to neighborhood change, could prevent segregation. Suppose that a household made a mistake and moved to a less desirable neighborhood. This decreased the desirability of the new neighborhood to the same in-group households located everywhere, but also increased the desirability of it for out-group neighbors already located there. This in turn increased the odds that a relatively satisfied out-group household in the neighborhood in question made a mistake and left. By assuming there were households that adjusted their decision even to a slight modification of their neighborhood composition, this caused over time a domino effect until the perfect integration of neighborhoods was locally achieved (Bruch and Mare 2006, p. 694; Van de Rijt, Siegel and Macy 2009, p.1174).

Bruch and Mare (2009, p. 1187) summarized this point as follows:

> Even a small number of individuals, who by chance move into areas with few own-group members, increase the desirability of those areas to members of their group, thereby increasing the probability that more own-group members subsequently move there. Threshold functions, in contrast, have large intervals of proportion own group across which individuals are indifferent. Thus, a small number of individuals who move to an area with few own-group members are unlikely to increase the desirability of that area for future movers.

The model was replicated by Van de Rijt, Siegel and Macy (2009). They discovered an error in one crucial simulation parameter which defined how randomness entered the choice of new neighborhoods by unsatisfied households. They rewrote the original model and more thoroughly explored the possibility of random mistakes by households. They focused particularly on two key parameters of the model, that is, preference and choice. While the first parameter indicated when a location was desirable for each household given the proportion of in-group neighbors, the second defined that the probability of moving to an empty location for each household was dependent upon the weight of a coefficient β which represented the desirability relative to random chance. When $\beta = 0$, ethnic composition of neighborhoods was irrelevant and the random choice by households was dominant. When $\beta = 1$, Schelling's rule entered the picture as in this case households always moved to or remained in their most preferred location.

The problem with this was that Bruch and Mare failed to explore the whole continuum of coefficient β, so that even when randomness and mistakes should have been expunged from their model, household choice was biased by mistakes. As outlined by Van de Rijt, Siegel and Macy (2009, p. 1169), in the case of supposing no random choice, in the original model it was as if people picked neighborhoods 'by throwing darts at a map of the city – not completely random, but with substantial room for error'.

To explore this point more thoroughly, Van de Rijt, Siegel and Macy examined a variety of situations where continuous and threshold functions were compared. By generalizing and extending the model, they also contributed to the debate on 'segregation versus integration' suggested by Pancs and Vriend (2007) and Zangh (2004).

Results showed that in a multicultural population with integrative preferences (i.e., to live in a half-white, half-black neighborhood), threshold preferences at the micro level might help to prevent tipping at the population level, on condition that agents make mistakes and move to neighborhoods which do not correspond to their preferences. This mimics the realistic situation in which agents do not have complete information about the real composition of their new neighborhood where they move.

Their findings revealed that individual preferences and social outcome could be paradoxically in stark contrast. Indeed, once agents have a clear preference toward diversity, move to undesirable neighborhoods and promptly react to their neighborhood's changes, segregation is likely to occur. On the contrary, once agents have a clear preference toward ethnicity, they promptly react to their neighborhood's changes and rarely make mistakes in selecting their new neighborhood, so integration is more likely. Therefore, by providing a more abstracted analytic version of Bruch and Mare's model, Van de Rijt, Siegel and Macy showed that social integration with continuous preferences was possible only when neighborhood choice was sufficiently random, so that households were likely to move into less-preferred locations.

This replication suggested that the validity of Bruch and Mare's findings was restricted to very special circumstances. The original article suggested that the special circumstance was the typical threshold function assumed by Schelling. The replication indicated that what was really special was the narrow parameter space of coefficient β explored by the replicators. Indeed, they took into account only a special window at the boundary of randomness where coefficient β was neither too low to look at an integration of linear and threshold functions (i.e., $\beta = 0$), nor too high so both functions segregate (i.e., $\beta = 1$). Van de Rijt, Siegel and Macy (2009, p. 1178) found that 'above this window [which Bruch and Mare focussed on], the effect of thresholds reverses, with less segregation than observed with linear preferences'.

Their conclusion was as follows:

Schelling did not overstate the tendency toward segregation. Populations with linear preferences also segregate, as do those with more empirically plausible preferences. If anything, Schelling *understated* the tendency toward segregation, which can emerge not only in a population that tolerates diversity (as Schelling demonstrated), but even among multi-culturalists who actively seek diversity, so long as they are also sensitive to small changes in ethnic composition Van de Rijt, Siegel and Macy (2009, p. 1180).

It is worth noting that the mistake was honorably admitted by Bruch and Mare (2009) in their reply and most importantly that the first replication gave the original authors the chance to develop their model further and to pinpoint relevant aspects which were not so clear in the first version. They more thoroughly investigated the impact of randomness over choice, the relevance of mistakes and their cumulative effect on outcomes, as well as the speed with which integrated communities converged to segregation. They examined the impact of the preference function shape (i.e., threshold vs. linear) on randomness and confirmed that threshold functions were less susceptible to random variations than linear ones, as small changes in neighborhood composition rarely resulted in changes in neighborhood desirability, if not around the threshold point. The point was that with threshold functions, mistakes could be absorbed and would have a small and circumscribed impact. The same was not true with linear functions, where mistakes and randomness cumulated over time.

Moreover, they provided further empirical support for their argument, by relying on empirical surveys on ethnic preferences for integration that showed that black preferences for integration could even sustain segregation. They found that black preference for diversity and their willingness to tolerate a range of diverse neighborhoods could create integrated neighborhoods where there was more resilience to small perturbations in the racial make-up. This meant that threshold functions included a region of relative indifference which could prevent random perturbations from destabilizing residential patterns (Bruch and Mare 2009, pp. 1193–1994).

Obviously, here I have reported the detail about this *querelle* only briefly. It is more important to outline that these discussions are of general interest not because they ultimately fixed a given issue or said the last word about it. The point is that thanks to replication and the subsequent debate, now we know more about the topics involved.

To sum up, this *querelle* testifies that replication is not only a means to evaluate the precision of peer work and circumscribe generalization, nor is a 'spot the error' game. Rather, it is a means to motivate new intuition, help new achievement and generally improve our understanding of the issue at stake.

4.2.2   The querelle about trust and mobility

This second *querelle* is interesting as it revolves around a model which aimed at explaining an empirical puzzle with large theoretical implications for sociology. It created an intense debate sometimes even punctuated with sarcastic remarks, revealing that while replication is a difficult undertaking for various reasons, the overall result is, again, highly productive to discipline collaboration.

The *querelle* originated from an article published by Michael W. Macy and Yoshimichi Sato in *PNAS* (Macy and Sato 2002). The article's key point was an attempt to explain a challenging empirical puzzle of cross-national differences in trust originally highlighted by Yamagishi and Yamagishi (1994; see also Yamagishi, Cook and Watabe 1998) in their comparative investigations on trust and cultural differences in the US and Japan. Why are individualistic Americans more trusting than collectivistic Japanese? Although received wisdom is that a collectivistic culture is expected to nurture high trust, empirical surveys and laboratory experiments showed that Americans were more likely to trust strangers than Japanese.

This puzzle is a good example of the divorce between common sense and sociological explanations, a long list which has recently been reported by Duncan Watts (2011). On the one hand, in this case, common sense predicted that people embedded in collectivistic cultures were expected to trust each other more. However, Yamagishi's findings supported the idea that people in more individualistic cultures were more sensitive to trustworthiness and detected trust signals from others to enlarge their social circles and benefit from larger opportunities of social and economic exchange.

Macy and Sato (2010, 1.6) summarized this point as follows:

> Yamagishi argues that populations tend toward either a parochial equilibrium that minimizes the transaction costs of being cheated, or toward a global-market equilibrium that minimizes the opportunity costs of a small pool of possible exchange partners. The outcome depends decisively on whether agents acquire the 'social intelligence' needed to effectively navigate a global market. The argument has the counter-intuitive implication that trust in strangers will be lower in collectivistic societies like Japan. Yamagishi's empirical findings are consistent with this hypothesis, but because the argument is highly counter-intuitive, many scholars have remained sceptical. Demonstrating this dynamic with a forma model is therefore important in showing that the theory is logical even though it violates intuition.

Following previous work on trust between strangers (e.g., Macy and Skvoretz 1998), the idea was to use an ABM to examine whether Americans developed social norms which allowed them to take advantage of the greater opportunities of a global market, and particularly the willingness and ability to judge who could and could not be trusted (Macy and Sato 2010, 1.2). Obviously, this question was implicitly expected also to cast light on the question of the bridge between 'community' and 'society'.

The model was based on a population of N agents ($N = 1000$) playing an iterated Prisoner Dilemma with an exit option. Exit meant that agents could decide not to continue in the game. The assumption was that if one of all matched agents did not trust any other, interaction did not take place and agents would lose game opportunities (i.e., trust was symmetrical and exit gave negative payoffs). Agents had two environments, neighborhoods of varying degrees where they interacted only with neighbors and a global market where they interacted with strangers. At each iteration, agents could randomly change their neighborhoods and choose to interact on a global market. When they interacted on the market, agents were capable of detecting trustworthy agents and adopting conditional cooperation strategies. Reinforcement learning was assumed so that agents could learn from their experience whether to trust (i.e., play or exit), when to be trustworthy (cooperate or defect) and where to play (within neighborhoods or on the global market). There were transaction costs and opportunity costs related to the global market or neighborhoods.

Simulations were used to test certain hypotheses about the role of mobility for trust. First, by testing the effect of mobility, they found a curvilinear effect of mobility on trust. More specifically, with low mobility, agents rarely encountered strangers and were victims of parochialism, trusting only similar agents and avoiding transactions on the global market. As mobility grew moderately, agents learnt how to detect trust signals and to treat strangers appropriately, so that they were active on the global market, thus achieving greater economic opportunities. When mobility increased further, trust dissolved, because agents could not appropriately discriminate between each other. Furthermore, they did not find any significant correlation between mobility and neighborhood size.

The conclusion was that differences in parochialism between Japan and the US could be explained by higher rates of mobility in the latter. However, findings on the negative impact of higher social mobility were used by the authors to claim that:

> Although American society enjoys relatively high trust and participation in global markets, there is no guarantee that this will continue indefinitely. Rapid advances in telecommunications could undermine the embeddedness of social relationships needed to make trust and trustworthiness self-reinforcing (Macy and Sato 2002, p. 7220).

Attracted by this interesting case and the claims of the explanatory power of this model, Will and Hegselmann (2008) replicated the model starting from the paper as their sole information. They documented the difficulty of replicating the model without a full description and access to model instructions and codes. They re-implemented the model in two different languages (i.e., NetLogo and Fortran 95). They carefully tested the model to identify results and found criticalities in various parts of the original model, for example, the reinforcement learning mechanisms and the transaction and opportunity costs.

Above all, they found that the most interesting finding of the model, that is, the non-monotonic effect of mobility increase on trust, was difficult to be replicated exactly. More specifically, their replication matched the positive effect of mobility on trust in strangers on a global market generated by the expansion in opportunity costs for parochial agents, but not the reverse effect of transaction costs, which were expected to increase with the increase in social mobility (Will and Hegselmann 2008, 4.8). Unlike the original version, they also found that neighborhood size could have a positive effect on market interaction and that this depended on opportunity costs and the heterogeneity assumed in the market. As a result, their conclusion was that their replication failed to validate Macy and Sato's findings.

Macy and Sato (2008) replied point by point and made the original code available. They defended themselves by outlining that complicating the transaction and opportunity costs too much was outside their scope as they wanted to examine the effect of mobility on the emergence of trust and trustworthiness. However, it was the availability of the code source that made the difference.

Indeed, Will (2009) took the opportunity to replicate Macy and Sato's model exactly. He rewrote the model, fully describing its building blocks and re-run simulations. He found that the original reinforcement learning assumption stated that newcomers (i.e., new agents entering neighborhoods because of mobility) did not update their propensity to enter the market via learning as other agents did. He suggested that this rule was largely unnecessary and counter-intuitive, nor was it mentioned by the authors in the original article. He corrected this by assuming that agents could immediately update their propensity to enter the market so that learning could take place uniformly. Results showed that unlike Macy and Sato (2002), the rise in social mobility did not imply *per se* any more trust in strangers.

Macy and Sato (2010) eventually took the chance to re-run and manipulate Will's version and revised their own model. They acknowledged that Will correctly identified an unnecessary assumption in their model and that he rewrote their model in a simpler and more elegant way. They admitted that had they published their paper today, they would have used Will's version (1.4). More importantly, they acknowledged that this further exercise increased their 'understanding of the causal mechanisms through which mobility affects the levels of trust and cooperation in social and economic exchanges' (1.1).

On the other hand, they contested the conclusion that Will took from his new results. They observed that Will correctly contended that the assumption that newcomers did not update their propensity to enter the market was unnecessary and confusing and agreed on his idea to allow newcomers to update their propensity immediately. However they also observed that, by keeping the learning rate at the maximum level, as in the original version, Will did not fully explore the learning rate parameter space, for example, by assuming lower rates.

Macy and Sato did this to compensate for the removal of the one-iteration delay in updating newcomers' propensity to enter the market, and intriguingly found again a non-monotonic effect of mobility on trust. Results showed that as mobility increased from 0 to 0.2, trust in strangers nearly doubled, but that this effect reversed above mobility at 0.2. The point was that this reversal seemed even more empirically plausible than the reversal obtained by the original model (i.e., mobility at 0.9). This made them conclude that paradoxically Will's revised version brought more grist to the original mill and so further extended the generalization of their arguments. They finally ended their article praising the added value of replication.

Apart from the pleasures of reading well-documented and disciplined dialog between scholars, this replication confirmed once more that understanding and explanation can increase when discussion strictly focuses on well-structured research, models and details. Probably none of the scholars involved in this *querelle* (but this holds also for the previous one) would have reached the same understanding of the issue at stake if they had not being able to exercise the other's criticism.

4.3   Multi-level empirical validation

Multi-level empirical validation is *the process through which relevant model parameters are informed by and simulation findings are evaluated against empirical data*. It consists of two different components, namely empirical specification and validation, which are logically distinct but substantively correlated.

More precisely, empirical specification deals with assumptions (i.e., model input) and validation with findings (i.e., model output). I have kept these two intuitively different concepts together in the idea of multi-level validation because I want to emphasize that for ABMs in sociology, it is important not only to replicate/generate empirical regularities and observed statistical patterns at the macro level. If possible, models should be informed by empirically grounded specifications of micro behavior. Although difficult and not always at hand, the injection of empirical data into models is especially important in our field. This is because we do not have all-embracing theories about micro level processes and the descriptive adequacy of 'situations' where agents interact (i.e., context-specific macro constraints) is often decisive in discriminating between alternative explanations.

This has convinced me that empirical validation also includes problems of realism in model construction. Obviously, this is just a best case scenario, as sociologists often lack empirical data about micro processes. However, this does not disqualify the importance of this multi-level validation approach for sociology models.

Specification may include direct or indirect data (i.e., data explicitly designed and gathered for the model or derived from existing sources), as well as more loose reference to second-hand empirical knowledge and stylized facts. Data can be used to fine-tune important model parameters. They could be both qualitative and quantitative. For instance, data could allow us to define features such as number and types of agents or the typology of the interaction network. However, they could also inform us about agent behavioral rules, as in some examples described in Chapter 2 and in general in experimentally grounded models (e.g., Duffy 2006).

As reported in Boero and Squazzoni (2005), there are various means of gathering first-hand data for ABMs. Even the typology of models (e.g., abstract or case-based) poses constraints and challenges to this, as well as to output validation.

First, we suggest that specification can be achieved by various strategies. There is no unique, standard procedure. First-hand data can be gathered with various tools, even with a mix of them:

   (a) experimental methods (i.e., laboratory or field experiments with real agents, or mixed experiments with real and artificial agents);

   (b) stakeholder approach (i.e., direct involvement of domain experts for model construction validation) (Moss 1998; Bousquet 2003; Moss and Edmonds 2005);

   (c) qualitative methods (i.e., interviews to involved agents, archival data, empirical case studies);

   (d) quantitative methods (i.e., statistical surveys on the target).

Here, we can say that there is no best method for specification. Each of them has its own pros and cons. They can help us to calibrate simulation parameters relating to agent behavior, structural constraints or network interaction in different ways, some more qualitative, others more quantitative. Let us take some examples of ABM research inspired by these methods, referring both to their respective pros and cons.

There are good examples of integration of experimental data and ABMs especially in agent-based computational economics (for a review, see Duffy 2006). In these cases, the laboratory and ABMs are used as a means of isolating sources of aggregate phenomena which are difficult to understand without entering into detail of agent behavior and interaction effects. In some cases, models have been used to extend evidence from the laboratory, as in our examples in Boero et al. (2010) and Boero, Bravo and Squazzoni (2010) illustrated in Chapter 2. In our examples, models perfectly replicated laboratory conditions, and agent behavior was calibrated according to subject behavior. This allowed us to explore implications of real behavior in more complex social structures. As such, simulation results reflected manipulated consequences of 'real' behavior.

In other cases, simulation results are used to support experimental design. Generally, experimental and simulation results have been combined to cross-validate findings and so reduce the problems of external validity typical of any experimental method. This is good progress, in my view. However, it is worth outlining that experimental data are not always at hand and require advanced knowledge and 'abstractedness' of the problem at stake. Unfortunately, it is not always feasible to translate the puzzle under investigation into a simplified and easily understandable interaction game to be played by human subjects in a well-controlled environment.

On the other hand, the stakeholder approach follows the idea that people involved in the field have more knowledge of the puzzle under investigation than researchers and so can bring information to specify relevant model components (e.g., Moss 1998; Etienne, Le Page and Cohen 2003; Moss and Edmonds 2005). Although this is a good strategy especially when there is poor knowledge of reality, it could confuse the explanation with the description. This means that researchers could be biased by taking on faith certain inaccurate interpretations which often people might have about the situation they live in.

A positive example of validation based on stakeholder approach was the water demand model built by Moss and Edmonds (2005). Their aim was to examine social mechanisms behind the unpredictably clustered volatility of water consumption in the UK. This issue also had important policy implications. First, understanding generative mechanisms which accounted for the unpredictability of water consumption patterns could help policy makers and authorities to regulate and manage this important resource more efficiently. Secondly, as water was privatized in the UK from the late 1980s, the hypothesis was that this may have caused an overall increase in water consumption and large deviations in consumption behavior. As we will see, this example shows not only the added value of collaboration with stakeholders and integration between various empirical knowledge sources, but also the importance of models to discover unrevealed insights of empirical reality.

Moss and Edmunds started from statistical data of changes in daily water consumption in the UK, which showed an abnormal thin-peaked distribution, due to values outside the mean. They wanted to understand whether social embeddedness of households could explain these empirical patterns. They collected data on environmental household water consumption (e.g., temperature, precipitation, evaporation) and used a pre-existing survey to model the distribution of different water-using devices used by households. The model consisted of a population of households adjusting their water consumption under the influence of neighbors. Moreover, they were constrained by the environment, their own water-using devices, and authority recommendations.

Domain experts, both from water supply companies and the UK Environment Agency, helped to fine-tune the model towards more realistic features. For instance, experts from the agency responsible for water quality and supply sufficiency, provided evidence that water-using devices were renovated on average every five years following ownership patterns. This helped to improve the realism for technology innovation (i.e., water-using devices). Domain experts from water supply companies evaluated an initial version of the model and suggested to correct it for aggregate water consumption patterns which unrealistically returned to pre-drought levels after a period of drought. This posed another crucial realistic constraint to be considered in the model.

Results showed first, that social embeddedness was responsible for fat-tailed time series with clustered volatility equal to the empirical regularities studied. Secondly, certain simulation scenarios where social embeddedness was removed indicated that there was a greater level of local oscillation in water demand and almost no systematic, collective response to droughts.

In short, by ruling out social embeddedness, the particular puzzle which attracted stakeholder attention disappeared. This was further confirmation of the explanatory importance of social embeddedness for water consumption patterns to understand real behavior. Indeed, Moss and Edmonds concluded that when the water industry was public, neighbor pressure had a social control function, that is, they helped to limit excessive water consumption as people observed and morally sanctioned each other. Water privatization in the late 1980s eroded this social sanction function and transformed water consumption into an economic good. This increased consumption, as well as the effect of knowing that half the water in the mains was lost through leakage while households were exhorted to save water.

An example of empirically calibrated quantitative parameters is the famous Anasazi model, already previously mentioned (e.g., Dean et al. 2000). Here, the authors used existing data and archeological evidence to calibrate certain crucial model parameters and to empirically validate simulation findings. Their study was focused on a particular area inhabited by the Kayenta Anasazi, the so-called Long House Valley in North Eastern Arizona. This area was chosen for its representativeness, its topological bounds and the quantity and quality of scientific evidence, from sociocultural, demographic and environmental aspects.

To reproduce realistic features of the environment, the authors extracted a quantitative index from available data that represented the annual potential production of maize in kilograms, for each hectare of the 180 km of land which characterized the area, and for each year from 382 to 1450 AD. They built an empirically grounded fertility index which represented the production landscape of Anasazi households. This was calibrated on different geographical areas within the Valley, created using a standard method to infer production data from climate data (the so-called 'Palmer Drought Severity Indices') and estimated according to data on the effect of hydrologic curves and aggradations. Data on soil composition, rain fall, and productivity of maize species available in that Valley at that time were used to mimic production opportunities for Anasazi households.

The idea was that nutrition determined fertility and subsequently population dynamics. Demographic variables, nutrition needs and household consumption were empirically calculated and rules for household composition were drawn from bio-anthropological, agricultural, ethnographic and archeological records (for details, see. Dean *et al.* 2000).

Simulation approximated available aggregate data of Anasazi history, especially location and the size of settlements. They showed that the Anasazi were capable of finding an efficient equilibrium between concentration and dispersion of settlements and low–high frequency of environmental changes. They also showed that, despite considering environmental conditions in the period of the so-called 'Great Drought' around 1200 AD, which caused their disappearance, the Anasazi could have still survived in the Valley if they had only decided to move north and disaggregated cluster settlements. After all, this solution was adopted by similar populations in other areas.

The conclusion was that if they had not done so, it was for reasons related to social ties and political power. In short, the Anasazi did not disappear from the Long House Valley around 1270 due to environmental constraints. Therefore, the findings falsified previous explanations and offered new insights for future research (e.g., examining power structures).

Another good example of how to use quantitative surveys to calibrate agent interaction to explain an interesting social puzzle was given by Ormerod and Wiltshire (2009). They built a simple and intuitive model to identify social mechanisms behind the rise of binge drinking among young people in the UK.

They started from a survey carried out by a market research company that interviewed 504 18- to 24-year-olds in the UK to understand problems of alcohol consumption. This sample group was believed to reflect demographic features strongly sensitive to problematic alcohol consumption. The results showed that there were around 950 000 young binge drinkers and about 1.5 million binge drinking events each week. They also showed that the proportion of heavy drinkers among females recently grew from 29 to 40%.

Although binge drinking has existed for many years, possibly in lower numbers, there is proof of its recent rise in the very large increase in admissions to hospital of young people with problems related to drinking and in police records of arrests of young people who have been binge drinking.

The authors extrapolated three types of social groups from the data which could influence a person's attitude towards drinking: the family, work colleagues, and friends. They found that binge drinkers had different types of social networks to non-binge drinkers. Indeed, friends were better predictors of binge drinking than family and work colleagues.

Then, they built a model which looked at a population of agents who decided whether becoming a binge drinker depended on the proportion of friends in their network who already were binge drinkers. At step 0, all agents were not binge drinkers. At step 1, a small percentage of agents (i.e., 2%) were assigned binge-drinker behavior.

Each agent had a heterogeneous threshold to convert behavior from not binge to binge drinking. Thresholds defined the proportion of binge-drinking friends needed to convert to binge drinking. Empirical data were used to calibrate threshold parameters. Certain initial model explorations showed that a percentage of 16.2% initial binge drinkers at step 1 was needed to reach the estimated number from the empirical data.

Then, the authors assumed three types of interaction structures, that is, random, scale-free and small-world networks. The idea was that these topologies could replicate various fashion-spreading mechanisms which could have possibly been responsible for the rise of binge drinking. For example, random networks mimicked fashion markets, where agent behavior depended on observation of unknown people, such as when one buys a pair of new fancy shoes after seeing them across the street worn by a lot of people. Scale-free networks mimicked a small group of influential people capable of influencing other behavior, such as VIPs on TV. Small-world networks mimicked a structure of overlapping groups of friends of friends who influenced each other locally.

The authors extensively explored the model parameter space to search for the best combination of relevant parameters in each of the three types of networks which helped to replicate the observed regularities. Simulation results showed that a small-world topology better approximated the observed behavior pattern. The authors suggested that the spread of imitative behavior across friendship networks was a sufficient condition to replicate real patterns.

Even if the authors acknowledged serious limitations in finding generalizations (e.g., lack of longitudinal data and no direct data on binge-drinking friends' behavior), their results are interesting and have important policy implications. The discovery that the relevant network of binge drinkers has a small-world topology suggests that policy makers should not think that there is a small number of influential people who play the crucial role of spreading this antisocial fashion. This means that the resolution of the problem cannot be achieved by addressing repressive action against specific targets. The conclusion is that binge drinking has more to do with structural aspects of social interaction, such as the way people group together to interact and influence each other locally.

Obviously, calibrating models does not mean only collecting quantitative data or exploiting existing surveys which might provide information about structural aspects of a model. Qualitative data which also look at behavioral aspects are important. The lack of this was seen as a weakness by the authors of the previous example.

A good example of qualitative work supporting an ABM is the Geller and Moss (2008) model of Afghan power structures. To empirically calibrate and validate their model, the authors conducted semistructured interviews with Afghan urban elites between 2006 and 2007 and various case studies on power and social structures in different regions. Unlike the previous case, here there were no data available from official surveys. Therefore, field research helped them to look at relevant aspects of Afghan society.

Geller and Moss' aim was to look at structural and processual features of Afghan power structures to understand their implications for various economic and social issues. They focused on the *qawm*, which is a dominant feature of Afghan society. *Qawm* means a complex interpersonal network of political, social, economic, military and cultural relationships within which people are informally stratified into different roles. Geller and Moss modeled this social context in detail. They were inspired by the attempt to find whether traditional categories of Weberian sociology such as *anomie* and neopatrimonialism, could explain relevant features of this particular social structure.

Their model was based on a population of 208 agents interacting in a two-grid space topology, which replicated the four ethnic regions characterizing Afghanistan. Agents were assigned 10 roles following evidence on *qawm*, as follows: politicians, religious leaders, businessmen, organized criminals, commanders, drug dealers, drug farmers, farmers, civilians, and warriors. These were the nodes of the *qawm* network.

To describe the complex web of mutual 'social exchange' relationships between these roles, the authors gave the following example:

> If a politician is in need of military protection, he approaches a commander. In return, a commander receives political appreciation by mere cooperation with a politician. If a businessman wants to be awarded a governmental construction contract, he relies on a politician's connections. In return, the politician receives a monetary provision, e.g., bribes. If a politician wants beneficial publicity, he asks a religious leader for support. The religious leader, in return, becomes perceived as a religious authority. If a warrior seeks subsistence for his family, he lends his services to a commander, who in return provides him with weapons, clothes, food and/or money. If an organised criminal wants to carry drugs, he relies on a businessman's transport business, and the businessman receives a share of the profit from the sold drugs. If a drug farmer needs protection for his poppy fields, he affiliates himself with a commander, who in return receives a tithe of the profit from the drugs sold to a drug dealer (Geller and Moss 2008, p. 324).

To mimic this situation, each agent was randomly assigned an ethnicity, a religion, a political-military background, a number of kinsfolk and neighborhoods. The authors assumed that more wealthy agents were better-informed. This meant that these agents could map a larger portion of the environment move across space, and create and break relationships.

All agents received and accumulated economic and social resources according to their position in the social hierarchy. Strong men, such as commanders, politicians, businessmen, religious leaders and organized criminals, had more chance to accumulate resources than ordinary people. For instance, businessmen could invest money and have revenue and commanders could profit from the patronage of certain warriors. At the same time, commanders could gain the reputation of being trustworthy by protecting a politician. Therefore, affiliations and patron–client relationships between agents fueled the flow of social and economic resources, including accumulation and decay. For instance, if a commander could not provide protection any more, he was viewed as incapable by other linked agents. If a politician could not pay his clients any more, he was viewed as untrustworthy and outperformed by others.

To do so, they used a declarative approach to represent agent behavior based on the idea of endorsement. This meant that agent behavior followed empirical data which indicated each agent's (endorser) reasoning about another agent's (endorsee). In empirical research, questions posed to interviewees were as follows: 'When is an agent powerful?', 'How does a powerful agent behave?', and so on. This was a logical way to trace roles empirically, reconstruct networks and map agent behavior. At the same time, it was useful to model agent behavior realistically, where quantification and numbers from the context were lacking.

Simulation results showed, first, that *qawm* consolidated over time thanks to dynamic properties of endorsements, relationships and resources, taking the form of a segregated network composed of small units where agent interaction was more intense. They also showed that *qawm* structures had typical properties of a small-world topology. More than homogenous power organizations, this structure contained heterogeneous concentrations of power generated by mutually dependent agents. As such, the Afghan social structure showed the typical high robustness capacities against environment exogenous perturbations which characterize any small-world topology. The authors suggested that this could account for the long-standing historical resilience of *qawm*.

Simulations also replicated empirical evidence on specific features of Afghan power holder networks as reported in empirical case studies. Empirical studies found a variety of power groups which consisted of political, economic and military agents cooperating in a limited and closed way. This was matched by simulation. Moreover, results showed that, despite what one would expect from an economy based on the accumulation and distribution of resource such as in Afghanistan, there was a strong correlation between neo-patrimonialism and a rentier economy, where a small number of agents cumulated resources, leaving others poor.

Results also provided insights into the influence of social structure on social conflict. Indeed, neopatrimonial behavior led to a segregated society where all-out war was the exception and constant noise and volatility of social conflict events were the rule. This was because this fragmented structure nurtured episodic clusters of cohesion building and dissolution which determined fragile alliances or conflict of unpredictable magnitude, duration and outcome.

In subsequent work, Geller *et al.* (2011) improved the veridicality of geographical and climate aspects of the model to examine the link of corruption and the drug industry. They empirically calibrated the main simulation parameters which represented climatic conditions for drug crops so as to reproduce its production cycle and realistically estimated parameter values for opium and heroin export from 1999 to 2009. They showed that corruption typical of these social structures blunted any eradication and interdiction policy and neutralized NATO counter-narcotic operations.

However, it is also worth noting that even empirical model specification and validation have their own problems and caveats (e.g., Windrum, Fagiolo and Moneta 2007). First, they might convey a message that description comes before explanation. Indeed, paradoxically, by emphasizing the primacy of validation procedures and especially in cases of large-scale empirical targets where data are not so cogent, a model could satisfy empirical specification and validation without explaining anything (Windrum, Fagiolo and Moneta 2007, 4.8). This brings our attention again to the primacy of explanation for this type of research. Empirical evidence is important to frame the *explanandum* and calibrate important simulation parameters which structure the *explananda*, but it cannot guarantee explanation *per se*.

Secondly, by putting empirical data first and data always being available for particular aspects involved, modelers could be biased in developing their models (Windrum, Fagiolo and Moneta 2007, 4.13). For instance, the availability of data could encourage modelers to focus on specific variables which are measurable, whereas there may be many potentially important ones for which data do not exist. Windrum, Fagiolo and Moneta (2007, 4.13) suggested that 'there is an inherent conservativeness here, a conservativeness which inhibits the search for new theories and new explanatory variables'. This means that 'pure' theoretical research is important when it allows us to look at new insights and guide us in new data search.

Furthermore, the possibility to empirically specify and validate a model requires high-quality data which are not always at hand. Certainly, there are reasons to believe that the new social media will become an incommensurable repository where a large amount of very detailed data on human behavior in many spheres will be found and that this will drastically change the perspective of social sciences, increasing realism (e.g., Watts 2011). However, we are still far from being capable of injecting appropriate data into models at present, nor are we used to designing large-scale experiments on social media to gather data for simulation. Therefore, at present we lack data and need models for this reason also.

Having shown this point, we must say that empirical validation is important and can make a difference especially for an empirical discipline such as sociology. Indeed, we do not have a cumulative or mainstream theoretical paradigm but rather a plethora of fragmented, contestable and difficultly testable explanations. Therefore, the recourse to empirical evidence is of paramount importance for good explanations. However, this does not mean that ABMs are merely data-driven exploration models in the usual statistical meaning. As argued by Brock (1999), in the case of economics (also in general), empirical regularities are mostly in forms of properties of stationary distributions and this does not provide information on the generative processes which have actually generated them. This is where explanation enters the picture. This is why models are necessary even if we have data available.

In conclusion, it is worth remembering that explanation is the core of agent-based computational sociology and precisely where ABMs can make a difference. Data are of paramount importance to validate explanation and provide interesting puzzles to be explained. They can also help us integrate ABMs with other research methods. As a result, certain limitations of the respective methods could be reduced.

References

Abdou, M. and Gilbert, N. (2009) Modelling the emergence and dynamics of social and workplace segregation. *Mind & Society*, **8**(2), 173–191.

Axelrod, R.M. (1986) An evolutionary approach to norms. *American Political Science Review*, **80**(4), 1095–1111.

Axelrod, R. (1997) Advancing the art of simulation in the social sciences. *Complexity*, **3**(2), 16–22.

Axtell, R., Axelrod, R.M., Epstein, J.M., and Cohen, M.D. (1996) Aligning simulation models: a case study and results. *Computational and Mathematical Organization Theory*, **1**(2), 123–141.

Bauer, B., Müller, J., and Odell, J. (2001) Agent UML: a formalism for specifying multiagent interaction, in *Agent-Oriented Software Engineering: First International Workshop AOSE 2000, Limerick, Ireland, June 10, 2000. Lecture Notes in Computer Science*, (eds P. Ciancarini and M. Wooldridge), Springer-Verlag, Berlin Heidelberg, pp. 91–103.

Boero, R. and Squazzoni, F. (2005) Does the empirical embeddedness matter? Methodological issues on agent-based models for analytical social science. *Journal of Artificial Societies and Social Simulation*, **8**(4), accessible at: http://jasss.soc.surrey.ac.uk/8/4/6.html.

Boero, R., Bravo, G., and Squazzoni, F. (2010) Trust and Partner Selection in Social Networks: An Experimentally Grounded Model, arXiv:1008.4705v1 [physics.soc-ph].

Boero, R., Bravo, G., Castellani, M., and Squazzoni, F. (2010) Why bother with what others tell you? An experimental data-driven agent-based model. *Journal of Artificial Societies and Social Simulation*, **13**(3), accessible at: http://jasss.soc.surrey.ac.uk/13/3/6 .html.

Bousquet, F., Barreteau, O., Antona, M., *et al.* (2003) Our companion modelling approach. *Journal of Artificial Societies and Social Simulation*, **6**(1), accessible at: http://jasss.soc. surrey.ac.uk/6/2/1.html.

Brock, W. (1999) Scaling in economics: a reader's guide. *Industrial and Corporate Change*, **8**, 409–446.

Bruch, E. and Mare, R.D. (2006) Neighborhood choice and neighborhood change. *American Journal of Sociology*, **112**, 667–709.

Bruch, E. and Mare, R.D. (2009) Preferences and pathways to segregation: reply to Van de Rijt, Siegel and Macy. *American Journal of Sociology*, **114**, 1181–1198.

David, N. (2009) Validation and verification in social simulation: patterns and clarification of terminology, in *Epistemological Aspects of Computer Simulation in the Social Sciences* (ed. F. Squazzoni), Springe Verlag, Berlin-Heidelberg, pp. 117–129.

Dean, J.S., Gumerman, G.J., Epstein, J.M., *et al.* (2000) Understanding Anasazi culture change through agent-based modeling, in *Dynamics in Human and Primate Societies: Agent-Based Modeling of Social and Spatial Processes* (eds T.A. Kohler and J.G. Gumerman), Oxford University Press, New York, pp. 179–205.

Dosi, G., Fagiolo, G., and Roventini, A. (2006) An evolutionary model of endogenous business cycles. *Computational Economics*, **27**(1), 3–34.

Duffy, J. (2001) Learning to speculate: experiments with artificial and real agents. *JEDC*, **25**, 295–319.

Duffy, J. (2006) Agent-based models and human subject experiments, in *Handbook of Computational Economics. Agent- Based Computational Economics. Volume II* (eds L. Tesfatsion and K.L. Judd), North Holland, Amsterdam, pp. 949–1011.

Edmonds, B. and Hales, D. (2003) Replication, replication, replication: some hard lessons from model alignment. *Journal of Artificial Societies and Social Simulation*, **6**(4), 11, accessible at: http://jasss.soc.surrey.ac.uk/6/4/11.html.

Epstein, J.M. (1998) Zones of cooperation in demographic prisoner's dilemma. *Complexity* **4**(2), 36–48.

Etienne, M., Le Page, C., and Cohen, M. (2003) A step-by-step approach to building land management scenarios based on multiple viewpoints on multi-agent system simulations. *Journal of Artificial Societies and Social Simulation*, **6**(2), accessible at: http://jasss.soc.surrey.ac.uk/6/2/2.html.

Frenken, K. (2006) Technological innovation and complexity theory. *Economics of Innovation and New Technology*, **15**(2), 137–155.

Galan, J.M. and Izquierdo, L.R. (2005) Appearances can be deceiving: lessons learned re-implementing Axelrod's 'Evolutionary Approach to Norms'. *Journal of Artificial Societies and Social Simulation*, **8**(3), accessible at: http://jasss.soc.surrey.ac.uk/8/3/2.html.

Geller, A. and Moss, S. (2008) Growing *Qawm*: an evidence-driven declarative model of Afghan power structures. *Advances in Complex Systems*, **11**(2), 321–335.

Geller, A., Mussavi Rizi, S.M., and Letek, M.M. (2011) How corruption blunts counternarcotic policies in Afghanistan: a multiagent investigation, in *Social Computing, Behavioral-Cultural Modeling and Prediction* (eds J. Salerno, S.Y. Yang, D. Nau, and S.-K. Chai), Springer-Verlag, Berlin Heidelberg, pp. 121–128.

Gilbert, N. (2008) *Agent-Based Models*, Sage Publications, London.

Gilbert, N. and Ahrweiler, P. (2009) The epistemologies of social simulation research, in *Epistemological Aspects of Computer Simulation in the Social Sciences* (ed. F. Squazzoni), Springer-Verlag, Berlin Heidelberg, pp. 12–28.

Gilbert, N. and Troitzsch, K.G. (2005) *Simulation for the Social Scientist*, 2nd edn, Open University Press, Maidenhead.

Gintis, H. (2009) Review of 'Handbook of Computational Economics, Volume II: Agent-Based Computational Economics'. *Journal of Artificial Societies and Social Simulation*, **10**(1), accessible at: http://jasss.soc.surrey.ac.uk/10/1/reviews/gintis.html.

Goldthorpe, J.H. (2007) *On Sociology. Volume One: Critique and Program*, Stanford University Press, Stanford.

Grimm, V., Berger, U., Bastiansen, F., *et al.* (2006) A standard protocol for describing individual-based and agent-based models. *Ecological Modelling*, **198**(1–2), 115–126.

Grimm, V., Berger, U., DeAngelis, D.L., *et al.* (2010) The ODD protocol: a review and first update. *Ecological Modelling*, **221**(23), 2760–2768.

Hammond, R.A. and Axelrod, R. (2006) Evolution of contingent altruism when cooperation is expensive. *Theoretical Population Biology*, **69**(3), 333–338.

Hedström, P. (2005) *Dissecting the Social. On the Principles of Analytical Sociology*, Cambridge University Press, Cambridge, MA.

Hegselmann, R. (1996) Cellular automata in the social sciences: perspectives, restrictions, and artefacts, in *Modelling and Simulation in the Social Sciences from the Philosophy Point of View* (eds R. Hegselmann, U. Mueller, and K.G. Troitzsch), Kluwer Academic Publishers, Dordrecht, pp. 209–233.

Izquierdo, S.S., Izquierdo, L.R., and Gotts, N. (2008) Reinforcement learning dynamics in social dilemmas. *Journal of Artificial Societies and Social Simulation*, **11**(2), accessible at: http://jasss.soc.surrey.ac.uk/11/2/1.html.

Janssen, M.A. (2009) Understanding artificial Anasazi. *Journal of Artificial Societies and Social Simulation*, **12**(4), accessible at: http://jasss.soc.surrey.ac.uk/12/4/13.html.

Janssen, M.A., Alessa, L.N., Barton, M., *et al.* (2008) Towards a community framework for agent-based modelling. *Journal of Artificial Societies and Social Simulation*, **11**(2), accessible at: http://jasss.soc.surrey.ac.uk/11/2/6.html.

Kaldor, N. (1961) Capital accumulation and economic growth, in *The Theory of Capital* (eds F.A. Lutz and D.C. Hague), St Martins Press, London, pp. 177–222.

Kiyotaki, N. and Wright, R. (1989) On money as a medium of exchange. *Journal of Political Economy*, **97**, 924–954.

Macy, M.W. and Flache, A. (2002) Learning dynamics in social dilemmas. *PNAS*, **99**(3), 7229–7236.

Macy, M.W. and Sato, Y. (2002) Trust, cooperation, and market formation in the U.S. and Japan. *PNAS*, **99**(3), 7214–7220.

Macy, M.W. and Sato, Y. (2008) Reply to Will and Hedgselmann. *Journal of Artificial Societies and Social Simulation*, **11**(4), accessible at: http://jasss.soc.surrey.ac.uk/11/4/11.html.

Macy, M.W. and Sato, Y. (2010) The surprising success of a replication that failed. *Journal of Artificial Societies and Social Simulation*, **13**(2), accessible at: http://jasss.soc.surrey.ac.uk/13/2/9.html.

Macy, M. and Skvoretz, J. (1998) The evolution of trust and cooperation between strangers: a computational model. *American Sociological Review*, **63**, 638–660.

Martensson, A. and Martensson, P. (2007) Extending rigor and relevance: towards credible, contributory and communicable research, in *ECIS 2007 Proceedings*, Paper 124, accessible at: http://aisel.aisnet.org/ecis2007/124.

Merali, Z. (2010) Computational science: ... error. *Nature*, **467**, accessible at: http://www.nature.com/news/2010/101013/pdf/467775a.pdf.

Moss, S. (1998) Critical incident management: an empirically derived computational model. *Journal of Artificial Societies and Social Simulation*, **1**(4), accessible at: http://jasss.soc.surrey.ac.uk/1/4/1.html

Moss, S. and Edmonds, B. (2005) Sociology and simulation: statistical and qualitative cross-validation. *American Journal of Sociology*, **110**(4), 1095–1131.

Ormerod, P. (2002) The US business cycle: power law scaling for interacting units with complex internal structure. *Physica A*, **314**, 774–785.

Ormerod, P. and Rosewell, B. (2009) Validation and verification of agent-based models in the social sciences, in *Epistemological Aspects of Computer Simulation in the Social Sciences* (ed. F. Squazzoni), Springer-Verlag, Berlin Heidelberg, pp. 130–140.

Ormerod, P. and Wiltshire, G. (2009) 'Binge' drinking in the UK: a social network phenomenon. *Mind & Society*, **8**(2), 135–152.

Pancs, R. and Vriend, N.J. (2007) Schelling's spatial proximity model of segregation revisited. *Journal of Public Economics*, **92**(1–2), 1–24.

Polhill, G. (2010) ODD updated. *Journal of Artificial Societies and Social Simulation*, **13**(4), 9, accessible at: http://jasss.soc.surrey.ac.uk/13/4/9.html.

Polhill, G., Parker, D., Brown, D., and Grimm, W. (2008) Using the ODD protocol for describing three agent-based social simulation models of land-use change. *Journal of Artificial Societies and Social Simulation*, **11**(2), 3, accessible at: http://jasss.soc.surrey.ac.uk/11/2/3. html.

Radax, W. and Rengs, B. (2010) Prospects and pitfalls of statistical testing: insights from replicating the demographic prisoner's dilemma. *Journal of Artificial Societies and Social Simulation* **13**(4), accessible at: http://jasss.soc.surrey.ac.uk/13/4/1.html.

Richiardi, M., Leombruni, R., Saam, N., and Sonnessa, M. (2006) A common protocol for agent-based social simulation. *Journal of Artificial Societies and Social Simulation* **9**(1), accessible at: http://jasss.soc.surrey.ac.uk/9/1/15.html.

Riolo, R.L., Cohen, M.D., and Axelrod, R. (2001) Evolution of cooperation without reciprocity. *Nature*, **414**, 441–443.

Rouchier, J. (2003) Re-implementation of a multi-agent model aimed at sustaining experimental economic research: The case of simulations with emerging speculation. *Journal of Artificial Societies and Social Simulation* **6**(4), 7, accessible at: http://jasss.soc.surrey. ac.uk/6/4/7.html.

Rouchier, J., Cioffi-Revilla, C., Polhill, J.G., and Takadama, K. (2008) Progress in model-to-model analysis. *Journal of Artificial Societies and Social Simulation*, **11**(2), 8, accessible at: http://jasss.soc.surrey.ac.uk/11/2/8.html.

Squazzoni, F. and Boero, R. (2005) Towards an agent-based computational sociology: good reasons to strengthen cross-fertilization between complexity and sociology, in *Advances in Sociology Research. Volume II* (ed. L.M. Stoneham), Nova Science Publishers, New York, pp. 103–133.

Van de Rijt, A., Siegel, D., and Macy, M. (2009) Neighborhood chance and neighborhood change: a comment on Bruch and Mare. *American Journal of Sociology*, **114**, 1166–1180.

Watts, D. (2011) *Everything is Obvious: Once You Know the Answer*, Crown Business, New York.

Welser, H.T., Gleave, E., and Vaughan, D.S. (2007) Cultural evolution, disproportionate prior exposure and the problem of cooperation. *Rationality and Society*, **19**(2), 171–202.

Wilensky, U. and Rand, W. (2007) Making models match. Replicating an agent-based model. *Journal of Artificial Societies and Social Simulation*, **10**(4), accessible at: http://jasss.soc. surrey.ac.uk/10/4/2.html.

Will, O. (2009) Resolving a replication that failed: news on the Macy & Sato model. *Journal of Artificial Societies and Social Simulation*, **12**(4), accessible at: http://jasss.soc.surrey. ac.uk/12/4/11.html.

Will, O. and Hegselmann, R. (2008) A replication that failed: on the computational model in 'Macy and Sato 2002'. *Journal of Artificial Societies and Social Simulation*, **11**(3), accessible at: http://jasss.soc.surrey.ac.uk/11/3/3.html.

Windrum, P., Fagiolo, G., and Moneta, A. (2007) Empirical validation of agent-based models. Alternatives and prospects. *Journal of Artificial Societies and Social Simulation*, **10**(2), accessible at: http://jasss.soc.surrey.ac.uk/10/2/8.html.

Wright, I. (2005) The social architecture of capitalism. *Physyca A*, **346**, 589–620.

Yamagishi, T. and Yamagishi, M. (1994) Trust and commitment in the United States and Japan. *Motivation and Emotion*, **18**, 129–166.

Yagamashi, T., Cook, K.S., and Watabe, M. (1998) Uncertainty, trust, and commitment formation in the United States and Japan. *American Journal of Sociology*, **104**(1), 165–194.

Zangh, J. (2004) Residential segregation in an all-integrationist world. *Journal of Economic Behavior and Organization*, **54**, 533–550.

5

Conclusions

I would hope that the foundations for the use of agent-based computational sociology have been laid even despite the early stage of its development. In this closing chapter, I would like to draw some lessons from its use, emphasize some challenges and the prospects of this type of research and suggest some measures to increase its recognition. In this way, we can trace a road map of where agent-based computational sociology is and where it is going.

From a concrete point of view, all the examples which have been given have shown the importance of social influence in determining the unpredictability of social outcomes and the contingent nature of social behavior. Unlike standard economic and rational choice models, here the key concept is the heterogeneity of social behavior and its interaction effects. Exploring the heterogeneity rather than bringing individual action back to a general rational choice model, not only is a means to base sociology on more realistic foundations but it also clears the way for understanding why and how agent interaction is responsible for complex social outcomes.

Generally, most of the authors quoted in this book have shown that considering agent behavior and social interaction and structures simultaneously are important for sociology. Their results have implicated that particular social structure features, which determine how agents interact by segmenting social systems into complex social networks, are generating mechanisms for social patterns.

Take for example, studies on the relevance of reciprocity and social sanctions to understand cooperation introduced in Chapter 2. Here, interaction implies that the way certain behavior is reciprocally linked dramatically affects social outcomes. The Bowles and Gintis study showed that the co-existence of strong reciprocators, cooperators and free riders is functional to social order and that the presence of strong reciprocators inside groups is essential to guarantee the survival of these groups in a selective environment. Therefore, mutual interaction between various types of agent behavior is important to provide a precise picture of social behavior.

Agent-Based Computational Sociology, First Edition. Flaminio Squazzoni.
© 2012 John Wiley & Sons, Ltd. Published 2012 by John Wiley & Sons, Ltd.

However, social structure can really matter in this picture by influencing who interacts with whom. This means that important sociological aspects will be lost if we do not look at agent heterogeneity and social structures simultaneously.

Most sociological problems arise from the fact that individual action aggregation is nonlinear, due to agent interaction (e.g., Granovetter 1978; Miller and Page 2007; Salganik and Watts 2009). As I have tried to show, understanding this effect is difficult without modeling. Neither quantitative macro outlooks which examine social aggregates, which in their turn take for granted micro generative processes, nor qualitative and interpretative approaches, which lose sight of the complex aggregate dynamics, are sufficient for this challenge. ABMs here can help us observe the interaction effects in large-scale social systems.

The first lesson to draw is that we cannot escape from the microscopic nature of sociology. In most cases, at least those we are interested in, social patterns originate locally from agent interaction and are caused by the amplification processes across the system (Martin 2009). To understand this, rather than looking at the macroscopic scale, we need to discover behavioral and interactional details that really matter. It is hard to do this without the tools to study the micro scale where social processes originate in depth. Furthermore, there is a dramatic mismatch between observation scales in social systems, that is, between people's behavior and social outcomes. This is one of the most pressing problems in sociology. Agent interaction is the dominant force which distorts aggregation, so that what we see at the local scale is mostly a poor predictor of what we see at the global scale and vice versa.

Most of the examples we have looked at, such as Schelling's segregation model and its subsequent developments, described in Chapter 3, as well as game-theory oriented models presented in Chapter 2, have shown that looking at agent interaction is essential to fill the observational gap between individual motivation and collective patterns. On this note, I hope to have shown that agent-based computational sociology has something to say, especially to clarify this dichotomy.

This mismatch has made many sociologists believe that there is an isomorphism between complexity and the macro and micro scales of social interaction. A consequence of this is to believe that complex social puzzles are the result of complicated and impenetrable agent behavior. Agent-based computational sociology shows that this is not always true. Indeed, complex and unpredictable social outcomes, such as racial segregation in urban areas, the emergence of a riot or of political extremism, can be generated by relatively simple and rational individual action influenced by social interactions.

The consequence of these interactions is that postulating impenetrable causes at a micro level is not required to understand complex social puzzles (e.g., Miller and Page 2007; Watts 2011). It is agent interaction which is mostly responsible for analytical scale-transmigration from simple behavior to complex outcomes (e.g., Buchanan 2007; Martin 2009). Therefore, there is a *traît d'union* between agent-based computational sociology and complex systems theory which should be investigated in detail (e.g., Byrne 1998; Castellani and Hafferty 2009; Macy and Flache 2009).

This point has serious implications for sociological theory. Furthermore, it also poses a challenge for ABM research in the future. The crucial effect of social interaction in terms of the social embeddedness of individual behavior requires us to seriously consider how people behave, what they do, under what motivation they do it, and why they are heterogeneous and different. This also requires us to link behavior to contingent and structural features of social interaction, by understanding who influences whom, who is more influential, what framework do agents have and how this could influence their behavior.

Jointly considering these two aspects could imply injecting more empirical details into models, especially focusing on the cogency of institutional contexts in determining opportunities and influencing agent behavior. Indeed, bizarre though they may seem at a first glance from a 'purely' abstract point of view, certain agent behavior can only be fully understandable when related to particular institutional settings where agent behavior takes place (e.g., Gigerenzer and Selten 2001; Elster 2007).

This is where agent-based computational sociology should allow us to make some progress. For instance, in being more accurate in linking social behavior, social structures and institutional contexts and discovering/classifying behavioral taxonomies which truly reflect the heterogeneity of social behavior. This could help especially in integrating theory and observation, behavior and contexts.

This is why agent-based computational sociology requires a Mertonian 'middle-range theory' approach (Merton 1968). As argued by Hedström and Udehn (2009, p. 31), one of the main challenges for current sociology is to develop clear, precise, and simple theories. These would allow us to explain a well-specified range of different empirical phenomena, would not support reductionism in terms of *explananda*, and would favor finding cumulativeness.

In my view, this does not disqualify the importance of abstraction as a means of looking at social mechanisms in a 'pure' manner, nor does it deny the relevance of case-based investigations. However, being truly Mertonian on this point means that models should include details of behavior and the social situation which means that we must translate abstract theories into empirically verified constructions. As I have tried to show in Chapter 4, it is reasonable to say that, unlike economists who are interested only in abstraction and generalization, sociologists do venture into such an unexplored middle ground between /abstraction/generalization and empirical detail/specification.

Being more concrete at an empirical level and finding ways to combine theory and observation more closely, would require us to integrate ABMs and other sociological methods better. Indeed, integration can help us to gather data at various levels (e.g., agents and social structures) and improve the validity of our simulation analysis (e.g., matching artificial and empirical output data). This is why I have insisted on this point in many parts of this book.

However, this should not lead us to the conclusion that theoretical abstraction and simplification are bad and that embracing descriptive realism is a panacea. Empirical description without good theory is a poor sociological guide and cannot solve the most urgent problem of sociology, which is its analytical weakness. Therefore, empirical models and theoretical investigation, adherence and abstraction should work together as best they can. This 'working together' is the challenge for future agent-based computational sociologists.

This challenge is even more complicated by the fact that we should approach it by avoiding the so-called 'kitchen sink' temptation, that is, the idea that models should map the complexity of reality one-to-one.[1] As argued by Macy and Flache (2009, p. 263), this temptation obscures the analysis of social mechanisms, makes models opaque to peer scrutiny and limits our ability to seriously test simulation robustness. Hedström (2005) was right in arguing that the flexibility of ABMs could tempt modelers to increase model sophistication, especially at an agent behavior level, without achieving any explanatory sociological advantage. This could however, erode model transparency and the ability to generalize.

However, for the reason I have already mentioned, unlike economists and rational choice modelers who underestimate the advantage of empirical research, sociologists are doomed to face a permanent trade-off between simplification and 'complexification' of models. There is not an ontological preference or a best way here, although preference should be given to simplification. Indeed, abstraction is always useful in providing theoretical insights. Empirical investigation is important in revealing interesting puzzles and testing theoretical findings. The most important point is that scholars are aware of the respective constraints of these approaches and that they devote their efforts towards models capable of finding a synthesis between the two.

Here, we come to the methodological side of this argument. As argued in Chapter 4, without fixing stable and socially shared standards in documenting, publishing, replicating and validating models, agent-based computational sociology cannot achieve its full potential. For this reason, also best practices for including various types of empirical data into models are of paramount importance to integrate theory and observation cumulatively (e.g., Yang and Gilbert 2008; Hassan et al. 2010). Only by fostering methodological standards, can cumulativeness be really strengthened. This would help to resolve one of the most serious deficiencies of sociology, that is, theoretical fragmentation.

Unfortunately, there is little awareness of this even in more advanced sociological communities, such as analytical sociology (e.g., Bearman and Hedström 2009), where emphasis is only given to explanatory achievements. As I have claimed in Chapter 4, these achievements may be important in themselves. However, without methodology, they are poor measures of developing knowledge critically, collectively and cumulatively. This is what is needed to improve sociology as a discipline.

There is no doubt that this is an even more complicated challenge than the previous one, if this is possible. Data are often fragmented, partial or completely lacking and models are so different and specific that a standard approach is difficult to achieve. However, as I illustrated in Chapter 4, progress has been made on this and there are serious reasons to expect that there will be further developments in the future.

Another reason to plead for tighter integration of theory and observation and more serious methodology development is one aspect I have deliberately excluded from my considerations here, that is, policy applications. Policy models often require the capability to look at contingent details. As I suggested in Squazzoni and Boero

---

[1] I owe this definition to Gérard Weisbuch. I would like to thank him for his stimulating discussions in a couple of meetings in 2008 about the good and bad ways of approaching social sciences through ABMs.

(2010), there is proof that ABM research can promote change in policy approach to social and economic issues. Although excluded from this book, this point is worth at least considering here.

First, following Epstein (2006) there are serious advantages in thinking about policy not as a problem of setting up incentives for rational individuals but as a means to exploit well-established social interaction mechanisms. Usually, policy makers are incentivized by the vulgate of mainstream economists to think that individuals are atomized, rational self-interest agents who respond to stimuli without being influenced by what others do and by pre-existing social and moral norms. This has proved to be wrong in most cases.

By underestimating the impact of pre-existing social norms and the mechanisms of social interaction, policy makers prearrange policies on weak foundations and even encourage free riding of the people targeted. Secondly, they overestimate the importance of prediction against understanding and set-up policies which take place 'offline' and outside the system involved. On the contrary, they should be considering themselves as a constitutive part of it. This makes the traditional policy models prescribe only *ex-ante* solutions and recipes which dramatically underestimate the entire process of policies. This often includes the reaction of agents to policy decisions, the aggregate effect of their interactions and their systemic consequences on large spatial-temporal scales.

As suggested by Durlauf (1997), when the role of social interaction is seriously considered for policy purposes, policy makers can come to different conclusions. First, they can realize that multiple types of internally consistent aggregate behavior easily occur which are difficult to predict. Furthermore, they can also see that the effect of different policies might be nonlinear as they are dependent on social interaction effects. The former makes history a poor guide for evaluating policy effectiveness, while the latter makes identifying effective policy options depend less on abstract conventional theoretical models and more on empirical detail of the social context.

Agents are not considered as fully rational utility maximizers who behave independently of each other, but rather as adaptive agents who are context-dependent, following heterogeneous preferences. Therefore, it is difficult to predict how small changes in incentives can cause a given behavior at a micro level. If this is so, as shown by Moss (2002), aggregate outcomes are highly sensitive to unpredictable details that are impossible to understand within *ex-ante* statistical data and macro analyses.

The ABM concept is that even if an agent's behavior is in principle predictable at any given time, concrete interactions among multiple agents can cause unexpected outcomes, such as self-fulfilling prophecies and local optimum traps (e.g., Frydman and Goldberg 2007). Therefore, the challenge for policy in a complex world is not to predict the future state of a given system. It is to understand the system's properties and dissect its generative mechanisms and processes. Policy decisions can therefore be better informed and embedded within the system's behavior, thus becoming part of it (Squazzoni and Boero 2010).

We can say that a new conceptualization of policy as part of a social system interacts with other components and consequently needs to be flexible and adaptive to the behavior of other systems' components, even by benefiting from exploiting social interaction mechanisms. This is an idea which agent-based computational sociologists should try to advance. Of course, this has not been concentrated on in this book, which was intended more as a 'pure' analytical exercise, but these ideas seem to me to be a natural by-product for future research.

There is another point we need to consider here. By looking at the various examples included here, the more astute readers will agree with historians in arguing that any innovation in science is a creature of its times. Agent-based computational sociology is not an exception. We just need to look at our present society: the increasing relevance and power of individuals, a strong tendency towards self-regulation of social interaction in a variety of fields such as urban neighborhoods, professional communities, social media and global markets and the erosion of traditional social order institutions. Therefore, agent-based computational sociology is appropriate when it underlines the importance of understanding the bottom-up emergence of social norms and structures from decentralized agent interaction.

On the other hand, as it defends the primacy of agency on social structures, certain critical and philosophically oriented sociologists could argue that this type of research does not look at society critically enough. They could suggest that it is even instrumental in exacerbating underlying social master trends leading to growing individualization. This would mean that one could consider agent-based computational sociology as an example of a 'conservative' or 'non-progressive' approach to society issues.

I have no intention of discussing philosophical or political implications here. For the moment, the only thing that matters is the pleasure of working with sociology capable of providing sound explanations of certain puzzles in our society. Certainly, compared with grand theories and philosophies of society which deal with the key of life, the universe and everything, this type of sociology could imply a restriction in the pretension and power of sociological investigation. This is true and I am proud to say that agent-based computational sociology should take a step backwards today to develop more rigorous science tomorrow.

Finally, I would like to emphasize the fact that there is also a pedagogical challenge. To increase the possibility that this type of research will be recognized in our community, we need to improve educational initiatives of teaching programming languages to sociology students. Up to the point when the only required skill for young sociologists is a couple of statistics courses as it is today, it will be difficult to institutionalize ABM research in sociology. Obviously, institutional change is subject to path dependency so innovation will always be difficult. However, leaders in the ABM community should do more to change this situation.

Fortunately, the digital generation divide implies that the next wave of students will be more accustomed than we are to computing. This gives me confidence that even without systematic and 'political' initiatives, this type of research will still attract young scholars. The situation could be improved if we marketed advanced sociology research (e.g., PhD programs and postdoctoral positions) also to young scientists from various backgrounds such as physics, engineering, computer science, and biology. Now, in many cases, these disciplinary crossovers are difficult. This may be because a sociology career is not so appealing to others, but I believe above all that sociology is not particularly open to outsiders. This is a serious limitation which reduces the richness of cross-fertilization, without protecting our disciplinary identity.

So I would very much like to make a more general point, which underlies the discussion in this book. Everybody knows that research funding agencies will probably continue in the future to support laboratory-based, large-scale, issue-based experimental and modeling oriented research on a strong competitive basis. This is a global trend and not only restricted to the US alone. In doing so, competition and funding increasingly determine the reproduction success of each species of scientists which inhabits this landscape we call science. How can a species, such as sociologists, who mostly carry on individual, small-scale, traditional, anti-experimental and low technology research, survive and grow? There is little chance, I would say. Perhaps we could be substituted by other colleagues (even more distantly related cousins, such as physicists) who would like to apply the same kind of rigorous research to understand social puzzles? The worst possible nightmare, many of you will think; a real possibility, I would say (e.g., Buchanan 2007; Helbing 2010).

Honestly, I am not sure that agent-based computational sociology is a guarantee of being a part of this new trans-disciplinary competitive venture. I do not know whether it will favor the reproduction of our species – to continue the evolutionary analogy I have just made. However, I am confident that it inhabits the same scientific milieu of more advanced and competing sciences. It has its own peculiarity, which has something to say to other specialists and can be understood and appreciated by them and may favor common platforms for trans-disciplinary research. In some cases, this is what is already happening today.

To sum up, my message here is that sociologists are being called on to accept the challenge of large-scale, high-tech, trans-disciplinary research and they have to play this game in an increasingly global and competitive scientific landscape. Otherwise, it is probable that sociological research will be carried out mainly outside our discipline and by nonsociologists. Therefore, this book has looked both at positive outcomes (i.e., examples of innovative formalized research carried out by sociologists), but also potentially negative developments, at least for our discipline (i.e., examples of good sociology performed by nonsociologists).

In general, what I am sure of is that agent-based computational sociology is not sufficient *per se*. In some of my recent work (for examples see Chapter 2), cross-fertilization between ABMs and laboratory research has been put into practice. ABMs have been grounded on well-controlled experimental data on human behavior. Other good examples of empirically grounded models have been illustrated in Chapter 4.

From my understanding of the field, I believe that tighter integration of ABMs and quantitative, qualitative, empirical and experimental research is timely. This can both improve empirical evidence on which models are built and distinguish between potentially alternative theoretical findings through empirical scrutiny. Therefore, agent-based computational sociologists should welcome contributions from qualitative, quantitative and experimental sociologists. From these cross-fertilizations, future progress is expected with less parochialism and balkanization.

Agent-based computational sociology has a special position. Tighter links between observation and theory are productive, if and only if they are mediated by formalized models. If not, it is unlikely that theory and observation can work together. Of course, this 'working together' is not the rule at present. However, significant steps towards this end have already been undertaken.

References

Bearman, P. and Hedström, P. (eds) (2009) *The Oxford Handbook of Analytical Sociology*, Oxford University Press, Oxford.

Buchanan, M. (2007) *The Social Atom. Why the Rich Get Richer, Cheaters Get Caught, and Your Neighbor Usually Looks Like You*, Bloomsbury, New York.

Byrne, D. (1998) *Complexity Theory and the Social Sciences*, Routledge, London.

Castellani, B. and Hafferty, F.W. (2009) *Sociology and Complexity Science. A New Field of Inquiry*, Springer-Verlag, Berlin Heidelberg.

Durlauf, S. (1997) What should policymakers know about economic complexity? *The Washington Quarterly*, **21**(1), 157–165.

Elster, J. (2007) *Explaining Social Behavior: More Nuts and Bolts for the Social Sciences*. Cambridge University Press, New York.

Epstein, J.M. (2006) *Generative Social Science. Studies in Agent-Based Computational Modeling*, Princeton University Press, Princeton.

Frydman, R. and Goldberg, M.D. (2007) *Imperfect Knowledge Economics: Exchange Rates and Risk*, Princeton University Press, Princeton.

Gigerenzer, G. and Selten, R. (eds) (2001) *Bounded Rationality – The Adaptive Toolbox*, The MIT Press, Cambridge, MA.

Granovetter, M. (1978) Threshold models of collective behavior. *American Journal of Sociology*, **83**(6), 1420–1443.

Hassan, S., Pavón, J., Antunes, L., and Gilbert, N. (2010) Injecting data into agent-based simulation, in *Simulating Interacting Agents and Social Phenomena*, Vol. 7 (eds K. Takadama, C. Cioffi-Revilla, and G. Deffuant), Springer-Verlag, Berlin Heidelberg, pp. 173–185.

Hedström, P. (2005) *Dissecting the Social. On the Principles of Analytical Sociology*, Cambridge University Press, Cambridge, MA.

Hedström, P. and Udehn, L. (2009) Analytical sociology and theories of the middle range, in *The Oxford Handbook of Analytical Sociology* (eds P. Bearman and P. Hedström), Oxford University Press, Oxford, pp. 25–47.

Helbing, D. (2010) *Quantitative Sociodynamics. Stochastic Methods and Models of Social Interaction Processes*, 2nd edn, Springer-Verlag, Berlin Heidelberg.

Macy, M.W. and Flache, A. (2009) Social dynamics from the bottom up. agent-based models of social interaction, in *The Oxford Handbook of Analytical Sociology* (eds P. Bearman and P. Hedström), Oxford University Press, Oxford. pp. 246–268.

Martin, J.L. (2009) *Social Structures*, Princeton University Press, Princeton.

Merton, R.K. (1968) *Social Theory and Social Structure*, The Free Press, New York.

Miller, J.H. and Page, S.E. (2007) *Complex Adaptive System. An Introduction to Computational Models of Social Life*, Princeton University Press, Princeton.

Moss, S. (2002) Policy analysis from first principles. *PNAS*, **99** (3), 7267–7274.

Salganik, M.J. and Watts, D.J. (2009) Social influence. The puzzling nature of success in cultural markets, in *The Oxford Handbook of Analytical Sociology* (eds P. Bearman and P. Hedström), Oxford University Press, Oxford. pp. 315–341.

Squazzoni, F. and Boero, R. (2010) Complexity-friendly policy modelling, in *Innovation in Complex Social Systems* (ed. P. Arhweiler), Routledge, London, pp. 290–299.

Yang, L. and Gilbert, N. (2008) Getting away from numbers: using qualitative observation for agent-based modeling. *Advances in Complex Systems*, **11** (2), 175–185.

Watts, D. (2011) *Everything is Obvious: Once You Know the Answer*, Crown Business, New York.

Appendix A

This appendix aims at supplying additional information on how to do ABM research in sociology. The first section includes a list of research centers where educational initiatives and ABM research projects are regularly pursued. They are an ideal environment to learn ABMs and find colleagues who are doing this type of research. The second section lists the most important scientific associations. Details on models described in the book can be found in the book's supporting information web page at: www.eco.unibs.it/computationalsociology.

A.1 Research centers

Recently, several educational and research centers have been established where ABM research can be learnt and/or pursued. A list of the most influential ones (first those in the US and then those in Europe) is given below.

The **Santa Fe Institute** (SFI) (New Mexico, USA) is the worldwide leading research center on adaptive complex systems and computer simulation. Established in 1984, it aims at pursuing trans-disciplinary cutting-edge research. Note that agent-based modeling as a simulation technique was first started in the 1990s around a project at this institute. Each year, SFI organizes summer schools on complex systems and computational social sciences where it is possible to learn ABM techniques. Members of the institute are carrying out computational research in the following areas: cities, scaling and sustainability; decision making and cognitive systems; conflict; risk, innovation and markets; behavioral dynamics (e.g., cooperation and social norms). In order to be invited as a research fellow, you should personally contact a member of the institute resident faculty.

For information, see: www.santafe.edu/.

The **Center for Social Complexity** (George Madison University, Virginia, USA) aims at combining pure and applied research for new insights into the fundamental nature of social phenomena at all levels of complexity, for example, from cognitive to world-level social systems. It hosts a PhD program in 'Computational Social

---

Agent-Based Computational Sociology, First Edition. Flaminio Squazzoni.
© 2012 John Wiley & Sons, Ltd. Published 2012 by John Wiley & Sons, Ltd.

Sciences' headed by Claudio Cioffi-Revilla. Among the research projects, there is the development and maintenance of MASON, one of the most famous simulation libraries (see below).

For information, see: socialcomplexity.gmu.edu.

The **Center for Computational Analysis of Social and Organizational Systems** (CASOS) (Canergie Mellon, Pittsburgh, USA), headed by Kathleen M. Carkey, aims to bring together computer science, dynamic network analysis and empirical studies of complex sociotechnical systems. It runs a PhD Program on 'Computation, Organization and Society' and it often organizes summer institutes on the simulation of sociotechnical systems.

For information, see: www.casos.cs.cmu.edu/.

The **Center for the Study of Complex Systems** (CSCS) (University of Michigan, USA) is a broadly interdisciplinary center devoted to research on complex systems in a variety of fields. It is directed by Scott Page. Certain members are currently developing research projects on relevant sociological areas, such as neighborhood segregation, health, and contagion social networks. It has opportunities for postdoctoral positions.

For information, see: www.cscs.umich.edu/.

The **Center on Social Dynamics and Policy** (CSDP) of the Brookings Institution (Washington, USA), directed by Ross A. Hammond, is aimed at applying computational modeling techniques to study complex social dynamics for policy implications.

For information, see: www.brookings.edu/dynamics.aspx.

The **Social Dynamics Laboratory** (SDL) (Cornell University, USA), directed by Michael W. Macy, is aimed at studying the interplay between network topology and the dynamics of social interaction, by combining ABMs, online networks data and laboratory experiments.

For information, see: http://sdl.soc.cornell.edu/.

The **Centre for Research in Social Simulation** (CRESS) (University of Surrey, UK), directed by Nigel Gilbert and based at the Department of Sociology in the Faculty of Arts and Human Sciences, is the leading EU center on social simulation. The current projects include a couple on industrial ecosystems and innovation networks in business. It collaborates with a PhD program in sociology based in the same department.

For information, see: cress.soc.surrey.ac.uk/.

The **Centre for Policy Modelling** (CPM) (Manchester Metropolitan Business School University, UK), directed by Bruce Edmonds and founded by Scott Moss, is aimed at carrying out ABM research for policy purposes. It is interested especially in empirical approaches and regularly hosts PhD students.

For information, see: http://cfpm.org/.

The **Macaulay Land Use Research Institute** (Aberdeen, UK) concentrates on research and consultancy for socioecological systems and especially on the environmental and social consequences of rural land use.

For information, see: http://www.macaulay.ac.uk/.

The **Laboratory on Agent-Based Social Simulation** (LABSS) (CNR, Rome, Italy), directed by Rosaria Conte, is the leading center on ABM research in Italy, especially for those interested in studying cognition and social norms.

For information, see: labss.istc.cnr.it/?q=node/13.

The **Computable and Experimental Economics Laboratory** (CEEL) (Department of Economics, University of Trento, Italy) is aimed at studying cognitive aspects of action through laboratory experiments and computer simulation. It often organizes summer schools and workshops on ABMs in economics.

For information, see: http://www-ceel.economia.unitn.it/.

The **Research Group on Experimental and Computational Sociology** (GECS) (University of Brescia, Italy), headed by Flaminio Squazzoni, aims at combining experimental and computational methods to study socioeconomic phenomena. It collaborates with a PhD program in economic sociology based in the same department.

For information, see: www.eco.unibs.it/gecs.

Other departments and institutes where ABM sociological research is regularly carried out are the **Sociology Group at Nuffield College** at Oxford University, chaired by Diego Gambetta (see: http://www.nuffield.ox.ac.uk/sociology/; the contact is Peter Hedström), and the **Centre of Methods and Policy Application in the Social Sciences** (COMPASS) at the University of Auckland (see: http://www.arts.auckland.ac.nz/uoa/centre-of-methods-and-policy-application-in-the-social-sciences-compass/; the contact is Peter Davis).

A.2   Scientific associations

There are three regional associations for researchers doing ABM research in the social sciences and they include sociologists. They organize annual conferences and jointly co-organize a biannual world congress. Participating in the activities of one of these associations and attending their conferences is a good way for beginners to enter this field, build good contacts and collaboration, present preliminary work and know what is going on.

The associations are: **European Social Simulation Association** (ESSA) in Europe (see: http://www.essa.eu.org/); **Computational Social Science Society** (CSSS) in the USA (see: http://computationalsocialscience.org/; it follows the experience of NAACSOS, see: http://www.casos.cs.cmu.edu/naacsos/index.php); and **The Pacific Asian Association for Agent-Based Approach in Social Systems Sciences** (PAAA) in Asia (see: http://www.paaa-web.org/).

Moreover, a larger association that is active in promoting ABM research in a variety of fields is the **Complex Systems Society** (CSS) (see: http://cssociety.org/tiki-index.php).

A.3   Journals

There are two journals explicitly devoted to publishing ABM research in social sciences. These are *Journal of Artificial Societies and Social Simulation* (*JASSS*) and *Computational and Mathematical Organization Theory* (*CMOT*). *JASSS* is an online journal published quarterly that has recently achieved a leading role. It is included in the ISI Journal Citation Report and is freely accessible at: http://jasss.soc.surrey.ac.uk/JASSS.html. The *CMOT* is a commercial Springer journal, has been included in the ISI Journal Citation Report from 2011 and is accessible at: www.springerlink.com/content/1381-298X.

More economics-oriented specialized journals are: *Computational Economics* (see: www.springerlink.com/content/0927-7099), the *Journal of Economic Dynamics and Control* (see: www.elsevier.com/wps/find/journaldescription.cws_home/505547/description#description) and the *Journal of Economic Interaction and Coordination* (see: www.springerlink.com/content/1860-711X).

Other related journals that regularly have special issues, reviews or articles that have ABM research as their key theme are as follows: *Advances in Complex Systems* (see: www.worldscinet.com/acs/acs.shtml); *Autonomous Agents and Multi-Agent Systems* (see: www.springerlink.com/content/1387-2532); *Complexity* (see: www3.interscience.wiley.com/journal/38804/home); *Computational Management Science* (see: www.springerlink.com/content/1619-697X); *Ecology and Society* (see: www.ecologyandsociety.org/); *Emergence: Complexity and Organization* (see: http://emergence.org/); *Journal of Economic Behavior and Organization* (see: www.elsevier.com/wps/find/journaldescription.cws_home/505559/description#description); *Journal of Conflict Resolution* (see: jcr.sagepub.com/); *Journal of Evolutionary Economics* (see: www.springerlink.com/content/0936-9937); *Mind and Society* (see: www.springer.com/economics/journal/11299); *Physica A* (see: www.elsevier.com/wps/find/journaldescription.cws_home/505702/description#description); *Rationality and Society* (see: rss.sagepub.com/); *Social Networks* (see: www.elsevier.com/wps/find/journaldescription.cws_home/505596/description#description); and *Social Science Computer Review* (see: hcl.chass.ncsu.edu/sscore/sscore.htm).

A.4   Simulation tools

There are various tools for building ABMs. With the exception of Mathematica, that is, a commercial software (see: http://www.wolfram.com/mathematica/) which allows equation-based computer simulation, they are all open source and have large user communities. Basically, they provide simulation tools and libraries which help to create models of various types and complexity with various programming languages. A comparison of the technical features of the most used platforms can be found in Gilbert (2008).

Here is a list of the most well-known and their respective web sites:

Swarm: www.swarm.org

MASON: cs.gmu.edu/~eclab/projects/mason/

Repast: repast.sourceforge.net/

NetLogo: ccl.northwestern.edu/netlogo/.

Developed by an interdisciplinary team at the Santa Fe Institute in the early 1990s, Swarm has become the origin of all these tools and can be developed from Objective C and Java. Other toolkits, such as Repast and MASON, have borrowed many concepts and technical features from Swarm. Not easy as a first entry to ABMs, it requires advanced programming skills, but is still powerful and effective.

Repast is Swarm's successor, has been developed by a team at the University of Chicago and may be developed from various languages, such as Java, C++, Microsoft .NET and Python. GIS is supported and it is easy to create sophisticated visualizations. It is well-documented and is followed by a large and growing user community.

MASON was developed by a team at George Mason University. It is a Java platform, now migrating to Google Code.

Developed by a team at Northwestern University (Chicago, USA), NetLogo is the most famous ABM toolkit, as it is user friendly and has a large set of ready-to-use models. As a result, it is the most commonly used platform for educational purposes. It is also the ideal tool to start ABMs. It is based on a Logo dialect and is relatively easy to learn.

Reference

Gilbert, N. (2008) *Agent-Based Models*, Sage Publications, London.

Appendix B

This appendix includes instructions and codes to run the model on partner selection and dynamic networks (Boero, Bravo and Squazzoni 2010) and the reputation model of Boero *et al.* (2010) described, respectively, in Sections 2.5 and 2.6. It is aimed at helping the reader to understand, manipulate and extend the work presented. It is supported by a web page (www.eco.unibs.it/computationalsociology), where the complete simulation packages, including these instructions and tools needed to run the simulation, are available in files.

Both models rely on JAS (see: http://jaslibrary.sourceforge.net/), which is an open-source Java external library that allows us to manage efficiently the simulation schedule. To run the simulation, please run the JAS desktop (it does not include the Java Environment, so you have to download and install Java JRE package from http://www.oracle.com/technetwork/java/javase/downloads/index-jsp-138363.html) and then load the simulation as a project. You must modify the path (i.e., the path between <Path>...</Path>) variable inside in the model's .sprj.xml files included in the package.

An alternative is to run the simulation in batch mode (see JAS supporting material). In this case, you must add a static main method in the model and then the command that, depending on your OS, should look as follows: *java -cp JAS.jar;. BaselineModel*, in the case of Boero, Bravo and Squazzoni (2010) and *SocrateSIMModel 0* (the last number is the parameter which communicates to the model what experimental set is to be run), in the case of Boero *et al.* (2010).

Before running the simulation, please remember that, in order to access and modify the code, you must have a code editor (it can be a text editor like Notepad, or even better PSPAD, NetBeans or Eclipse) to be manually added to JAS (go to Tools menu → JAS Options → Code Editor Path). After each simulation run you can see the simulation output by opening the output files you find in the project folder. See below for details on the data format.

Other material, examples and codes are available at: <www.eco.unibs.it/computationalsociology>.

Agent-Based Computational Sociology, First Edition. Flaminio Squazzoni.
© 2012 John Wiley & Sons, Ltd. Published 2012 by John Wiley & Sons, Ltd.

B.1   Example I: Partner selection and dynamic networks (Boero, Bravo and Squazzoni 2010)

This is an experimentally grounded ABM that investigates the link between social interaction and social structure in trust situations. It works on a database in Excel format where we reported data on 108 subjects who played a repeated version of an investment game in the laboratory. As explained in the text, we used these data to calibrate an ABM that reproduced the behavior of the subject in the laboratory to investigate the impact of more complex interaction structures on cooperation.

It is essential to remember that agent behavior was based on experimental data, these data were statistically elaborated according to the model explained in the text to derive investor/trustee behavior for each agent over time, the model replicated the structure of the experiment (i.e., roles, interaction and payoff) in the 'baseline' file and then we manipulated network structures. While in some cases, the networks were fixed, in dynamic network settings (see Table 2.5), we added a threshold happiness function to agent behavior that broke the ties. This was in order to provide a dynamical nature to social network formation. Considering these assumptions helped us to understand the model design features.

The structure of the simulation package, which is available on the supporting material web page mentioned above, consists of:

1. the *model*, where the methods to create agents and their schedule are included;

2. the *observer*, where tools to observe the simulation on the run inside the JAS desktop are included (please note that visualization and graphs have not been developed in this case as outputs have been saved as raw data to be statistically analyzed);

3. the *agent*, which is the class for representing agents inside a simulation and receives inputs and initial parameters from the model;

4. the *network factory*, which contains the code to build the various network structures (and others if you prefer) described in the text.

Figure B.1 shows the simulation parameter consol, where values can be easily changed. For example, by clicking on the 'networkStructure' window, various network structures can be selected and run.

The output data labels are as follows: run ID, partnerID, round, type, sent, counterAs_A_or_B and degree (see Figure B.2.). Run is the number of simulation run and ID indicates the agent under observation, partner ID is the ID of the agent with whom the agent under observation interacted, Round is the number of interaction within the Run, Type is the agent role in the game (i.e., investor or trustee), CounterAs_A_or_B allows to count each agent role during the simulation and Degree measures the agent network connectivity. This format can be easily exported into statistical analysis software, such as Excel, SPSS or R.

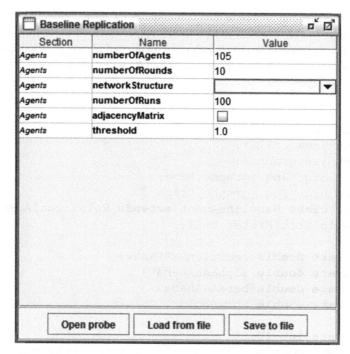

Figure B.1   The simulation parameter consol.

```
run ID partnerID round type sent counterAs_A_or_B degree
1 78 309 1 B 2.2349604318929797 1 103
1 59 288 1 A 3.590909091 1 103
1 90 304 1 B 2.1530413811543556 1 103
1 59 300 1 A 2.85130073210342 2 103
1 75 292 1 B 2.271995315698773 1 103
1 57 247 1 B 0.8757894700000001 1 103
1 34 267 1 A 0.0 1 103
1 31 254 1 B 0.21590908999999997 1 103
1 34 241 1 A 0.0 2 103
1 97 233 1 B 0.7186845399999999 1 103
1 55 314 1 B 0.842105264 1 103
1 61 265 1 A 2.0 1 103
1 11 285 1 B 3.97292442369512 1 103
1 61 221 1 A 3.1578947360000003 2 103
1 88 290 1 B 2.1564631023677916 1 103
```

Figure B.2   The output data format.

Here, there is the complete code. It consists of agent, model, observer and network factory codes, which can be found, respectively, in the following files in the package available at the book web page mentioned above: *BaselineAgent.java*, *BaselineModel.java, BaselineObserver.java* and *NetworkFactory.java*.[1]

This is the agent code:

```java
import java.io.*;
import java.util.*;
import jas.graph.*;
import org._3pq.jgrapht.Edge;
import org._3pq.jgrapht.Graph;
public class BaselineAgent extends RelationalAgent{
  public PrintWriter buff;

  private double reactionAsBBehav;
  private double alphaAsABehav;
  private double betaAsABehav;
  private double threshold;

  private int ID;
  private double submissionA, returnA, submissionB,
receivedB, endowment, oldSubmissionA, oldReturnA;

  private int degree;

  private BaselineAgent partner;
  private int counterAsA;
  private int counterAsB;
  private int agentType;
  private int sessionTime;
  private int run;
  private boolean[] happy;
  private Random randomGenerator;

  private ArrayList<BaselineAgent> agentList;

  private int linksToBuild;
  /*
  * The list of group members if groups are networks
and not neighbors */
```

[1] The code of this model is copyrighted by Riccardo Boero (riccardo.boero@unito.it). I gratefully acknowledge permission for its use by the author.

```
    private ArrayList<BaselineAgent> neighboursList;

    public BaselineAgent(Graph arg0, Random r, int
ii, ArrayList<BaselineAgent> aglist, int noAgents,
double ts) {
      super(arg0);
      this.randomGenerator = r;
      this.ID = ii;
      this.agentList = aglist;
      neighboursList = new ArrayList<BaselineAgent>();
      happy = new boolean[noAgents];
      this.threshold = ts;
      this.reset();
      agentType = 0;
    }
    public void setBuffer (PrintWriter buff){
      this.buff = buff;
    }
    public void act(){
      updateNeighboursList();
      if (neighboursList.size() > 0){
        for (Iterator<BaselineAgent> iterator =
neighboursList.iterator(); iterator.hasNext();) {
          BaselineAgent agent = (BaselineAgent) iterator.
next();
          partner = agent;
          if (agentType == 0){
            actAsA();
          }
        }
      }
    }

    public void actAsA(){
      updateEndowmentAsA();
      if (counterAsA == 0 | oldSubmissionA == -1)
        submissionA = alphaAsABehav;
      else
        submissionA = (alphaAsABehav +
(betaAsABehav*(oldReturnA - oldSubmissionA)));
      if (submissionA < 0) submissionA = 0;
      if (submissionA > endowment) submissionA =
endowment;
      setReturnA(partner.setReceivedB(submissionA,
this));
```

```
   if (counterAsA > 1) {
     if (returnA >= oldReturnA) happy[partner.getId()]
 = true;
     else happy[partner.getId()] = false;
   }
   updateOldReturnValue();
   oldSubmissionA = submissionA;
   counterAsA++;
   writeDataAsA();
 }
 public void actAsB(){
   updateNeighboursList();
   updateEndowmentAsB();
   submissionB = (reactionAsBBehav * endowment);
   if (submissionB < 0) submissionB = 0;
   counterAsB++;
   writeDataAsB();
 }

 public void updateOldReturnValue(){
   oldReturnA = returnA;
 }

 public void writeDataAsA(){
     buff.println(run+" "+(ID+1)+" "+(partner.getId()
+1)+" "+sessionTime+" A "+submissionA+"
"+counterAsA+" "+degree);
     buff.flush();
 }

 public void writeDataAsB(){
     buff.println(run+" "+(ID+1)+" "+(partner.getId()
+1)+" "+sessionTime+" B "+submissionB+"
"+counterAsB+" "+degree);
     buff.flush();
 }

 public int rr() {
   return randomGenerator.nextInt(5);
 }

 private void updateEndowmentAsA (){
   endowment = 10;
 }
```

```java
   private void updateEndowmentAsB (){
      endowment = 10 + (receivedB * 3);
    }

   public void reset(){
      counterAsA = 0;
      counterAsB = 0;
      oldSubmissionA = -1;
      updateNeighboursList();
      for (int i = 0; i < happy.length; i++) {
        happy[i] = true;
      }
   }

   public void setReactionAsBBehav(double
reactionAsBBehav) {
      this.reactionAsBBehav = reactionAsBBehav;
   }
   public void setAlphaAsABehav(double
alphaAsABehav) {
      this.alphaAsABehav = alphaAsABehav;
   }
   public void setBetaAsABehav(double betaAsABehav) {
      this.betaAsABehav = betaAsABehav;
   }
   public void setAgentType(int agentType) {
      this.agentType = agentType;
   }
   public void setReturnA(double returnA) {
      this.returnA = returnA;
   }
   public double setReceivedB(double receivedB,
BaselineAgent ag) {
      this.receivedB = receivedB;
      partner = ag;
      actAsB();
      return submissionB;
   }
   public int getAgentType() {
      return agentType;
   }
   @SuppressWarnings("unchecked")
   public void updateNeighboursList() {
      neighboursList.clear();
      for (Iterator i = getIncidentOutEdges().
```

```
iterator(); i.hasNext(); ){
      Edge link = (Edge) i.next();
      BaselineAgent agent = (BaselineAgent) link.
oppositeVertex(this);
      if (agent != null){
        neighboursList.add(agent);
        partner = agent;
        checkBidirectionalLink(agent);
      }
    }
    degree = neighboursList.size();
  }

  public void checkBidirectionalLink(BaselineAgent ag){
    if (ag.getRelation(this) == null) {
      ag.addRelation(this, 1);
    }
  }

  public void updateUnhappiness () {
    for (Iterator<BaselineAgent> iterator =
neighboursList.iterator(); iterator.hasNext();) {
      BaselineAgent agent = (BaselineAgent) iterator.
next();
      if (happy[agent.getId()] & agent.getHappy(this)
== false)
        happy[agent.getId()] = false;
    }
  }

  public void meet() {
    if (happy[partner.getId()] == false) {
      this.removeRelation(partner);
      partner.removeRelation(this);
      for (Iterator <BaselineAgent> iterator =
agentList.iterator(); iterator.hasNext();) {
        BaselineAgent ag = (BaselineAgent)
iterator.next();
        if (ag != this & ag.getHappy(this) == false) {
          this.addRelation(ag, 1);
          partner = ag;
          happy[partner.getId()] = true;
          ag.removeRelation(ag.getPartner());
          ag.addRelation(this, 1);
```

```java
        ag.addPartner(this);
        partner.setHappy(true, this);
        break;
      }
    }
  }
}
public void searchAndMeet_fix() {
  if (neighboursList.size() != 0) {
    for (Iterator<BaselineAgent> iterator =
neighboursList.iterator(); iterator.hasNext();) {
      BaselineAgent aPartner = (BaselineAgent)
iterator.next();
      if (happy[aPartner.getId()] == false) {
        this.removeRelation(aPartner);
        aPartner.removeRelation(this);
      }
    }
  }
  updateNeighboursList();
  if (neighboursList.size() == 0) {
    int i = randomGenerator.nextInt(agentList.size());
    BaselineAgent ag = agentList.get(i);
    if (ag == this){
      if (i != agentList.size()-1)
        ag = agentList.get(i+1);
      else
        ag = agentList.get(i-1);
    }
    this.addRelation(ag, 1);
    ag.addRelation(this, 1);
    partner = ag;
    happy[partner.getId()] = true;
    if (ag.getHappy(this) == false){
     ag.setHappy(true, this);
    }
    ag.addPartner(this);
  }
  updateNeighboursList();
}

public void searchAndMeet_var() {
  for (Iterator<BaselineAgent> iterator = agentList.
iterator(); iterator.hasNext();) {
    BaselineAgent aPartner = (BaselineAgent)
```

```
iterator.next();
      if (happy[aPartner.getId()] == false) {
        this.removeRelation(aPartner);
        aPartner.removeRelation(this);
        happy[aPartner.getId()] = true;
        int i = randomGenerator.nextInt(agentList.
size());
        BaselineAgent ag = agentList.get(i);
        if (ag == this){
          if (i != agentList.size()-1)
            ag = agentList.get(i+1);
          else
            ag = agentList.get(i-1);
        }
        this.addRelation(ag, 1);
        ag.addRelation(this, 1);
        partner = ag;
        happy[partner.getId()] = true;
        if (ag.getHappy(this) == false){
          ag.setHappy(true, this);
        }
        ag.addPartner(this);
      }
    }
  }

  public void removeLink_unhappy(){
    linksToBuild = 0;
    updateNeighboursList();
    for (Iterator<BaselineAgent> iterator = agentList.
iterator(); iterator.hasNext();) {
      BaselineAgent aPartner = (BaselineAgent)
iterator.next();
      if (happy[aPartner.getId()] == false) {
        this.removeRelation(aPartner);
        aPartner.removeRelation(this);
        linksToBuild++;
      }
    }
  }
  public void removeLink_threshold(){
    linksToBuild = 0;
    updateNeighboursList();
    for (Iterator<BaselineAgent> iterator = agentList.
iterator(); iterator.hasNext();) {
```

```
        BaselineAgent aPartner = (BaselineAgent)
iterator.next();
        if (happy[aPartner.getId()] == false) {
          if (this.isClose(aPartner)) {
            this.removeRelation(aPartner);
            aPartner.removeRelation(this);
            if (randomGenerator.nextDouble() <
threshold)
              linksToBuild++;
          }
        }
      }
   }


  public void searchAndMeet_unhappy() {
    updateNeighboursList();
    if (linksToBuild == 0 & neigh-
boursList.size() == 0)
      linksToBuild++;
    for (int i = 0; i < linksToBuild; i++) {
      int r = randomGenerator.nextInt(agentList.
size());
      BaselineAgent ag = agentList.get(r);
      if (ag == this){
        if (r != agentList.size()-1)
          ag = agentList.get(r+1);
        else
          ag = agentList.get(r-1);
      }
      this.addRelation(ag, 1);
      ag.addRelation(this, 1);
      partner = ag;
      happy[partner.getId()] = true;
      if (ag.getHappy(this) == false){
        ag.setHappy(true, this);
      }
      ag.addPartner(this);
    }
  }


  public void searchAndMeet_threshold() {
    updateNeighboursList();
    for (int i = 0; i < linksToBuild; i++) {
      int r = randomGenerator.nextInt(agentList.
size());
```

```java
        BaselineAgent ag = agentList.get(r);
        while (ag == this | isClose(ag))
          ag = agentList.get(randomGenerator.nextInt
(agentList.size()));
        this.addRelation(ag, 1);
        ag.addRelation(this, 1);
        partner = ag;
        happy[partner.getId()] = true;
        if (ag.getHappy(this) == false){
          ag.setHappy(true, this);
        }
        ag.addPartner(this);
      }
    }

  public Boolean getHappy(BaselineAgent agent) {
    return happy[agent.getId()];
  }
  public void setHappy(Boolean happy, BaselineAgent
agent) {
    this.happy[agent.getId()] = happy;
  }
  public void addPartner(BaselineAgent partner) {
    updateNeighboursList();
  }

  public BaselineAgent getPartner() {
    return partner;
  }
  public void setSessionTime(int sessionTime) {
    this.sessionTime = sessionTime;
  }
  public void setRun(int run) {
    this.run = run;
  }
  public boolean isClose(BaselineAgent agent){
    updateNeighboursList();
    agent.updateNeighboursList();
    if (neighboursList.contains(agent) | agent.
neighboursList.contains(this))
      return true;
    else
      return false;
    }
  }
```

This is the model code:

```
import java.io.*;
import java.util.*;
import org._3pq.jgrapht.graph.
DirectedWeightedMultigraph;
import jas.engine.*;
import jas.events.SimGroupEvent;
import jas.io.ParameterFrame;
public class BaselineModel extends SimModel
{
  //Model parameters
  public int numberOfAgents;
  public int numberOfRounds;
  public int numberOfRuns;
  public double threshold;
  public Random randomGenerator;
  public long seed;

  private String dataFile;
  private PrintWriter buff;
  private FileWriter file;

  private int sessionTime;
  private int run;
  //Simulation agents
  public ArrayList <BaselineAgent> agentList;
  public ArrayList <BaselineAgent> originalAgentList;
  public ArrayList<BaselineAgent> getAgentList() {
    return agentList;
  }
  //Technical
  private ParameterFrame parameterFrame;
  public DirectedWeightedMultigraph graph;

  //Network structures
  private static final int DENSE = 0;
  private static final int SMALLWORLD = 1;
  private static final int SCALEFREE = 2;
  private static final int COUPLES = 3;
  private static final int DYN_COUPLES = 4;
  private static final int EXPERIMENT = 5;
  private static final int DYNAMIC_ZERO = 6;
  private static final int DYNAMIC_GROW = 7;
  private static final int RND_COUPLES = 8;
```

```java
private static final int DYNAMIC_UNHAPPY = 9;
private static final int DYNAMIC_THRESHOLD = 10;
private static final int DYNAMIC_THRESHOLD_5 = 11;

// for networks
private int networkStructure;
// for printing the adjacency matrix
private boolean adjacencyMatrix;
private NetworkFactory netFactory;

public void setParameters()
{
  numberOfAgents  = 105;
  numberOfRounds = 10;
  numberOfRuns = 100;
  seed = 0;
  sessionTime = 0;
  run = 0;
  //fileSource = "";
  threshold = 0.0;
  networkStructure = DENSE;
  adjacencyMatrix = false;
  parameterFrame = new ParameterFrame(this,
"Baseline Replication", path + "BaselineParams.
pForm.xml");
  addSimWindow(parameterFrame);
}
public void shuffleLists()
{
  Collections.shuffle(agentList, randomGenerator);
}
public void simulationEnd()
{

}
public void buildModel()
{
  buildAgents();
  buildSchedule();
}
private void buildAgents()
{
  dataFile = "output.txt";
  try {
    // file for output data
```

```
      file = new FileWriter (dataFile);
      }
   catch (IOException e){
      System.err.println ("Exception in building
FileWriter object: " + e.toString ());
      }
      // build buffered stream for output data
      buff = new PrintWriter (file);
      buff.println("run ID partnerID round type sent
counterAs_A_or_B degree");
      buff.flush();

      graph = new DirectedWeightedMultigraph();
      double [] reactionAsBBehav =
{0.263214286,0.602030817,0.145073369,0.29041769,
0.233286767,0.23805235,0.298571429,0.130808974,
0.200503373,0.08,0.204015038,0.161264971,0.086405405,
0.08,0.09712605,0.091504966,0.140312368,0.113973717,0,
0.095157895,0,0.15,0.124105263,0.0125,0.098545455,0,
0.352631579,0.073026316,0.148785425,0.041669173,
0.021590909,0.263289474,0.055384615,0.113556876,
0.0285,0.049052632,0.234121457,0.05410642,0.258799227,
0.030769231,0.266158184,0.087348178,0.089068826,0.056,
0.167896104,0.153583916,0.102631579,0.057142857,
0.082267732,0.219259109,0.214947552,0.0405,0,
0.087578947,0.052631579,0.046590909,0.087578947,0.036,
0.444336288,0.198214286,0.09493007,0.190460066,
0.0939698,0.06148555,0.04217033,0.094478908,
0.265669856,0.122662139,0.117340659,0.180789474,
0.049090909,0.146709291,0.193066802,0.114089664,
0.11574026,0.065,0.033910931,0.107591093,0.084631579,
0.175023923,0.093269231,0.103181818,0.076821862,
0.074285714,0,0.113598901,0.154201681,0.159090909,
0.131444976,0.11604251,0,0.224464115,0.12,0,
0.064172457,0.035526316,0.071868454,0.213339658,
0.537937063,0.170882353,0.538684211,0.097226006,
0.187012987,0.111542111,0.121199853};
      double [] alphaAsABehav =
{8.48744186,7.923076923,2.705544933,3,8.734482759,
8.111111111,4.416666667,4.543478261,4,10,6.191780822,
4.660377358,3.793814433,2.31372549,1.748201439,
3.711864407,3.323741007,1.720588235,5.384615385,
3.41509434,0,7.504672897,2.995073892,2.823529412,
0.736842105,0,11.51666667,0.666666667,3.263157895,
4.75,5.181818182,9.691176471,5.117647059,-
```

```
0.083333333,2.205882353,2.603448276,0.666666667,
0.74137931,3.692307692,2.463414634,3,1.107142857,5.83,
6.474576271,6.388888889,2.25,2.461538462,4,2.246575342,
5.307692308,1.5,0,0,3.176470588,5.178571429,2,4,
0.75,3.590909091,3.561576355,2,1.783454988,4.590361446,
3.833333333,1.97979798,2.039215686,7.642857143,
7.033412888,2.75,4.663551402,5.7,9,0.526315789,
5.459183673,2.75,3.285714286,1.111111111,4.5,
2.518072289,1.777777778,1.645418327,2.5,0.636363636,
1.266666667,5.061728395,4.881516588,5.964285714,
1.222222222,5,3.422535211,3.539130435,5.377259475,
7.747524752,0,1,1.141315015,3.5,4.736486486,
9.970760234,6.25,3.307692308,3,1.909090909,
3.090909091,3.25};


    double [] betaAsABehav = {-0.005581395,
-0.102564103,0.10707457,-
2,0.031034483,0.144444444,0.666666667,0.456521739,
0.447368421,0,0.255707763,0.051212938,0.082474227,
0.37254902,0.007194245,0.847457627,0.568345324,
0.029411765,1.153846154,-
0.066037736,0,0.261682243,0.113300493,0.470588235,
0.052631579,0,0.466666667,0.333333333,1.684210526,
0.333333333,0.636363636,-0.058823529,0.607843137,
-0.333333333,-0.088235294,0.293103448,-
0.333333333,0.172413793,1.115384615,0.073170732,
0,0.142857143,0.08,0.63559322,0.222222222,-0.75,
-0.038461538,0.333333333,0.143835616,0.318681319,-
0.115384615,0,0,0.078431373,0.714285714,-4.19E
-17,0.4,1,0.545454545,0.246305419,-1,0.143552311,-
0.361445783,0.30952381,-
0.131313131,0.156862745,0.785714286,0.133651551,0.5,
0.551401869,-0.1,0.35,-0.105263158,0.183673469,0.5,
0.285714286,0.555555556,1,-
0.024096386,0.111111111,0.083665339,1,0.454545455,-
0.013333333,1.049382716,0.502369668,
0.357142857,0.555555556,7.74E-
17,0.345070423,0.156521739,-0.056559767,0.099009901,
0,-0.333333333,-
0.053974485,0.5,0.013513514,0.625730994,-0.073529412,
-1.076923077,0.127659574,-0.272727273,-0.227272727,
0.052631579};
```

```
    randomGenerator = new Random(seed);

    agentList = new ArrayList<BaselineAgent>();
    originalAgentList = new ArrayList<
BaselineAgent>();
    netFactory = new NetworkFactory (graph, this,
randomGenerator);
    for (int i = 0; i < numberOfAgents; i++)
    {
      BaselineAgent agent = new BaselineAgent(graph,
randomGenerator, i, agentList, numberOfAgents,
threshold);
      originalAgentList.add(agent);
      agent.setBuffer(buff);
      agent.setAlphaAsABehav(alphaAsABehav[i]);
      agent.setBetaAsABehav(betaAsABehav[i]);
      agent.setReactionAsBBehav(reactionAsBBehav[i]);
    }
    resetNetwork();
  }

  public void setRole(){
    if (sessionTime == 0){
      for (Iterator<BaselineAgent>
iterator = agentList.iterator(); iterator.
hasNext();) {
        BaselineAgent agent = (BaselineAgent)
iterator.next();
        agent.setAgentType(-1);
      }
      for (Iterator<BaselineAgent> iterator =
agentList.iterator(); iterator.hasNext();) {
        BaselineAgent agent = (BaselineAgent)
iterator.next();
        if (agent.getAgentType() == -1) {
          agent.setAgentType(0);
          agent.updateNeighboursList();
          agent.getPartner().setAgentType(1);
        }
      }
    } else {
      for (Iterator<BaselineAgent> iterator =
agentList.iterator(); iterator.hasNext();) {
        BaselineAgent agent = (BaselineAgent)
iterator.next();
```

```
        if (agent.getAgentType() == 0)
          agent.setAgentType(1);
        else
          agent.setAgentType(0);
        }
      }
    }


  private void buildSchedule()
  {
    SimGroupEvent g = eventList.scheduleGroup(0, 1);
    g.addEvent(this, "updateSessionTime");
    g.addCollectionEvent(agentList, BaselineAgent.
  class, "act");
    if (networkStructure == DYN_COUPLES |
  networkStructure == DYNAMIC_ZERO | networkStructure ==
  DYNAMIC_GROW) {
      g.addEvent(this, "shuffleLists");
      g.addCollectionEvent(agentList, BaselineAgent.
  class, "updateUnhappiness");
      }
    if (networkStructure == EXPERIMENT |
  networkStructure == RND_COUPLES){
      g.addEvent(this, "mixCouples");
      }
    if (networkStructure == DYN_COUPLES)
      g.addCollectionEvent(agentList, BaselineAgent.
  class, "meet");
    if (networkStructure == DYNAMIC_ZERO)
      g.addCollectionEvent(agentList, BaselineAgent.
  class, "searchAndMeet_fix");
    if (networkStructure == DYNAMIC_GROW)
      g.addCollectionEvent(agentList, BaselineAgent.
  class, "searchAndMeet_var");
    if (networkStructure == DYNAMIC_UNHAPPY){
      g.addEvent(this, "shuffleLists");
      g.addCollectionEvent(agentList, BaselineAgent.
  class, "removeLink_unhappy");
      g.addCollectionEvent(agentList, BaselineAgent.
  class, "searchAndMeet_unhappy");
      }
    if (networkStructure == DYNAMIC_THRESHOLD |
  networkStructure == DYNAMIC_THRESHOLD_5){
      g.addEvent(this, "shuffleLists");
      g.addCollectionEvent(agentList, BaselineAgent.
```

```
class, "removeLink_threshold");
   g.addCollectionEvent(agentList, BaselineAgent.
class, "searchAndMeet_threshold");
   }
   if (adjacencyMatrix){
   SimGroupEvent g2 = eventList.scheduleGroup
(numberOfRounds-1, numberOfRounds);
      g2.addEvent(this, "writeAdjacencyMatrix");
   }
   SimGroupEvent g3 = eventList.scheduleGroup
(numberOfRounds, numberOfRounds);
   g3.addCollectionEvent(originalAgentList,
BaselineAgent.class, "reset");
   g3.addEvent(this, "resetSessionTime");
   g3.addEvent(this, "resetNetwork");
   eventList.scheduleSystem((numberOfRounds*number
OfRuns),
   Sim.EVENT_SIMULATION_END);
   }

   public void buildNetwork(){
   // NETWORK
   if (networkStructure == DENSE)
netFactory.setDense();
   else {
      if (networkStructure == SMALLWORLD) netFactory.
setSmallWorld();
      else {
      if (networkStructure == SCALEFREE) netFactory.
setScaleFree();
      else {
        if (networkStructure == COUPLES |
networkStructure == DYN_COUPLES
           | networkStructure == EXPERIMENT
           | networkStructure == DYNAMIC_GROW |
networkStructure == DYNAMIC_ZERO
           | networkStructure == RND_COUPLES |
networkStructure == DYNAMIC_UNHAPPY
           | networkStructure == DYNAMIC_THRESHOLD)
         netFactory.setCouples();
        else {
        if (networkStructure == DYNAMIC_THRESHOLD_5)
         netFactory.setFiveLinks();
      }
     }
```

```
      }
    }
  }
  public void decreaseAgentsPopulation(){
    Collections.shuffle(originalAgentList);
    agentList.clear();
    for (int i = 0; i < (numberOfAgents-1); i++) {
      agentList.add(originalAgentList.get(i));
    }
  }

  public void mixCouples() {
    if (networkStructure == EXPERIMENT) {
      setRole();
      netFactory.mixCouples();
    } else {
      if (networkStructure == RND_COUPLES)
        netFactory.setCouples();
    }
  }

  public void resetNetwork(){
    decreaseAgentsPopulation();
    buildNetwork();
    if (networkStructure == EXPERIMENT)
      setRole();
    run++;
  }
  public void updateSessionTime() {
    sessionTime++;
    for (Iterator<BaselineAgent> iterator =
agentList.iterator(); iterator.hasNext();) {
      BaselineAgent agent = (BaselineAgent) iterator.
next();
        agent.setSessionTime(sessionTime);
        agent.setRun(run);
    }
  }

  public void resetSessionTime() {
    sessionTime = 0;
  }
  public void writeAdjacencyMatrix(){
    String matrixFile = "adjacencyMatrixAtRun"
+run+".txt";
```

```
    FileWriter aFile = null;
    try {
      aFile = new FileWriter (matrixFile);
    }
    catch (IOException e){
      System.err.println ("Exception in building
matrix FileWriter object: "
          + e.toString ());
    }
    PrintWriter aBuffer = new PrintWriter (aFile);
    String heading = "";
    for (Iterator<BaselineAgent> iterator =
agentList.iterator(); iterator.hasNext();) {
      BaselineAgent agent = (BaselineAgent) iterator.
next();
      heading+=","+(agent.getId()+1);
    }
    aBuffer.println(heading);
    for (Iterator<BaselineAgent> iterator =
agentList.iterator(); iterator.hasNext();) {
      BaselineAgent agent = (BaselineAgent) iterator.
next();
      String newLine = (agent.getId()+1)+"";
      for (int i = 0; i < agentList.size(); i++) {
        if (agent.isClose(agentList.get(i)))
          newLine += ",1";
        else
          newLine += ",0";
      }
      aBuffer.println(newLine);
    }
    aBuffer.flush();
    aBuffer.close();
  }
```

This is the observer code:

```
import jas.engine.*;
public class BaselineObserver extends SimModel{

  //Model parameters
  public BaselineModel  model;
  //Technical
  private double[] statCollection;
  //private TimePlot countPlotter;
```

```java
public void setParameters()
{
    model = (BaselineModel) Sim.engine.getModelWithID
("BaselineModel");
    if (model == null)
        Sim.fatalError("The Observer did not find a Model
instance in memory!", null);
}
public void buildModel()
{
}
}
```

This is the network factory code:

```java
import java.util.*;
import org._3pq.jgrapht.Edge;
import org._3pq.jgrapht.Graph;
public class NetworkFactory {
    private Graph graph;
    private ArrayList<BaselineAgent> agentList;
    private double intensity;
    private BaselineModel model;
    public Random randomGenerator;
    public NetworkFactory(Graph g, BaselineModel a,
Random r) {
        graph = g;
        model = a;
        agentList = model.getAgentList();
        intensity = 1.0;
        randomGenerator = r;
    }
    public void setDense() {
        eraseEdges();
        shuffleList();

        for (Iterator<BaselineAgent> iter =
agentList.iterator(); iter.hasNext();) {
            BaselineAgent element = (BaselineAgent) iter.
next();
            for (Iterator<BaselineAgent> iterator =
agentList.iterator(); iterator
                .hasNext();) {
                BaselineAgent ele = (BaselineAgent) iterator.
next();
```

```java
      if ((element != ele) & element.
getRelation(ele)==null){
          element.addRelation(ele, intensity);
          ele.addRelation(element, intensity);
        }
      }
    }
  }

  public void setCouples() {
    eraseEdges();
    shuffleList();
    int numGroups = agentList.size()/2;
    for (int i = 0; i < numGroups; i++) {
      List<BaselineAgent> groupList = agentList.
        subList(2*i,2*(i+1));
      for (Iterator<BaselineAgent> iter =
groupList.iterator(); iter.hasNext();) {
        BaselineAgent element = (BaselineAgent)
iter.next();
        for (Iterator<BaselineAgent> iterator =
            groupList.iterator(); iterator.
            hasNext();) {
        BaselineAgent ele = (BaselineAgent)
iterator.next();
        if ((element != ele) & element.
getRelation(ele)==null){
            element.addRelation(ele, intensity);
            ele.addRelation(element, intensity);
          }
        }
      }
    }
  }
  /*
   * Creates a small world network topology inside
groups by following the Newman Watts
   * model derived by the Watts-Strogatz
   * model, with parameter k = 2, p = 0.01, minimum
group size = 5.
   */
  public void setSmallWorld (){
    eraseEdges();
    shuffleList();
    double prob = 0.1;
```

```java
    int numGroups = 1;
    int groupSize = agentList.size();
    for (int i = 0; i < numGroups; i++) {
      List<BaselineAgent> groupList = agentList.
          subList(groupSize*i,groupSize*(i+1));
      // create links to the neigbours
      for (Iterator<BaselineAgent> iter = groupList.
iterator(); iter.hasNext();) {
        BaselineAgent element = (BaselineAgent) iter.
next();
        // if groups are networks:
        //element.setGroupList(groupList);
        if (groupList.indexOf(element) == 0) {
        BaselineAgent neighbour1 = groupList.get
(groupList.size()-1);
        BaselineAgent neighbour2 = groupList.get
(groupList.size()-2);
        BaselineAgent neighbour3 =
groupList.get(1);
        BaselineAgent neighbour4 =
groupList.get(2);
          if ((element != neighbour1) &
element.getRelation (neighbour1)==null)
             element.addRelation(neighbour1,
intensity);
          if ((element != neighbour2) &
element.getRelation(neighbour2)==null)
             element.addRelation(neighbour2,
intensity);
          if ((element != neighbour3) &
element.getRelation (neighbour3)==null)
             element.addRelation(neighbour3,
intensity);
          if ((element != neighbour4) &
element.getRelation(neighbour4)==null)
             element.addRelation(neighbour4,
intensity);
          }
        else {
          if (groupList.indexOf(element) == 1) {
             BaselineAgent neighbour1 = groupList.get
(groupList.size()-1);
             BaselineAgent neighbour2 = groupList.
get(0);
```

```
                BaselineAgent neighbour3 =
groupList.get(2);
                BaselineAgent neighbour4 =
groupList.get(3);
                    if ((element != neighbour1) &
element.getRelation(neighbour1)==null)
                    element.addRelation(neighbour1,
intensity);
                    if ((element != neighbour2) &
element.getRelation(neighbour2)==null)
                    element.addRelation(neighbour2,
intensity);
                    if ((element != neighbour3) &
element.getRelation(neighbour3)==null)
                    element.addRelation(neighbour3,
intensity);
                    if ((element != neighbour4) &
element.getRelation(neighbour4)==null)
                    element.addRelation(neighbour4,
intensity);
    }
    else {
    if (groupList.indexOf(element) ==
groupList.size()-1) {
        BaselineAgent neighbour1 = groupList.get
(groupList.size()-2);
        BaselineAgent neighbour2 = groupList.get
(groupList.size()-3);
        BaselineAgent neighbour3 = groupList.get(0);
        BaselineAgent neighbour4 = groupList.get(1);
        if ((element != neighbour1) &
element.getRelation(neighbour1)==null)
            element.addRelation(neighbour1, intensity);
        if ((element != neighbour2) &
element.getRelation(neighbour2)==null)
            element.addRelation(neighbour2, intensity);
        if ((element != neighbour3) &
element.getRelation(neighbour3)==null)
            element.addRelation(neighbour3, intensity);
        if ((element != neighbour4) &
element.getRelation(neighbour4)==null)
            element.addRelation(neighbour4, intensity);
    }
```

```
    else {
      if (groupList.indexOf(element) == groupList.
size()-2) {
        BaselineAgent neighbour1 = groupList.get
(groupList.size()-3);
        BaselineAgent neighbour2 = groupList.get
(groupList.size()-4);
        BaselineAgent neighbour3 = groupList.get
(groupList.size()-1);
        BaselineAgent neighbour4 = groupList.get(0);
        if ((element != neighbour1) &
element.getRelation(neighbour1)==null)
            element.addRelation(neighbour1, intensity);
        if ((element != neighbour2) &
element.getRelation(neighbour2)==null)
            element.addRelation(neighbour2, intensity);
        if ((element != neighbour3) &
element.getRelation(neighbour3)==null)
            element.addRelation(neighbour3, intensity);
        if ((element != neighbour4) &
element.getRelation(neighbour4)==null)
            element.addRelation(neighbour4, intensity);
      }

    else {
      BaselineAgent neighbour1 =
groupList.get(groupList.indexOf(element)-2);
      BaselineAgent neighbour2 =
groupList.get(groupList.indexOf(element)-1);
      BaselineAgent neighbour3 =
groupList.get(groupList.indexOf(element)+2);
      BaselineAgent neighbour4 =
groupList.get(groupList.indexOf(element)+1);
      if ((element != neighbour1) &
element.getRelation(neighbour1)==null)
          element.addRelation(neighbour1, intensity);
      if ((element != neighbour2) &
element.getRelation(neighbour2)==null)
          element.addRelation(neighbour2, intensity);
      if ((element != neighbour3) &
element.getRelation(neighbour3)==null)
          element.addRelation(neighbour3, intensity);
      if ((element != neighbour4) &
element.getRelation(neighbour4)==null)
```

```java
          element.addRelation(neighbour4, intensity);
          }
        }
      }
    }
  }
  // create long range links
  for (Iterator<BaselineAgent> iter = groupList.
iterator(); iter.hasNext();) {
    BaselineAgent element = (BaselineAgent)
iter.next();
      for (Iterator<BaselineAgent> iterator = groupList.
          iterator();iterator.hasNext();) {
      BaselineAgent ele = (BaselineAgent) iterator.
next();
        if ((element != ele) & !checkIfAlreadyConnected
          (element, ele) & model.randomGenerator.
nextDouble() <= prob){
          element.addRelation(ele, intensity);
          ele.addRelation(element, intensity);
          }
        }
      }
    }
  }

  /*
   * Creates a Scale Free Network with a power law
distribution like of degrees (order = 3),
   * according to the Barabasi-Albert SF model.
   */
  public void setScaleFree (){
    eraseEdges();
    shuffleList();
    int numGroups = 1;
    int groupSize = agentList.size();
    for (int i = 0; i < numGroups; i++) {
      List<BaselineAgent> groupList = agentList.subList
          (groupSize*i, groupSize*(i+1));
      int numEdges = 0;
      int numEdgesOld = 0;
      for (Iterator<BaselineAgent> iter =
groupList.iterator(); iter.hasNext();) {
        BaselineAgent element = (BaselineAgent)
iter.next();
```

```
      // if groups are networks:
      //element.setGroupList(groupList);
      if (groupList.indexOf(element) == 0){
         BaselineAgent ele = groupList.get(1);
         if ((element != ele) &
!checkIfAlreadyConnected(element, ele)){
         element.addRelation(ele, intensity);
         ele.addRelation(element, intensity);
         numEdges++;
         numEdgesOld++;
      }
   } else {
      if (groupList.indexOf(element) != 1){
      for (Iterator<BaselineAgent> iterator =
groupList.iterator(); iterator
            .hasNext();) {
      BaselineAgent ele = (BaselineAgent) iterator.
next();
      if (getNumOfLinks(ele) != 0.0){
         double prob = getNumOfLinks(ele)/(double)
numEdges;
         if ((element != ele) &
!checkIfAlreadyConnected(element, ele) &
model.randomGenerator.nextDouble() <= prob){
            element.addRelation(ele, intensity);
            ele.addRelation(element, intensity);
            numEdges++;
         }
      }
   }
}
   if (numEdges != numEdgesOld)
      numEdgesOld = numEdges;
   else {
      BaselineAgent ele = groupList.get(model.
randomGenerator.nextInt(groupList.size()));
      while (ele == element)
         ele =
groupList.get(model.randomGenerator.
nextInt(groupList.size()));
         element.addRelation(ele, intensity);
         ele.addRelation(element, intensity);
         numEdges++;
```

```
        numEdgesOld++;
      }
     }
    }
   }
  }
 }

 private boolean checkIfAlreadyConnected
(BaselineAgent a, BaselineAgent b){
   boolean temp = false;
     if (a.getRelation(b) != null)
       temp = true;
     if (b.getRelation(a) != null)
       temp = true;
   return temp;
 }

 private double getNumOfLinks (BaselineAgent a){
   if (a.getIncidentEdges() != null)
     return (double) (a.getIncidentInEdges().size());
   else
     return 0.0;
 }

 @SuppressWarnings("unchecked")
 private void eraseEdges(){
   ArrayList<Edge> edgeList = new ArrayList<Edge>();
   for (Iterator iter = graph.edgeSet().iterator();
iter.hasNext();)
      edgeList.add((Edge) iter.next());
   graph.removeAllEdges(edgeList);
 }

 private void shuffleList()
 {
   Collections.shuffle(agentList);
 }

 public void mixCouples() {
   eraseEdges();
   shuffleList();
   BaselineAgent[] playersA =
 new BaselineAgent[agentList.size()/2];
```

```java
    BaselineAgent[] playersB =
  new BaselineAgent[agentList.size()/2];
    int[] checkB = new int[playersB.length];
    for (int i = 0; i < checkB.length; i++) {
      checkB[i] = 0;
    }
    for (Iterator<BaselineAgent> iterator = agentList.
iterator(); iterator.hasNext();) {
      BaselineAgent agent = (BaselineAgent) iterator.
next();
      if (agent.getAgentType() == 0) {
        int i = 0;
        while (playersA[i] != null)
          i++;
        playersA[i] = agent;
      }
      else {
        int i = 0;
        while (playersB[i] != null)
          i++;
        playersB[i] = agent;
      }
    }
    for (int i = 0; i < playersA.length; i++) {
      int rB = randomGenerator.nextInt(playersB.
length);
      while (checkB[rB] != 0)
        rB = randomGenerator.nextInt(playersB.length);
      playersA[i].addRelation(playersB[rB],
intensity);
      playersB[rB].addRelation(playersA[i],
intensity);
      checkB[rB] = 1;
    }
  }

  public void setFiveLinks() {
    eraseEdges();
    shuffleList();
    for (int i = 0; i > 520; i++) {
      BaselineAgent candidate1 =
agentList.get(randomGenerator.nextInt(104));
      BaselineAgent candidate2 =
agentList.get(randomGenerator.nextInt(104));
      while ((candidate1 == candidate2) | candidate1.
```

```
getRelation(candidate2)!= null | candidate2.
getRelation(candidate1)!= null)
    candidate2 = agentList.get(randomGenerator.
nextInt(104));
    candidate1.addRelation(candidate2, intensity);
    candidate2.addRelation(candidate1, intensity);
  }
}
```

B.2   Example II: Reputation (Boero *et al.* 2010)

This model was based on data gathered from a laboratory experiment, where 64 individuals were asked to take investment decisions in an uncertain environment. This experiment was explicitly designed to generate a dataset to calibrate an ABM and derive macro implications in more complex systems from microscopic agent interaction. The purpose was to test the impact of other people's opinion on agent investment and the relevance of reputation as a learning scaffold in economic markets characterized by uncertainty.

As in the previous case, it is essential to remember that agent behavior was based on experimental data, these data were statistically elaborated through a cluster analysis (Table 2.8), where behavioral patterns were found, the model replicated the structure of the experiment, although with some minor modifications in the parameters (Table 2.9).

The structure of the simulation package, which is available on the supporting material web page mentioned above, consists of:

1. the model, which contains methods used to create agents and their schedule;

2. the observer, which contains tools to observe the simulation on the run;

3. the agent, which is a class for representing agents inside the simulation and receives input and initial parameters from the model.

The output data labels are as follows: ID, endowment, bestValueDiscovered, finalProfit, actionChoice, informationChoice. ID indicates the agent, endowment is the resource for each agent, bestValueDiscovered indicates the best yield discovered by agents, finalProfit is the expected final profit of the agent calculated for each simulation tick, actionChoice indicates the agent decision (i.e., exploring, exploiting, following hints) and informationChoice is the type of hint sent by the agent (i.e., best value, second best, and so on). The meaning of these variables has been specified in Chapter 2. This format can be easily exported into statistical analysis software, such as Excel, SPSS or R. Now, output is saved as *COLLECTIVE_J_NEG_output.text*. In this case, by running the simulation, two graphs are automatically generated which represent space exploration and agent behavior.

Here, is the code. It consists of agent, model and observer codes, which can be found, respectively, in the following files in the package available at the book web page mentioned above: *SocrateSIMAgent.java*, *SocrateSIMModel.java* and *SocrateSIMObserver.java*.[1]

The agent code is as follows:

```java
import java.io.*;
import java.util.*;
public class SocrateSIMAgent {
  public PrintWriter buff;
  private int endowment;
  private int actionChoice;
  private int informationChoice;
  private int bestValueDiscovered;
  private int bestValueDiscoveredName;
  private int finalProfit;
  private int actionBehaviour;
  private int informationBehaviour;
  private int partner;
  private SocrateSIMAgent[] agentArray;
  private int ID;
  private int explorationCost;
  private int[] space;
  private int[] explored;
  private int communicatedName;
  private int communicatedValue;
  private boolean[] isTrustworty;
  private ArrayList[] partnerEvaluations;
  private int averageFinalProfit;
  private int choice;
  private int lastChoice;
  private int imitatedAndLowerThanExpected;
  private int analyticSet;
  private Random randomGenerator;
  private boolean lemon;

  // values for action choices
  private static final int EXPLOITING = 0;
  private static final int EXPLORING = 1;
  private static final int LISTENING = 2;
  private static final int IMITATING = 3;

  // values for information choices
  private static final int FIRST_BEST = 0;
  private static final int OTHER_BEST = 1;
```

```java
    private static final int LOWER_HIGH = 2;
    private static final int HIGHER_LOW = 3;

    // values for action behaviour
    private static final int A1 = 0;
    private static final int A2 = 1;
    private static final int A3 = 2;

    // values for information behaviour
    private static final int I1 = 0;
    private static final int I2 = 1;
    private static final int I3 = 2;

    // analytic sets
    private static final int EXPLOIT_ONLY = 0;
    private static final int EXPLORE_ONLY = 1;
    private static final int INDIVIDUAL_J_POS = 2;
    private static final int COLLECTIVE_J_POS = 3;
    private static final int INDIVIDUAL_J_NEG = 4;
    private static final int COLLECTIVE_J_NEG = 5;
    private static final int LISTEN_ALWAYS = 6;

    /**
     * @param arg0
     */

    public SocrateSIMAgent(Random r,
SocrateSIMAgent[] a, int[] s, int ii, int as) {
        agentArray = a;
        randomGenerator = r;
        space = s;
        ID = ii;
        analyticSet = as;
        reset();
    }
    public void setBuffer (PrintWriter buff){
        this.buff = buff;
    }
    public void takeDecision(){
        if (analyticSet == INDIVIDUAL_J_POS |
    analyticSet == INDIVIDUAL_J_NEG |
            analyticSet == COLLECTIVE_J_POS | analyticSet
== COLLECTIVE_J_NEG | analyticSet == LISTEN_ALWAYS){
            switch (actionBehaviour) {
```

```
        case A1:
          if (randomGenerator.nextDouble() < 0.75) {
            if (randomGenerator.nextDouble() < 0.25)
actionChoice = EXPLORING;
              else actionChoice = LISTENING;
          } else
            actionChoice = EXPLOITING;
          break;
        case A2:
          // if partner is trustworthy
          if (isTrustworty[partner]){
            if (randomGenerator.nextDouble() < 0.75) {
              if (randomGenerator.nextDouble() < 0.75)
actionChoice = EXPLORING;
                else actionChoice = LISTENING;
            } else actionChoice = EXPLOITING;
          } else {
            if (randomGenerator.nextDouble() < 0.5) {
              if (randomGenerator.nextDouble()
< 0.75) actionChoice = EXPLORING;
                else actionChoice = LISTENING;
            } else actionChoice = EXPLOITING;
          }
          break;
        case A3:
          // if partner is trustworthy
          if (isTrustworty[partner]){
            if (randomGenerator.nextDouble() < 0.75)
              actionChoice = LISTENING;
            else actionChoice = EXPLOITING;
          } else {
            if (randomGenerator.nextDouble() < 0.25)
              actionChoice = LISTENING;
            else actionChoice = EXPLOITING;
          }
      }
    if (explored[communicatedName] != 0) {
      if (explored[communicatedName] !=
communicatedValue)
        worsenPartnerEvaluation();
      else
        improvePartnerEvaluation();
      if (actionChoice == LISTENING) actionChoice =
EXPLOITING;
      } else {
```

```
      if (communicatedValue <= bestValueDiscovered &
actionChoice == LISTENING)
        actionChoice = EXPLORING;
    }
  } else {
    if (analyticSet == EXPLOIT_ONLY)
      actionChoice = EXPLOITING;
    else {
      if (analyticSet == EXPLORE_ONLY){
        if (endowment >= explorationCost)
          actionChoice = EXPLORING;
      }
    }
  }
  if (endowment < explorationCost)
    actionChoice = EXPLOITING;
  execute();
}

public void communicateInfo(){
  switch (informationBehaviour) {
    case I1:
      if (randomGenerator.nextDouble() < 0.75)
        informationChoice = FIRST_BEST;
      else {
        if (randomGenerator.nextDouble() < 0.75)
          informationChoice = LOWER_HIGH;
        else informationChoice = HIGHER_LOW;
      }
      break;
    case I2:
      // if partner is trustworthy
      if (isTrustworty[partner]){
        if (randomGenerator.nextDouble() < 0.25)
informationChoice = FIRST_BEST;
        else informationChoice = OTHER_BEST;
      } else {
        if (randomGenerator.nextDouble() < 0.75) {
          if (randomGenerator.nextDouble() < 0.25)
informationChoice = FIRST_BEST;
          else informationChoice = OTHER_BEST;
        } else {
          if (randomGenerator.nextDouble() < 0.25)
informationChoice = LOWER_HIGH;
```

```
                else informationChoice = HIGHER_LOW;
              }
            }
            break;
          case I3:
            if (randomGenerator.nextDouble() < 0.25){
              if (randomGenerator.nextDouble() < 0.25)
informationChoice = FIRST_BEST;
              else informationChoice = OTHER_BEST;
            } else {
              if (randomGenerator.nextDouble() < 0.25)
informationChoice = LOWER_HIGH;
              else informationChoice = HIGHER_LOW;
            }
            break;
        }
        speak();
    }

    private void execute(){
      lastChoice = choice;
      lemon = false;
      switch (actionChoice) {
        case EXPLOITING:
          choice = bestValueDiscoveredName;
          endowment += bestValueDiscovered;
          break;
        case EXPLORING:
          choice = pickupNew();
          int value = space[choice];
          explored[choice] = value;
          if (value > bestValueDiscovered) {
            bestValueDiscovered = value;
            bestValueDiscoveredName = choice;
          }
          endowment = endowment - explorationCost +
value;
          break;
        case LISTENING:
          choice = communicatedName;
          int tempValue = space[choice];
          if (tempValue != communicatedValue) {
            worsenPartnerEvaluation();
            lemon = true;
          }
```

```
        else
          improvePartnerEvaluation();
        explored[choice] = tempValue;
        if (tempValue > bestValueDiscovered){
          bestValueDiscovered = tempValue;
          bestValueDiscoveredName = choice;
        }
        endowment = endowment - explorationCost +
tempValue;
        break;
      case IMITATING:
        int otherChoice = agentArray[partner].
getLastChoice();
        choice = otherChoice;
        if (explored[choice] != 0) {
          endowment += explored[choice];
        } else {
          int val = space[choice];
          explored[choice] = val;
          if (val > bestValueDiscovered) {
            bestValueDiscovered = val;
            bestValueDiscoveredName = choice;
          }
          endowment = endowment -
explorationCost + val;
        }
    }
    finalProfit = endowment +
(bestValueDiscovered*10);
  }

  private void speak(){
    switch (informationChoice) {
    case FIRST_BEST:
      agentArray[partner].tryOut(bestValue
DiscoveredName, bestValueDiscovered);
      break;
    case OTHER_BEST:
     if (ifOnlyOneKnown())
       agentArray[partner].tryOut
(bestValueDiscoveredName, bestValueDiscovered);
      else {
        int temp = randomGenerator.nextInt(space.
length);
        while (explored[temp] == 0 | temp ==
```

```
bestValueDiscoveredName)
         temp = randomGenerator.nextInt(space.length);
       agentArray[partner].tryOut(temp,
explored[temp]);
     }
     break;
  case LOWER_HIGH:
     agentArray[partner].tryOut
(bestValueDiscoveredName, bestValueDiscovered -
(20 + randomGenerator.nextInt (20)));
     break;
  case HIGHER_LOW:
     if (ifOnlyOneKnown())
       agentArray[partner].tryOut(bestValueDiscovered
Name, bestValueDiscovered - (20 + randomGenerator.
nextInt (20)));
     else {
     int temp = randomGenerator.
nextInt(space.length);
       while (explored[temp] == 0 | temp ==
bestValueDiscoveredName)
         temp = randomGenerator.nextInt(space.length);
       agentArray[partner].tryOut(temp,
explored[temp]+ (20 + randomGenerator.nextInt (20)));
     }
     break;
    }
  }

  public int getEndowment() {
    return endowment;
  }
  public int getFinalProfit() {
    return finalProfit;
  }
  public void writeData(){
    buff.println(ID+" "+endowment+"
"+bestValueDiscovered+" "+finalProfit+"
"+actionChoice+" "+informationChoice);
    buff.flush();
  }

  public void setActionBehaviour(int b){
    actionBehaviour = b;
  }
```

```java
public void setInformationBehaviour(int b){
  informationBehaviour = b;
}

public void setExplorationCost(int c){
  explorationCost = c;
}

public void reset(){
  endowment = 1000;
  averageFinalProfit = 0;
  explored = new int[space.length];
  for (int i = 0; i < explored.length; i++) {
    explored[i]=0;
  }
  choice = pickupNew();
  explored[choice] = space[choice];
  bestValueDiscovered = space[choice];
  bestValueDiscoveredName = choice;
  if (analyticSet > EXPLORE_ONLY){
    if (analyticSet == INDIVIDUAL_J_POS |
analyticSet == COLLECTIVE_J_POS
          | analyticSet == LISTEN_ALWAYS){
      isTrustworty = new boolean[agentArray.length];
      for (int i = 0; i < isTrustworty.length;
i++) {
        isTrustworty[i] = true;
      }
    } else {
      isTrustworty = new boolean[agentArray.length];
      for (int i = 0; i < isTrustworty.length;
i++) {
        isTrustworty[i] = false;
      }
    }
  }
  if (analyticSet == INDIVIDUAL_J_POS |
analyticSet == INDIVIDUAL_J_NEG){
    partnerEvaluations = new ArrayList[agentArray.
length];
    for (int i = 0; i < partnerEvaluations.length;
i++) {
```

```java
      partnerEvaluations[i] = new
ArrayList<Integer>();
    }
  }
}

  private int pickupNew(){
    int a = randomGenerator.nextInt(space.length);
    while (explored[a] != 0)
      a = randomGenerator.nextInt(space.length);
    return a;
  }

  public void tryOut(int name, int value){
    communicatedName = name;
    communicatedValue = value;
  }

  private void worsenPartnerEvaluation() {
    if (analyticSet != LISTEN_ALWAYS){
      partnerEvaluations[partner].add(new Integer(0));
      updatePartnerTrustworthiness();
    }
  }

  private void improvePartnerEvaluation() {
    if (analyticSet != LISTEN_ALWAYS){
      partnerEvaluations[partner].add(new Integer(1));
      updatePartnerTrustworthiness();
    }
  }

  private void updatePartnerTrustworthiness() {
    int tempSum = 0;
    for (Iterator iterator =
partnerEvaluations[partner].iterator(); iterator.
hasNext();) {
      Integer eval = (Integer) iterator.next();
      tempSum += eval.intValue();
    }
    if (analyticSet == INDIVIDUAL_J_POS |
analyticSet == COLLECTIVE_J_POS){
      if ((double) tempSum >= ((double)
partnerEvaluations[partner].size())/ 2.0)
        isTrustworty[partner] = true;
```

```java
        else
            isTrustworty[partner] = false;
      }
      if (analyticSet == INDIVIDUAL_J_NEG |
analyticSet == COLLECTIVE_J_NEG){
        if ((double) tempSum > ((double)
partnerEvaluations[partner].size())/ 2.0)
            isTrustworty[partner] = true;
        else
              isTrustworty[partner] = false;
      }
   }
   private boolean ifOnlyOneKnown() {
     int temp = 0;
     for (int i = 0; i < explored.length; i++) {
       if (explored[i] != 0)
           temp++;
     }
     if(temp>1)
       return false;
     else
       return true;
   }

   public int getBestValueDiscovered() {
     return bestValueDiscovered;
   }
   public void setPartner(int partner) {
   this.partner = partner;
   }
   public int getID() {
     return ID;
   }

   public boolean isExploiting (){
     if (actionChoice == EXPLOITING)
       return true;
     else return false;
   }

   public boolean isExploring (){
     if (actionChoice == EXPLORING)
       return true;
     else return false;
   }
```

```java
public boolean isListening (){
  if (actionChoice == LISTENING)
    return true;
  else return false;
}
public void setPartnerEvaluations(ArrayList[]
partnerEvaluations) {
  this.partnerEvaluations = partnerEvaluations;
}
public int getLastChoice() {
  return lastChoice;
}
public int getInformationChoice() {
  return informationChoice;
}
public int getLemon() {
  int a = 0;
  if (lemon)
    a = 1;
  return a;
}
```

The model code is as follows:

```java
import java.io.*;
import java.util.*;
import jas.engine.*;
import jas.events.*;
import jas.io.*;
public class SocrateSIMModel extends SimModel
{
  //Model parameters
  public int numberOfAgents;
  public int numberOfBonds;
  public int maxReturnInSpace;
  public int explorationCost;
  public int[] space;
  public Random randomGenerator;
  public long seed;
  public static int analyticSet;

  private String dataFile;
  private PrintWriter buff;
  private FileWriter file;
```

```
//Simulation agents
public ArrayList <SocrateSIMAgent> agentList;
//Technical
private ParameterFrame parameterFrame;
public ParametersBag parametersBag;

// for batch only
private boolean batch = false;
private static SimEngine eng;
private int tick;

// for information about lemons and information
choices
private int numOfFirstBest, numOfOtherBest,
numOfLowerHigh, numOfHigherLow, numOfLemons;
private int totalFPOfFirstBest, totalFPOfOtherBest,
totalFPOfLowerHigh, totalFPOfHigherLow;
private double averageFPOfFirstBest,
averageFPOfOtherBest, averageFPOfLowerHigh,
averageFPOfHigherLow;
private boolean infoOnInformationChoices = true;

// values for action behaviour
private static final int A1 = 0;
private static final int A2 = 1;
private static final int A3 = 2;

// values for information behaviour
private static final int I1 = 0;
private static final int I2 = 1;
private static final int I3 = 2;

// values for information choices
private static final int FIRST_BEST = 0;
private static final int OTHER_BEST = 1;
private static final int LOWER_HIGH = 2;
private static final int HIGHER_LOW = 3;

// analytic sets
private static final int EXPLOIT_ONLY = 0;
private static final int EXPLORE_ONLY = 1;
private static final int INDIVIDUAL_J_POS = 2;
private static final int COLLECTIVE_J_POS = 3;
private static final int INDIVIDUAL_J_NEG = 4;
private static final int COLLECTIVE_J_NEG = 5;
```

```java
  private static final int LISTEN_ALWAYS = 6;
  public void setParameters()
  {
    numberOfAgents  = 100;
    numberOfBonds = 1000000;
    maxReturnInSpace = 500;
    explorationCost = 8000;

    if (isBatch()){
      tick = 1;
      parametersBag = new ParametersBag("./
SocrateSIMParams.pForm.xml");
      parametersBag.mapToObject(this);
    } else {
      analyticSet = COLLECTIVE_J_NEG;
      parameterFrame = new ParameterFrame(this,
"Socrate Simulation", path + "SocrateSIMParams.
pForm.xml");
      addSimWindow(parameterFrame);
    }
  }
  public void shuffleList()
  {
    Collections.shuffle(agentList);
  }
  public void simulationEnd()
  {
    buff.close();
    if (isBatch())
      eng.quit();
  }
  public void buildModel()
  {
    buildAgents();
    buildSchedule();
  }
  private void buildAgents()
  {
    String scen = "";
    switch (analyticSet){
      case EXPLOIT_ONLY:
        scen = "EXPLOIT_ONLY";
        break;
      case EXPLORE_ONLY:
        scen = "EXPLORE_ONLY";
```

```
      break;
    case INDIVIDUAL_J_POS:
      scen = "INDIVIDUAL_J_POS";
      break;
    case COLLECTIVE_J_POS:
      scen = "COLLECTIVE_J_POS";
      break;
    case INDIVIDUAL_J_NEG:
      scen = "INDIVIDUAL_J_NEG";
      break;
    case COLLECTIVE_J_NEG:
      scen = "COLLECTIVE_J_NEG";
      break;
    case LISTEN_ALWAYS:
      scen = "LISTEN_ALWAYS";
}

dataFile = scen+"_output.txt";
try {
  // file for output data
  file = new FileWriter (dataFile);
}
catch (IOException e){
  System.err.println ("Exception in building
FileWriter object: "
      + e.toString ());
}
// build buffered stream for output data
buff = new PrintWriter (file);
if (isBatch()) {
  if (infoOnInformationChoices)
    buff.println("time avEndowment
avBestValueDiscovered avFinalProfit numOfFirstBest
numOfOtherBest numOfLowerHigh numOfHigherLow
numOfLemons avFinalProfitFirstBest
avFinalProfitOtherBest avFinalProfitLowerHigh
avFinalProfitHigherLow");
    else
      buff.println("time avEndowment
avBestValueDiscovered avFinalProfit");
  } else
    buff.println("ID endowment bestValueDiscovered
finalProfit actionChoice informationChoice");
  buff.flush();

  randomGenerator = new Random();
```

```java
// behaviour distribution across agents population
for action decisions and information
int [] actionBehav = new int[numberOfAgents];
for (int i = 0; i < actionBehav.length; i++) {
  double rr = randomGenerator.nextDouble();
  if (rr < 0.3125)
    actionBehav[i] = A1;
  else {
    if (rr < 0.453125)
      actionBehav[i] = A2;
    else
      actionBehav[i] = A3;
  }
}
int [] informationBehav = new int[numberOfAgents];
for (int i = 0; i < informationBehav.length; i++) {
  if (actionBehav[i] == A1){
    double rr = randomGenerator.nextDouble();
    if (rr < 0.4)
      informationBehav[i] = I1;
    else {
      if (rr < 0.95)
        informationBehav[i] = I2;
      else
        informationBehav[i] = I3;
    }
  } else {
    if (actionBehav[i] == A2){
      double rr = randomGenerator.nextDouble();
      if (rr < 0.111111111)
        informationBehav[i] = I1;
      else {
        if (rr < 0.444444444)
          informationBehav[i] = I2;
        else
          informationBehav[i] = I3;
      }
    } else {
      double rr = randomGenerator.nextDouble();
      if (rr > 0.228571429)
        informationBehav[i] = I1;
      else {
        if (rr > 0.742857143)
          informationBehav[i] = I2;
        else
```

```
          informationBehav[i] = I3;
      }
    }
  }
}

// building space
space = new int[numberOfBonds];
for (int i = 0; i < space.length; i++) {
  double rr = Math.abs(randomGenerator.
nextGaussian());
    space[i] = (int) (rr * (double) maxReturnInSpace);
  }
  agentList = new ArrayList<SocrateSIMAgent>();
  SocrateSIMAgent[] agentArray = new SocrateSIMAgent
[numberOfAgents];
  for (int i = 0; i < numberOfAgents; i++)
  {
    SocrateSIMAgent agent = new SocrateSIMAgent
(randomGenerator, agentArray, space, i, analyticSet);
    agentList.add(agent);
    agentArray[i] = agent;
    agent.setBuffer(buff);
  }
  for (int i = 0; i<numberOfAgents> i++){
    agentArray[i].setActionBehaviour(actionBehav[i]);
    agentArray[i].setInformationBehaviour
(informationBehav[i]);
    agentArray[i].setExplorationCost(explorationCost);
  }
  if (analyticSet == COLLECTIVE_J_POS | analyticSet ==
COLLECTIVE_J_NEG)
    setPartnerEvaluations();
  }
  private void buildSchedule()
  {
    eventList.scheduleSystem(49501, Sim.EVENT_
SIMULATION_END);
    SimGroupEvent g = eventList.scheduleGroup(0, 1);
    g.addEvent(this, "shuffleList");
    if (analyticSet > EXPLORE_ONLY){
      g.addEvent(this, "setPartners");
      g.addCollectionEvent(agentList, SocrateSIMAgent.
  class, "communicateInfo");
    }
```

```
      g.addCollectionEvent(agentList, SocrateSIMAgent.
   class, "takeDecision");
     if (isBatch()) {
       if (infoOnInformationChoices)
          g.addEvent(this,
 "computePopInformationChoices");
         g.addEvent(this, "writeData");
       } else
         g.addCollectionEvent(agentList, SocrateSIMAgent.
   class, "writeData");
       SimGroupEvent g2 = eventList.
 scheduleGroup(495, 495);
       g2.addCollectionEvent(agentList, SocrateSIMAgent.
   class, "reset");
       if (analyticSet == COLLECTIVE_J_POS |
 analyticSet == COLLECTIVE_J_NEG)
         g2.addEvent(this, "setPartnerEvaluations");
     }

   public synchronized void setPartners (){
       ArrayList<SocrateSIMAgent> agents =
 new ArrayList<SocrateSIMAgent>();
       for (Iterator<SocrateSIMAgent> iterator =
 agentList.iterator(); iterator.hasNext();) {
         SocrateSIMAgent pippo = (SocrateSIMAgent)
 iterator.next();
         agents.add(pippo);
       }
       int numCouples = agentList.size() / 2;
       for (int i = 0; i < numCouples; i++) {
         int rnd1 = randomGenerator.
 nextInt(agents.size());
         int rnd2 = randomGenerator.
 nextInt(agents.size());
         while (rnd1 == rnd2)
           rnd2 = randomGenerator.nextInt(agents.size());
         SocrateSIMAgent tizio = agents.get(rnd1);
         SocrateSIMAgent caio = agents.get(rnd2);
         tizio.setPartner(caio.getID());
         caio.setPartner(tizio.getID());
         agents.remove(tizio);
         agents.remove(caio);
       }
     }
```

```java
  public double getAverageBestValueDiscovered(){
    double a = 0.0;
    for (Iterator iterator = agentList.iterator();
iterator.hasNext();) {
      SocrateSIMAgent pippo = (SocrateSIMAgent)
iterator.next();
        a += (double) pippo.getBestValueDiscovered();
      }
    a = a / (double) agentList.size();
    return a;
  }
  public double getExploringPercentage() {
    double a = 0.0;
    for (Iterator iterator = agentList.iterator();
iterator.hasNext();) {
      SocrateSIMAgent pippo = (SocrateSIMAgent)
iterator.next();
      if (pippo.isExploring())
      a += 1.0;
    }
    a = a / (double) agentList.size();
    return a;
  }

  public double getExploitingPercentage() {
    double a = 0.0;
    for (Iterator iterator = agentList.iterator();
iterator.hasNext();) {
      SocrateSIMAgent pippo = (SocrateSIMAgent)
iterator.next();
      if (pippo.isExploiting())
        a += 1.0;
    }
    a = a / (double) agentList.size();
    return a;
  }

  public double getListeningPercentage() {
    double a = 0.0;
    for (Iterator iterator = agentList.iterator();
iterator.hasNext();) {
      SocrateSIMAgent pippo = (SocrateSIMAgent)
iterator.next();
      if (pippo.isListening())
```

```java
        a += 1.0;
    }
    a = a / (double) agentList.size();
    return a;
}

public void setPartnerEvaluations(){
    ArrayList[] pE = new ArrayList[numberOfAgents];
    for (int i = 0; i < pE.length; i++) {
        pE[i] = new ArrayList<Integer>();
    }
    for (Iterator iterator = agentList.iterator();
         iterator.hasNext();) {
        SocrateSIMAgent agent = (SocrateSIMAgent)
iterator.next();
        agent.setPartnerEvaluations(pE);
    }
}
public static void main(String[] args)
{
    if (args.length != 0){
        analyticSet = Integer.parseInt(args[0]);
        SocrateSIMModel p = new SocrateSIMModel();
        p.setBatch(true);
        p.setParameters();

        eng = new SimEngine();
        eng.addModel(p);
        eng.buildModels();
        eng.start();
    } else

        System.out.println("SYNTAX ERROR:
SocrateSIMModel [numScenario]");
    }
    /**
     * @return Returns the batch.
     */
    public boolean isBatch() {
        return batch;
    }

    /**
     * @param batch The batch to set.
     */
```

```
    public void setBatch(boolean batch) {
    this.batch = batch;
    }

    public void writeData(){
      if (tick > 495)
        tick = 1;
      double endowment = 0.0;
      double bestValueDiscovered = 0.0;
      double finalProfit = 0.0;
      for (Iterator iterator = agentList.iterator();
iterator.hasNext();) {
        SocrateSIMAgent agent = (SocrateSIMAgent)
iterator.next();
        endowment += (double) agent.getEndowment();
        bestValueDiscovered += (double) agent.
getBestValueDiscovered();
        finalProfit += (double) agent.getFinalProfit();
      }
      endowment = endowment / (double) numberOfAgents;
      bestValueDiscovered = bestValueDiscovered /
(double) numberOfAgents;
      finalProfit = finalProfit / (double)
numberOfAgents;
      if (infoOnInformationChoices)
        buff.println(tick+" "+endowment+"
"+bestValueDiscovered+" "+finalProfit+" "
            +numOfFirstBest+" "+numOfOtherBest+"
"+numOfLowerHigh+" "
            +numOfHigherLow+" "+numOfLemons+"
"+averageFPOfFirstBest+" "
            +averageFPOfOtherBest+"
"+averageFPOfLowerHigh+" "+averageFPOfHigherLow);
      else
        buff.println(tick+" "+endowment+"
"+bestValueDiscovered+" "+finalProfit);
      buff.flush();
      tick++;
    }

  public void computePopInformationChoices(){
    numOfFirstBest = 0;
    numOfOtherBest = 0;
    numOfHigherLow = 0;
```

```
numOfLowerHigh = 0;
numOfLemons = 0;
totalFPOfFirstBest = 0;
totalFPOfOtherBest = 0;
totalFPOfHigherLow = 0;
totalFPOfLowerHigh = 0;
averageFPOfFirstBest = 0.0;
averageFPOfOtherBest = 0.0;
averageFPOfHigherLow = 0.0;
averageFPOfLowerHigh = 0.0;
int temp = 0;
for (Iterator iterator = agentList.iterator();
iterator.hasNext();) {
    SocrateSIMAgent agent = (SocrateSIMAgent)
iterator.next();
    numOfLemons += agent.getLemon();
    temp = agent.getInformationChoice();
    if (temp == FIRST_BEST){
      numOfFirstBest++;
      totalFPOfFirstBest += agent.getFinalProfit();
    } else {

      if (temp == OTHER_BEST){
        numOfOtherBest++;
        totalFPOfOtherBest += agent.getFinalProfit();
      } else {
        if (temp == HIGHER_LOW) {
          numOfHigherLow++;
          totalFPOfHigherLow +=
agent.getFinalProfit();
        } else {
          if (temp == LOWER_HIGH) {
          numOfLowerHigh++;
          totalFPOfLowerHigh +=
agent.getFinalProfit();
          }
        }
      }
    }
  }
}
if (numOfFirstBest > 0)
  averageFPOfFirstBest = (double)
totalFPOfFirstBest / (double) numOfFirstBest;
  if (numOfOtherBest > 0)
    averageFPOfOtherBest = (double)
```

```
totalFPOfOtherBest / (double) numOfOtherBest;
    if (numOfHigherLow > 0)
      averageFPOfHigherLow = (double)
totalFPOfHigherLow / (double) numOfHigherLow;
    if (numOfLowerHigh > 0)
      averageFPOfLowerHigh = (double)
totalFPOfLowerHigh / (double) numOfLowerHigh;
    }
  }
```

The observer code is as follows:

```
import jas.engine.*;
import jas.events.SimGroupEvent;
import jas.graphics.plot.*;
public class SocrateSIMObserver extends SimModel{

  //Model parameters
  public SocrateSIMModel  model;
  private TimeSeriesPlotter bestDiscoveredPlotter;
  private TimeSeriesPlotter actionChoicePlotter;
  public void setParameters()
  {
    model = (SocrateSIMModel) Sim.engine.
getModelWithID("SocrateSIMModel");
    if (model == null)
      Sim.fatalError("The Observer did not find a
Model instance in memory!", null);
  }
  public void buildModel()
  {
    bestDiscoveredPlotter =
new TimeSeriesPlotter("BestDiscoveredValue");
    bestDiscoveredPlotter.addSeries("Average Value",
model,
"getAverageBestValueDiscovered", true);
    addSimWindow(bestDiscoveredPlotter);
    actionChoicePlotter =
new TimeSeriesPlotter("Action Choices");
    actionChoicePlotter.addSeries("Exploiting", model,
"getExploitingPercentage", true);
    actionChoicePlotter.addSeries("Exploring", model,
"getExploringPercentage", true);
    actionChoicePlotter.addSeries("Listening", model,
"getListeningPercentage", true);
```

```
addSimWindow(actionChoicePlotter);
SimGroupEvent g = eventList.scheduleGroup(0, 1);
g.addEvent(bestDiscoveredPlotter,
Sim.EVENT_UPDATE);
      g.addEvent(actionChoicePlotter, Sim.EVENT_UPDATE);
}
```

References

Boero, R., Bravo, G., and Squazzoni, F. (2010) Trust and Partner Selection in Social Networks: An Experimentally Grounded Model, arXiv:1008.4705v1 [physics.soc-ph].

Boero, R., Bravo, G., Castellani, M., and Squazzoni, F. (2010) Why bother with what others tell you? An experimental data-driven agent-based model. *Journal of Artificial Societies and Social Simulation*, **13**(3), accessible at: http://jasss.soc.surrey.ac.uk/13/3/6.html.

Index

Agent-Based Computational Sociology, First Edition. Flaminio Squazzoni.
© 2012 John Wiley & Sons, Ltd. Published 2012 by John Wiley & Sons, Ltd.

Printed and bound by CPI Group (UK) Ltd, Croydon, CR0 4YY

16/04/2025

14658543-0003